Israel: the History of an Idea

By the same author:

The Jews of Canterbury

On Earth as it is in Heaven: Jews, Christians and Liberation
    Theology

The Jewish Heritage

Jewish Petitionary Prayer: A Theological Exploration

Holocaust Theology

Rabbinic Perspectives on the New Testament

Issues in Contemporary Judaism

Dictionary of Judaica

A Dictionary of Judaism and Christianity

The Crucified Jew: Twenty Centuries of Christian Anti-Semitism

Exodus: An Agenda for Jewish–Christian Dialogue

Exploring Reality (co-editor)

The Canterbury Papers: Essays on Religion and Society (editor)

The Salman Rushdie Controversy in Interreligious Perspective
    (editor)

Tradition and Unity: Sermons Published in Honour of Robert
    Runcie (editor)

The Sayings of Moses (editor)

A Traditional Quest: Essays in Honour of Louis Jacobs (editor)

Using the Bible Today: Contemporary Interpretations of Scripture
    (editor)

Islam in a World of Diverse Faiths (editor)

Torah and Revelation (editor)

World Religions and Human Liberation (editor)

Religion in Public Life (co-editor)

Experiencing the Divine (editor)

Problems of Contemporary Jewish Theology (editor)

Many Mansions: Interfaith and Religious Intolerance (editor)

Israel: the History of an Idea

Dan Cohn-Sherbok

First published in Great Britain 1992

SPCK
Holy Trinity Church
Marylebone Road
London NW1 4DU

British Library Cataloguing in Publication Data
A catalogue record for this book is available
from the British Library

ISBN 0-281-04577-1

Typeset by Rowland Phototypesetting Ltd,
Bury St Edmunds, Suffolk
Printed and bound in Great Britain by
Mackays of Chatham PLC, Chatham, Kent

For Lavinia

Contents

Acknowledgements

I would like to acknowledge my indebtedness to a number of important books from which I obtained information as well as source material: Robert M. Seltzer, *Jewish People, Jewish Thought: The Jewish Experience in History*, London 1980; John Drane, *The Old Testament Story*, London 1983; Abba Hillel Silver, *A History of Messianic Speculation in Israel*, Gloucester, Mass., 1978; Shlomo Avineri, *The Making of Modern Zionism: The Intellectual Origins of the Jewish State*, New York 1981; Arthur Hertzberg, *The Zionist Idea: A Historical Analysis and Reader*, New York 1969; Walter Laqueur, *A History of Zionism*, New York 1972; Robert Wistrich, *Antisemitism: The Longest Hatred*, London 1991; Paul Johnson, *A History of the Jews*, London 1987; Joseph Klausner, *The Messianic Idea in History*, London 1956. I would also like to thank Judith Longman and Brendan Walsh of SPCK for their help and encouragement.

A Note on Dates: Throughout this work I have used the terminology BC or AD (rather than BCE and CE) since it is more familiar. The term AM refers to *Anno Mundi*. In the case of rulers, all dates refer to the years of their reign; dates for other individuals indicate life-spans.

Introduction

Throughout history Jews have longed to return to the Holy Land they inhabited in ancient times, and this quest has animated messianic aspirations through the centuries as well as the creation of a Zionist movement in the nineteenth century. In the years following the Holocaust Jews increasingly looked to the State of Israel as their refuge and hope. Facing mounting Arab aggression, world Jewry rallied in support of their beleaguered coreligionists who were struggling to preserve a Jewish presence in the Middle East. Dedicated to Jewish survival, Jews today see the Jewish state as fundamental to the continued existence of Judaism and the Jewish people.

Over the years there has been a wide variety of books dealing with various aspects of this Jewish quest, yet there has not yet appeared a succinct historical survey of this 4000-year-old longing for a Jewish homeland. The purpose of this study is to provide such an account. Chapter 1 begins with God's call to Abraham to leave the country of his birth and travel to Canaan where God promised to make of him a great nation. This same declaration was repeated to his grandson Jacob who, after wrestling with God's messenger, was renamed Israel (meaning 'he who struggles with God'). After Jacob's son Joseph became vizier in Egypt, the Israelite clan settled in Egypt for several hundred years. Eventually Moses led them out of Egyptian bondage, and the people settled in the Promised Land. There they established a monarchy, but, due to the corruption of the nation, God punished his chosen people through the instrument of the foreign powers who devastated the northern kingdom in the eighth century BC and the southern kingdom two centuries later.

This account of biblical history continues in Chapter 2 with a depiction of the return of the Jewish people to Judah in the sixth century BC. Though the Temple lay in ruins and Jerusalem was destroyed, the Babylonian exiles had not lost their faith in God. Sustained by their belief that God would deliver them from exile, a number of Jews sought permission to return to their former home. In 538 BC King Cyrus of Persia allowed them to leave. Under the leadership of Joshua and Zerubbabel, restoration of the Temple began. Encouraged in their efforts the nation strayed from the religious faith of their ancestors. To combat such laxity, the prophet Nehemiah asserted that the community must purify itself; in this effort he was joined by the priest Ezra. Although religious reforms were accordingly carried out, the people continued to abandon their Torah and the Temple was destroyed a second time in the first century AD by the Romans.

After Jerusalem and the Temple were devastated, the Jews were bereft of a homeland. The glories of ancient Israel had come to an end, and the Jews were destined to live among the nations. As Chapter 3 explains, in their despair the nation longed for a messianic figure of the House of David who would lead them back to Zion. Basing their beliefs on prophecies in Scripture, the Jewish people foresaw a period of redemption in which earthly life would be transformed and all nations would bow down to the one true God. Such a utopian vision animated rabbinic reflection about God's providential plan for his chosen people. According to rabbinic speculation, this process would involve the coming of a messianic figure (Messiah ben Joseph) who would serve as the forerunner of a second Messiah. This second Messiah would bring back all the exiles to Zion and complete earthly existence. Eventually at the end of the messianic era, all human beings would be judged: the righteous would enter into heaven whereas the wicked would be condemned to eternal punishment. This eschatological vision served as a means of overcoming the nation's trauma at suffering the loss of its sacred home and institutions.

Chapter 4 continues this narrative with an account of early messianic expectations. During the years after Herod's death (AD 4), a number of Jews believed that Jesus, the son of Joseph and Mary, would usher in the period of messianic redemption. After attracting followers from Galilee and elsewhere Jesus was put to death during the reign of Pontius Pilate – only a few of the faithful continued to accept him as their redeemer. Although mainstream Judaism rejected such claims, the Jewish community continued to long for deliverance, and in AD 132 the military leader, Simon bar Kochba, was acclaimed by many Jews as the Davidic Messiah. However, when the rebellion he led was crushed Jews put forward the year of redemption until the fifth century. In about the middle of this century another messianic pretender, Moses from Crete, declared that he would lead Jewish inhabitants from the island back to their homeland. After this plan failed, Jews continued to hope for a future return and their aspirations are recorded in a number of midrashic collections. In the ninth century Saadia Gaon attempted to determine the date of the final redemption on the basis of scriptural texts. In addition, during this period a number of pseudo-Messiahs appeared, and the traveller Eldad Ha-Dani brought news of the ten lost tribes which further stimulated messianic longing.

Such messianic speculation continued into the medieval period. As Chapter 5 shows, the year of the First Crusade (1096) was viewed by many Jews as the year of deliverance: when Jews were slaughtered during this period, their suffering was viewed as the birth pangs of the Messiah. In later years the same yearning for a return to Zion was expressed by Jews who continued to be persecuted by the Christian population. During the next two centuries various Jewish writers attempted to predict the date of the final redemption on the basis of scriptural verses in the Book of Daniel. In addition, during these years a number of pseudo-Messiahs appeared on the Jewish scene. As time passed other calculators continued to speculate about the coming of the Messiah, frequently employing various mystical devices in their computations. Prominent among the mystical works of this period was the *Zohar* which contains numerous calculations about the advent of the messianic era. Finally in the thirteenth century another messianic figure, Abraham Abulafia, evoked a wide following from Jews who longed for a return to the Holy Land. Thus medieval Jews, like their ancestors, yearned for release from the bondage of exile, and in their misery looked to God's promises of messianic fulfilment as the means of deliverance.

The early modern period witnessed this same aspiration for messianic redemption. As Chapter 6 demonstrates, during the fourteenth and fifteenth centuries various messianic treatises were produced and in the next century the tradition of messianic calculation was continued by numerous rabbinic scholars. During this century several false Messiahs also appeared claiming to bring about a new age. Undaunted by their failure, messianic calculators of the seventeenth century persisted in their computations. At the middle of the seventeenth century the Cossack Rebellion that devastated Polish Jewry heightened Jewish yearning for deliverance, and in 1665 the arrival of Shabbatai Tzevi electrified the Jewish world. Claiming to be the Messiah, Shabbatai attracted a large circle of followers; however his conversion to Islam evoked widespread despair.

Chapter 7 illustrates that with the apostasy of Shabbatai Tzevi, the Jewish preoccupation with messianic calculation diminished: many Jews became disillusioned with messianic anticipation and disappointment and the belief in the Messiah–king receded in significance. Instead many Jews looked to the Enlightenment as their salvation. Yet despite this shift in orientation, a number of religious Jews continued to believe in the coming of the Messiah and linked this yearning to an advocacy of Zionism. Prominent among such individuals was Yehuda hai Alkalai who maintained that Jewish settlers should establish Jewish colonies in Palestine in anticipation of the Messiah. A similar view was adopted by Zwi Hirsch Kalischer who argued that the messianic era will occur gradually through the ingathering of the Jewish nation in its ancestral home. A later religious Zionist, Abraham Isaac Kook, attempted to harmonize messianic aspirations with the efforts of secularist pioneers in the Holy Land. According to Kook, God's providential plan is manifest in their sacrifices.

Paralleling these religious aspirations to establish a Jewish settlement in the Holy Land prior to the coming of the Messiah, modern secular Zionists who are discussed in Chapter 8 encouraged such a development in order to solve the problem of anti-Semitism. An early precursor of Zionism was Moses Hess who maintained that Jew-hatred is inevitable in the diaspora. According to Hess the only remedy for this ancient scourge is the creation of a Jewish state. Similarly Leon Pinsker argued that anti-Semitism is an inextricable aspect of Western culture; the only solution to Judeophobia is for the Jewish people to reconstitute themselves in their own country. The foremost Zionist leader Theodor Herzl reached the same conclusion in his classic work, *The Jewish State*, and engaged in a ceaseless struggle for political recognition of this aim among world powers. Other Jewish activists of this period included Ber Borochov who attempted to integrate Jewish nationalism with Marxist ideology, and Vladmir Jabotinsky who championed the Jewish cause through armed struggle.

As Chapter 9 exemplifies, the Zionist movement was met with considerable opposition both within and without the Jewish community. Ultra-Orthodox critics of Zionism believed the creation of a Jewish state was a betrayal of traditional Judaism. It is forbidden, they asserted, to accelerate the coming of the Messiah through human effort. At the opposite end of the spectrum Reform Judaism attacked Zionism as misguided utopianism. According to these progressives, only emancipation could serve as a solution to the Jewish state; Zionism however is a reactionary delusion. In place of a national homeland, they advanced socialism as a remedy to anti-Semitism. Within the Arab world, the influx of settlers in Palestine evoked widespread fear and hostility. After the establishment of a Jewish state, such Arab reactions led to the creation of the Palestinian Liberation Organization which promoted armed struggle. In their opposition to a Jewish state Arabs throughout the world have promoted virulent Jew-hatred based on previous stereotypes of the Jewish people.

Despite such anti-Zionist attitudes, the Zionist cause has gained increasing acceptance in the Jewish world. As Chapter 10 explains, the first steps towards creating a Jewish homeland were taken at the end of the nineteenth century with the First Zionist Congress. Subsequently Zionists attempted to persuade the British government to permit the creation of a Jewish homeland in Palestine. Although Britain eventually approved of such a plan, the British government insisted that the rights of the Arab population be protected. After the First World War British representatives attempted to oversee this policy (which was enshrined in the Balfour Declaration) but were met with considerable opposition by militant Zionists. In 1939 a White Paper was published which set limits on the number of Jewish emigrants who could be allowed into Palestine. The Jewish populace rejected this policy and inaugurated a campaign of terror against the British. After the Second World War the creation of a Jewish state was approved by the United Nations. Despite such an official endorsement, this plan was rejected by the Arabs. In subsequent years Arabs and Jews have engaged in a series of conflicts, and in recent times Arabs in the Occupied Territories have engaged in extensive resistance. Arab-Israeli antagonism thus continues to undermine the Jewish quest for a homeland in the land of their ancestors.

The book concludes with a number of reflections about the Jewish quest for a homeland through the centuries. From this study it is clear that the yearning for a Jewish presence in the Holy Land is a fundamental feature of Judaism. For nearly 4000 years the Jewish people have looked to Zion as a source of hope and through the ages have steadfastly awaited the advent of the Messiah who would release them from exile. This aspiration was at all times motivated by a utopian vision of the future, whether it took the form of a theocracy or the miraculous transformation of earthly life. Now that the state of Israel has become a reality, Jewry must not lose sight of the moral and spiritual dimensions of the Jewish tradition. As the Jewish people stand on the threshold of the third millennium they must attempt to reconcile the political, social and economic concerns of everyday life with an idealistic vision of God's Kingdom on earth.

one

Patriarchs, Kings and Prophets

According to Scripture, Abraham was the father of the Israelites. Responding to God's decree, he left the country of his birth and travelled to Canaan where he was succeeded by his son Isaac and grandson Jacob. After Jacob's son Joseph became a vizier in Egypt, the Israelite clan settled there for the next few hundred years. Eventually Moses led the people out of Egyptian bondage; for forty years they travelled through the desert, finally entering the Promised Land. Under Joshua the Israelites subdued the inhabitants of Canaan, and the people were ruled over by a series of judges. Despite Samuel's misgivings about the establishment of a monarchy, Saul became the first king of the country, followed by David and Solomon. In the tenth century BC, however, the Israelites divided into two rival kingdoms: Israel in the north and Judah in the south. In the northern kingdom a succession of kings incorporated Canaanite religious practices into the cult, thereby evoking the wrath of such prophets as Elijah and Elisha. Although the country prospered during this period, the people had become morally corrupt. Such prophets as Amos and Hosea predicted that God would punish the nation unless the inhabitants embraced the ethical demands of the covenant. At the end of the eighth century BC these predictions were fulfilled when the Assyrian forces devastated the kingdom. In Judah, southern prophets such as Isaiah issued similar pronouncements. Despite several attempts at religious reform, the kings ultimately relied on political alliances to save the nation, and at the beginning of the sixth century BC Judah was conquered by the invading Babylonian army.

The Patriarchs

The story of the Israelite people begins in the fertile lowlands alongside the Tigris and Euphrates rivers. It was here in Mesopotamia that successive empires of the ancient world flourished and decayed before the Israelites arose as a separate people. Some writers maintain that the patriarchs (Abraham, Isaac and Jacob) were real persons – chiefs or founders of tribal units; others argue that the names of the patriarchs refer not to individuals but to families, clans or tribes. In either case, these ancestors of the Israelite nation appear to have been part of a wave of north-western Semitic-speaking peoples who moved into Canaan in the second millennium BC. They and their descendants were semi-nomadic groups with small bands of sheep and goats, coming from the desert in search of pasture and intermingling with the local inhabitants. It has been suggested that these immigrants and sojourners were part of a larger social stratum living on the fringes of settled society referred to in Near Eastern sources as *Habiru* – a term which resembles the biblical word 'Hebrew'. The patriarchal clans may have been part of this *Habiru* element in ancient Canaan.

In any event the Genesis narrative depicts Abraham as the father of the Israelite nation. Originally known as Abram, he came from Ur of the Chaldeans – a Sumerian city of Mesopotamia near the head of the Persian Gulf. Together with his father Terah, his wife Sarai, and his nephew Lot, he travelled to Haran, a trading centre in northern Syria. There his father died, and God called upon him to go to Canaan: 'Go from your country and your kindred and your father's house to the land that I will show you. And I will make of you a great nation' (Genesis 12.1–2). During a famine in Canaan, he went first to Egypt and then proceeded to the Negev, finally settling in the plain near Hebron. Here he experienced a revelation which confirmed that his deliverance from Ur was an act of providence: 'I am the LORD who brought you from Ur of the Chaldeans to give you this land to possess' (Genesis 15.7).

Since Sarai had not given birth to children, Abram had relations with her servant girl, Hagar, who bore Ishmael. But when Abram was ninety-nine and Sarai ninety, God granted them a son, Isaac. It was then that Abram was given his new name Abraham ('the father of a multitude'), and Sarai was renamed Sarah ('princess'). When Isaac was born, Abraham sent Hagar and Ishmael away at Sarah's request. During this time God made a covenant with Abraham, symbolized by an act of circumcision: 'You shall be circumcised in the flesh of your foreskins, and it shall be a sign of the covenant between me and you' (Genesis 17.11). Later God tested Abraham's dedication by ordering him to sacrifice Isaac, telling him only at the last moment to refrain. When Isaac became older, Abraham sent a servant to his kinsfolk in Hebron to find a wife, and the messenger returned with Rebecca. After many years, God answered Isaac's prayers for a son, and twins – Esau and Jacob – were born. Jacob bought his brother's birthright for food, and with his mother's help secured Isaac's blessing thereby incur-

ring Esau's wrath. Fleeing from his brother, Jacob travelled north-
wards towards Haran; en route he had a vision of a ladder rising
to heaven and heard God speak to him promising that his offspring
would inherit the land and fill the earth:

> And he dreamed that there was a ladder set up on the earth,
> and the top of it reached to heaven . . . and behold, the LORD
> stood above it and said, 'I am the LORD, the God of Abraham
> your father and the god of Isaac; the land on which you lie I
> will give to you and to your descendants; and your descendants
> shall be like the dust of the earth.' (Genesis 28.12–14)

After arriving in Haran, Jacob worked for twenty years as a
shepherd for his uncle Laban. There he married Laban's daugh-
ters, Rachel and Leah, and they and their maids (Bilhah and
Zilpah) bore twelve sons and a daughter. When he eventually
returned to Canaan, Jacob wrestled with a mysterious stranger in
the gorge of the Jabbok river, a tributary of the Jordan, where God
bestowed upon him the new name 'Israel':

> When the man saw that he did not prevail against Jacob, he
> touched the hollow of his thigh; and Jacob's thigh was put out
> of joint as he wrestled with him. Then he said, 'Let me go, for
> the day is breaking.' But Jacob said, 'I will not let you go, unless
> you bless me.' . . . Then he said, 'Your name shall no more be
> called Jacob, but Israel, for you have striven with God and with
> men, and have prevailed.' (Genesis 32.25–8)

Jacob was welcomed by Esau in Edom, but then the brothers
parted. Jacob lived in Canaan until one of his sons, Joseph, invited
him to settle in Egypt, where he died at the age of 147.

The history of the three patriarchs is followed by the cycle of
stories about Jacob's son Joseph. As a young boy, Joseph was
presented with a special coat (or a long-sleeved robe) as a sign
that he was his father's favourite. When he was in Shechem helping
the brothers tend his family's flocks, he angered them by
recounting dreams in which they bowed down before him. They
reacted by plotting his death, but one of the brothers (Reuben)
persuaded them to wait, and another (Judah) suggested that they
should sell him as a slave rather than kill him. Eventually Joseph
was taken to Egypt; his brothers dipped his coat in a kid's blood
and declared to their father that he had been mauled by a wild
animal.

In Egypt Joseph served in the house of Potiphar but was falsely accused by Potiphar's wife of rape and incarcerated. Some time later he was set free by the reigning Pharaoh to interpret his dreams, and subsequently became chief minister of the land. After a famine, he made the country rich and later encountered his brothers who came before him to buy grain. Movingly he revealed to them his true identity, and God's providential care: 'I am your brother Joseph', he declared, 'whom you sold into Egypt. And now do not be distressed, or angry with yourselves, because you sold me here; for God sent me before you to preserve life' (Genesis 45.4–5). Joseph died when he was 110, and his family remained and flourished in Egypt. But with the reign of a new Pharaoh 'who did not know Joseph' (Exodus 1.8) the Jewish people were oppressed and persecuted and forced to work as slaves on the construction of the royal cities of Pithom and Raamses. Finally the Pharaoh declared that all male offspring should be killed at birth: 'Every son that is born to the Hebrews you shall cast into the Nile, but you shall let every daughter live' (Exodus 1.22).

Exodus to monarchy

The biblical narrative continues with an account of the deliverance of the Jews from Egyptian bondage. Exodus relates that a son had been born to Amram of the house of Levi and his wife Jochebed. When he was three months old his parents concealed him among the reeds growing on the banks of the Nile to save him from Pharaoh's decree. Pharaoh's daughter found the child and adopted him as her son, Moses. When he became older, he attacked and killed a taskmaster who was oppressing a Hebrew slave, and fled to the desert. There he dwelt with Jethro (a priest of Midian) and married his daughter Zipporah. Eventually God revealed himself to Moses, commanding that he deliver the chosen people from Pharaoh's harsh bondage:

> I am the God of your father, the God of Abraham, the God of Isaac, and the God of Jacob . . . I have seen the affliction of my people who are in Egypt, and have heard their cry because of their taskmasters; I know their sufferings . . . Come, I will send you to Pharaoh that you may bring forth my people, the sons of Israel, out of Egypt. (Exodus 3.6–7, 10)

To persuade Pharaoh that he should let the Jewish people go, God inflicted ten plagues on the Egyptians culminating in the slaying of every Egyptian first-born son. The first-born of the

Israelites were spared as each family slaughtered a lamb and smeared its blood on the doorposts. Seeing this, the angel of death passed over that household. After this final plague, Pharaoh released the Israelites, and they fled without even waiting for their bread to rise. However the perils were not over; Pharaoh changed his mind and sent his forces in pursuit. When the Israelites came to an expanse of water, it seemed they were trapped. Miraculously it was converted to dry land by a strong wind so that they were able to escape. The Egyptians however were drowned as they chased after them: 'The Egyptians pursued, and went in after them into the midst of the sea, all Pharaoh's horses, his chariots, and his horsemen . . . The waters returned and covered the chariots and the horsemen and all the host of Pharaoh that had followed them into the sea; not so much as one of them remained' (Exodus 14.23, 28).

The band of free people entered the wilderness of Sinai where Moses performed miracles to provide them with food and water (Exodus 16—17). After travelling for about ninety days, they encamped before Mt Sinai. God called Moses up to the top of the mountain and told him that if his people would listen to him and keep his covenant, they would become God's special people. They were commanded to wash and purify themselves for two days; on the third day they came to the foot of the mountain amongst thunder, lightning, and the sound of a ram's horn to hear God's voice. Alone Moses climbed the mountain again where he remained for forty days. At the end of this period, he returned with two tablets of stone on which were inscribed God's laws. But on his return Moses found the people had forsaken him and their God, and in anger he smashed the tablets of stone (only later carving new ones). Subsequently the Jews moved on and came to Kadesh Barnea (near the border of Canaan). There Moses saw the Promised Land from a distance:

And Moses went up from the plains of Moab to Mount Nebo, to the top of Pisgah, which is opposite Jericho. And the LORD showed him all the land . . . And the LORD said to him, 'This is the land of which I swore to Abraham, to Isaac, and to Jacob, "I will give it to your descendants." I have let you see it with your eyes, but you shall not go over there.' (Deuteronomy 34.1, 4)

After Moses died, Joshua the son of Nun was commanded by God to lead the children of Israel into the Promised Land. After crossing the Jordan, he captured Jericho and went on to take Ai (near Bethel). Subsequently he defeated both southern and northern kings. The second part of the Book of Joshua begins with a list of areas which had not as yet been conquered in the plain and valley regions as well as on the coast. To encourage the people, Joshua delivered speeches enjoining them to remain steadfast in their faith: recalling God's past mercies, he ordered them to be obedient to the covenant. After Joshua's death at the age of 110, the people began to form separate groups. At first there were twelve tribes named after the sons of Jacob: Joseph and Benjamin (the sons of Rachel); Levi, Simeon, Reuben, Judah, Issachar and Zebulun (the sons of Leah); Dan and Naphtali (the sons of Bilhah); and Gad and Asher (the sons of Zilpah). When Levi became a special priestly group excluded from this territorial division, the tribe of Joseph was divided into two named after his sons, Ephraim and Manasseh.

The Book of Judges also tells the story of the twelve national heroes who served as judges of the nation after Joshua's death. The sagas of five major judges – Ehud, Deborah, Gideon, Jephthah and Samson – are recounted at length. The judges were tribal rulers attached to particular regions; their fragmented reign continued for more than 150 years during the twelfth and eleventh centuries BC. During quiet periods, the tribes were governed by councils of elders; it was only at times of emergency that the judges took control. From a religious perspective, the era of the judges was of central significance in the life of the people. The covenant between God and the Israelites – the first formulated by Moses – was repeatedly proclaimed at gatherings in such national shrines as Shechem. Such an emphasis on covenantal obligation reinforced the belief that the Jews were the recipients of God's loving-kindness; they were his chosen people, a dedicated and separate nation.

During the period of the judges, God was conceived of as the supreme monarch. When some tribes suggested to Gideon that he deserved a formal position of power, he declared it was impossible for the nation to be ruled by both God and a human king (Judges 8.22-3). The political association of the Israelites has been described as an amphictyony – a loose confederation united for common welfare. During Samuel's lifetime, however, the people found tribal alliance and simple trust in God's power inadequate. Politically and militarily Israel was less well organized than the Philistines (who occupied southern Canaan) and could offer no effective resistance to invading armies. After a defeat at Aphek, the leaders of the nation realized that they were powerless and decided to make certain God would be with them in battle: 'Let us bring the ark of the covenant of the Lord here from Shiloh', they declared, 'that he may come among us and save us from the power of our enemies' (1 Samuel 4.3). This plan was unsuccessful: the ark was captured, its shrine at Shiloh demolished and the Israelite army overcome.

Though the ark was later returned, this defeat crushed the people's confidence. The Israelites needed a king, but in the chapters which describe Saul's election to kingship (1 Samuel 8—12), there appear to be at least two strands of tradition. The first (1 Samuel 9.1—10.16) represents Saul as God's instrument for deliverance as evidenced by his leadership of the Israelite army against the Ammonites who had threatened Jabesh-Gilead. As a mark of his office, he was anointed by Samuel and was filled with God's power. The other strand (1 Samuel 8.10–17; 12), however, presents the people's desire for a king as a rejection of God's authority. According to this account, the king was selected by means of a sacred lot at a national assembly convened by Samuel; it is in this context that Samuel's warning against the dangers of kingship was expressed:

> And now behold the king whom you have chosen, for whom you have asked; behold, the LORD has set a king over you. If you will fear the LORD and serve him and hearken to his voice and not rebel against the commandment of the LORD, and if both you and the king who reigns over you will follow the LORD your God, it will be well; but if you will not hearken to the voice of the LORD, but rebel against the commandment of the LORD, then the hand of the LORD will be against you and your king. (1 Samuel 12.13–15)

From Saul to the two kingdoms

Samuel's forebodings about kingship proved to be correct: Saul's reign was plagued by a number of difficulties. His first problem was that he soon lost the support of Samuel. When Saul was instructed to take neither prisoners nor spoil in a campaign against the Amalekites, these instructions were not strictly followed. As a consequence, Samuel denounced the king and declared he had been rejected by God (1 Samuel 15). The second problem concerned Saul's moods of gloom and violence. After his anointing, God's spirit came upon Saul and imparted to him prophetic frenzy so that he could lead Israel to victory. For Saul such emotional activity took a toll on his mental state. To relieve him from depression, David joined his retinue so that he might bring relief through music. Yet this proved to be no solution. Saul became jealous of David's popularity and success. Saul's reign thus began with a successful military action reminiscent of the exploits of the judges, but it ended in madness and defeat.

After joining Saul's entourage, David quickly gained a reputation as a successful warrior, as is reflected in the account of his victory over the giant Goliath. Later, he married Saul's daughter Michal, buying her hand with the foreskins of a hundred slaughtered Philistines. But David's military exploits and general popularity evoked Saul's anger. On the advice of Saul's son Jonathan, David fled for safety to the cave of Adullam in the southern wilderness. When Saul, along with his son Jonathan, was killed at Mt Gilboa, David became the leader of the southern tribes; at Hebron he was anointed king of Judah. In the north, Saul's son Ishbaal was appointed king. Later however David supplanted Ishbaal and became king over the entire country.

One of David's first victories was over the Jebusites in Jerusalem, which he declared the new capital. Employing foreign craftsmen he built new fortifications and a palace. To Jerusalem he also brought the ark of the covenant, and by this act symbolically transferred power away from the tribes. Despite his glory as a conqueror and leader, Scripture bemoans David's moral failings. After he had committed adultery with Bathsheba and caused the death of her husband Uriah, the court prophet Nathan denounced David and demanded repentance. Towards the end of David's life, rivals for the throne battled against one another. Revolts led by his son Absalom and by Sheba from the tribe of Benjamin were suppressed; by the time of David's death, his son Adonijah seemed the likely successor. Although Adonijah was supported by the priest Abiathar and the army general Joab, another son, Solomon (970–930 BC) had still more powerful allies. Solomon's mother, Bathsheba, had been David's favourite wife, and was supported by the prophet Nathan, Zadok the priest, and Benaiah, another army commander. Eventually Solomon was victorious; Adonijah and his supporters were killed and Abiathar was exiled. But unlike David, Solomon was concerned more with his own security than the defence of the nation. Enormous resources were directed into a personal army consisting of 12,000 men and horses and 1,400 chariots.

In foreign affairs Solomon traded with Phoenicia, Arabia and Syria, Cilicia and probably with north and east Africa as well. By marrying an Egyptian princess he linked himself with Egypt. One of Solomon's close contacts was with Hiram, king of Tyre. The Phoenicians had extensive trading links in the Mediterranean, and through this alliance Solomon was able to develop his own trade in the Red Sea and the Indian Ocean. In all likelihood the Phoenicians also helped him build and operate his copper refineries on the Gulf of Aqaba. In addition, it appears that Solomon traded horses with the Egyptians in the south and the Hittites in the north.

As a result of this activity, Solomon was able to build a new palace for himself, another for his Egyptian wife, a hall for state occasions, a judgement chamber and, most importantly, the Temple. Originally David wanted to build a temple to house the ark of the covenant, but this became Solomon's greatest triumph. In addition to his architectural achievements, Solomon was universally recognized as a wise ruler. In the words of 1 Kings: 'Solomon's wisdom surpassed the wisdom of all the people of the east, and all the wisdom of Egypt' (1 Kings 4.30). According to tradition, he was able to recite 'three thousand proverbs; and his songs were a thousand and five. He spoke of trees, from the cedar that is in Lebanon to the hyssop that grows out of the wall; he spoke also of beasts, and of birds, and of reptiles, and of fish' (1 Kings 4.32–3).

To support Solomon's many projects, an elaborate system of taxation had been developed: each of the twelve districts of the territory was obliged to support the court for one month a year. Not surprisingly, this taxation evoked a strong reaction. The notion of a privileged élite supported by the general population conflicted with the egalitarian tribal organization. In place of twelve tribes serving God, twelve districts served the king. Moreover the fact that the Canaanites adopted a similar financial system emphasized the foreignness of this arrangement. But even such taxation was insufficient to support Solomon's projects; to meet his expenses he instituted forced labour. This provision provoked a revolt led by the northern army leader Jeroboam, but his plot was uncovered and he fled to Egypt. The northern tribes remained dissatisfied, but the southern were loyal to the house of David. Not only were David and his son southerners by birth, they also favoured the southern tribes: Judah and Benjamin seem to have been excluded from the taxation burden.

After Solomon's death, his son Rehoboam (930–908 BC) became king and sought the allegiance of the northern tribes. When he went to Shechem from Jerusalem to meet them, they outlined the terms on which they would accept the monarchy. Rehoboam refused to listen and arrogantly proclaimed, 'My father made your yoke heavy, but I will add to your yoke; my father chastised you with whips, but I will chastise you with scorpions' (1 Kings 12.14). As a consequence of Rehoboam's policies the northern tribes revolted against him and chose instead Jeroboam I as their monarch: 'When all Israel heard that Jeroboam had returned, they sent and called him to the assembly and made him king over all Israel' (1 Kings 12.20). Shechem initially served as Jeroboam's administrative centre, but he later made Tirzah his capital. No major battle appears to have taken place between the northern kingdom (Israel) and the southern kingdom (Judah), but border clashes resulted from Judah's retention of the territory of Benjamin.

As the kingdoms divided, the aggressor who threatened the nation was Shishak I, the first Pharaoh of the Twenty-Second Dynasty who invaded the land and forced Rehoboam to pay tribute. In the north the external danger was matched by an internal threat – the tribes keenly felt the loss of the Temple and desired to make pilgrimage to Jerusalem. To stem such disloyalty, Jeroboam I set up alternative shrines at old centres of Canaanite worship, Dan and Bethel. There he placed golden bulls in an attempt to reconcile the faith of Israel and features of Canaanite belief, a policy he believed to be necessary since there was a sizeable Canaanite population within this territory: the Canaanite elements would have no difficulty in associating these idols with their own god Baal (who was often represented as a bull); the Israelites could regard them as thrones for their God (like the throne in the Temple).

Jeroboam to the fall of Israel

Jeroboam I's successor was his son Nadab (910–909 BC) who was followed by Baasha (909–856 BC). Like Jeroboam I, he encouraged a mixture of Canaanite and Israelite religions or, as the biblical writers put it, he 'made Israel to sin' (1 Kings 15.34). When he died his son Elah (886 BC) attempted to succeed him, but was assassinated and Zimri (886 BC) the army commander usurped the throne. Zimri's reign lasted only seven days; he was followed by another general, Omri (885–874 BC), and his son Ahab (874–852 BC). Under the rule of these latter two kings, the position of the northern kingdom was greatly strengthened. They ended the conflict with Judah, and the alliance of the kingdoms was sealed by the marriage of Ahab's daughter, Athaliah, to Jehoram (851–843 BC), the son of Jehoshaphat, king of Judah. Israel also made peace with the powerful kingdom of Phoenicia and Ahab himself married the Phoenician princess, Jezebel. Further, Omri gained control over Moab. To consolidate his position, Omri built a new administrative centre and shrine in Samaria. Like Jeroboam, Ahab incorporated Canaanite religious features. He provided for the worship of Baal, and thereby incurred the condemnation of Scripture: he 'did evil in the sight of the LORD more than all that were before him. And as if it had been a light thing for him to walk in the sins of Jeroboam . . . went and served Baal and worshipped him' (1 Kings 16.31).

Such idolatrous practice was encouraged by Jezebel who wanted Baal to become the god of Israel. To combat this threat, the prophet Elijah was determined to prove the God of Israel was supreme. Thus he challenged 450 prophets of Baal and 400 prophets of Asherah to a contest on Mt Carmel, near Phoenician territory. This had once been the site of an altar to the Israelite God, but it had been displaced by a shrine to Baal. There he and the Canaanite prophets prepared sacrifices and prayed to their respective gods to send fire from heaven to ignite the offerings. Although the prophets of Baal and Asherah cried aloud in ecstatic frenzy and cut themselves with swords, no answer was forthcoming, but Elijah's supplication was successful: 'The fire of the LORD fell, and consumed the burnt offering, and the wood, and the stones, and the dust, and licked up the water that was in the trench. And when all the people saw it, they fell on their faces; and they said, "The LORD, he is God; the LORD, he is God"' (1 Kings 18.38–9). Despite Elijah's victory, Jezebel encouraged Ahab to follow Phoenician customs. She regarded the life and property of every subject as belonging to the king, and so had no hesitation in having the Israelite Naboth killed in order that Ahab could take possession of his property. But Elijah denounced the foreign queen, just as Nathan had previously rebuked David for similar unscrupulousness. For these early prophets, religion was bound up with life and politics, and not even the royal couple were above God's law.

Ahab was succeeded by his two sons, Ahaziah (852–850 BC)

and Joram (850–842 BC), but it was not long before those loyal to the faith of Israel rebelled. These devotees, inspired by the prophet Elisha, Elijah's successor, chose an army officer, Jehu (842–815 BC), to be the next king of Israel. During the battle between Israel and Syria, Joram was wounded and returned to recuperate in Jezreel. Jehu followed him there where he discovered Ahaziah (842 BC), king of Judah, who was paying a visit. Jehu assassinated both kings as well as Jezebel, the queen mother, and appealed to the city rulers of Samaria to pay allegiance to him. This they did by presenting him with the heads of seventy members of Ahab's family. But Jehu was less successful politically. Since he had killed the Phoenician princess Jezebel, he could no longer rely on the support of a Phoenician alliance. And by killing the king of Judah, he also lost the loyalty of the southern kingdom. In Judah Athaliah, Ahab's sister (842–824 BC) seized control and murdered all claimants to the throne except for one child, Joash (837–800 BC) who was rescued by the priest Jehoiada. Athaliah reigned for six years, but was deposed in a coup led by Jehoiada. Joash was then installed as king.

By the time Jehu's grandson Jehoash (801–786 BC) became king, Assyria had grown in power under King Shalmaneser III's grandson, Adad-Nirari III. According to Assyrian records, Israel was forced to pay tribute to Assyria along with the Edomites and Philistines. Damascus was devastated by the Syrian advance. When Scripture states, 'The LORD gave Israel a saviour, so that they escaped from the hand of the Syrians' (2 Kings 13.5), some scholars contend that this refers to Adad-Nirari. The Assyrian attack on Syria gave Jehoash the opportunity to recover Israel's lost territory; Amaziah the king of Judah (800–783 BC) similarly captured his land from the Edomites. At this stage Amaziah declared war also on the northern kingdom, but Judah was defeated and Jehoash raided Jerusalem. As a consequence, Amaziah lost favour and was assassinated, to be succeeded by his son Uzziah (783–742 BC).

Under Uzziah in Judah and Jeroboam II (786–746 BC) in Israel, the nation prospered for the next forty years. Uzziah repaired the fortifications in Jerusalem, reorganized the army, and equipped it with new weapons. He also instituted new agricultural methods and reopened parts of Solomon's copper refineries on the Gulf of Aqaba. In the northern kingdom Jeroboam II constructed new buildings and engaged in international trade. As the nation grew richer, the people became more religious – they believed their wealth was a sign of God's favour. Yet some dissenters thought that the quest for riches was incompatible with God's covenant. According to some scholars, a new edition of Israel's early history was written at this time as a reaction against such high living.

Towards the end of Jeroboam II's reign, Amos, a shepherd from Tekoa who firmly differentiated himself from the official cultic prophets, expressed his dissatisfaction; he proclaimed that Israelite society had become morally corrupt. Many Israelites had become rich, but at the expense of the poor. Israel had sinned, he declared:

> because they sell the righteous for silver,
> and the needy for a pair of shoes –
> they that trample the head of the poor
>   into the dust of the earth,
> and turn aside the way of the afflicted. (Amos 2.6–7)

Shrines like Bethel were full of worshippers, but such ritual was empty. The 'day of the LORD', Amos announced, would be a time of punishment for the nation's sinfulness:

> Woe to you who desire the day of the LORD . . .
> It is darkness and not light . . .
> I hate, I despise your feasts, and I take no delight in your
>   solemn assemblies.
> Even though you offer me your burnt offerings and cereal
>   offerings,
> I will not accept them . . .
> Therefore I will take you into exile beyond Damascus, says
>   the LORD, whose name is the God of hosts. (Amos 5.18,
>   21–2, 27)

His later contemporary, the prophet Hosea, echoed these dire predictions. Israel had gone astray and would be punished. Yet through personal tragedy – the infidelity of his wife Gomer – Hosea was able to offer words of consolation and hope. Just as his love for his wife had been rejected, so God's love for Israel had been despised. But despite the coming devastation, God would not cease to love his chosen people. Just as Hosea could not give up his wife, God could not abandon Israel: 'How can I hand you over, O Israel . . . My heart recoils within me, my compassion grows warm and tender' (Hosea 11.8).

It was not long before these prophecies of destruction were fulfilled. The Assyrian king Tiglath-Pileser III embarked on a policy of expansion during the reign of Menahem, king of Israel (746–

738 BC). Israel's government was unstable at the time anyway. Menahem's son Pekahiah (737–732 BC) held his throne for two years by paying tribute to the Assyrian king, but was overthrown by his rival Pekah. The new Israelite king formed an alliance with the king of Syria against the Assyrians. Together they attempted to persuade Jotham, king of Judah (742–735 BC) to join them; when he refused, they declared war on Judah. In face of this danger, the southern prophet Isaiah declared to Ahaz (735–715 BC), Jotham's successor, that this threat would come to naught: both Israel and Syria would collapse. But Ahaz was unconvinced. He attempted to placate the Assyrians and went to Damascus (which the Assyrians had just conquered) to pay homage to Tiglath-Pileser III. He returned with the plans for an altar to be erected in the Temple as a sign of Judah's submission.

In the northern kingdom, Pekah's position was weakened as the Assyrians pressed forward, and he was assassinated by Hoshea (732–722 BC) who surrendered to the Assyrians. When Shalmaneser V replaced Tiglath-Pileser III, Egyptian forces were powerless to help, and Shalmaneser V conquered Israel's capital, Samaria, after a siege of two years. The annals of Shalmaneser's successor Sargon II record that 27,290 Israelites were deported as a result of this conquest. This marked the end of the kingdom of Israel.

The collapse of Judah

With the collapse of the northern kingdom, Judah was under threat. To avoid a similar fate in the south, King Ahaz continued to pay tribute to Assyria to encourage the nation to worship Assyrian gods. However, the prophet Isaiah was deeply concerned about such idolatrous practices. He believed that the collapse of Israel was God's punishment for sinfulness, and he foresaw a similar fate for Judah. Echoing the words of Amos, Isaiah warned his countrymen that God was not satisfied with empty ritual:

> What to me is the multitude of your
>   sacrifices? says the LORD.
> I have had enough of burnt offerings of rams
>   and the fat of fed beasts;
> I do not delight in the blood of bulls,
>   or of lambs, or of he-goats. (Isaiah 1.11)

A contemporary of Isaiah, the prophet Micah, also criticized the people for their iniquity and foretold destruction:

Hear this, you heads of the house of Jacob
and rulers of the house of Israel,
who abhor justice and pervert all equity . . .
because of you Zion shall be ploughed as a field;
Jerusalem shall become a heap of ruins (Micah 3.9,12)

Ahab refused to listen to these words; trusting in his own political
alliances, he believed his kingdom was secure.

By the time Hezekiah (715–687 BC) succeeded Ahaz, the
Assyrian king, Sargon II, had turned his attention to problems
in other parts of the empire. This gave Egypt and Philistia an
opportunity to join ranks to throw off Assyrian domination. Seeking the help of Judah, the Philistine ambassadors tried to secure
Hezekiah's support. But the prophet Isaiah warned that such an
alliance would be of no avail. Assyria could not be stopped, and to
dramatize the inevitable devastation, Isaiah walked naked around
Jerusalem. 'So', he said, 'shall the king of Assyria lead away the
Egyptian captives, and the Ethiopian exiles, both the young and
the old, naked and barefoot, with buttocks uncovered, to the shame
of Egypt' (Isaiah 20.4). Fortunately Hezekiah heeded Isaiah's prediction. Assyria quickly conquered the Philistine and Egyptian
nations.

After the conquest Hezekiah attempted to establish his independence from Assyrian domination by reforming the religious practices of the people. As well as removing the altar to Assyrian gods
in the temple which his father Ahaz had erected, he tried to close
down local shrines in order to centralize the cult in Jerusalem.
Further, he sent a message to those who remained in the former
northern kingdom urging them to come south to worship. Hezekiah
also prepared his kingdom for the Assyrian onslaught: he created
new defences, restructured the army, established new store-cities,
and rationalized the civil service. In Jerusalem he excavated the
Siloam tunnel to ensure that the city would have a water supply if
it were besieged.

After the death of Sargon II, the kings of Babylon and Egypt
asked Hezekiah to help overthrow the Assyrians. Isaiah cautioned
against joining such an alliance, but Hezekiah took no notice.
Sargon's successor Sennacherib quickly acted to suppress this
revolt. He subdued Babylon, Phoenicia and Philistia, and then
moved against the kingdom of Judah in 701 BC. The next step in
the Assyrian campaign was the assault on Jerusalem. According
to Sennacherib's records, Hezekiah was shut up in the city like a

bird in a cage. Seeing no way of escape, he sent gold and silver as tribute to Sennacherib who was encamped at Lachish. 2 Kings contains an account of the siege of Jerusalem which ended in failure: the Assyrian army camped outside the city, but just as their victory seemed imminent the Assyrians withdrew.

Following the invasion of Judah, Sennacherib was succeeded by Esarhaddon who was a successful ruler. When he died the empire was divided between his two sons: Ashurbani-pal who reigned in Nineveh, and Shamash-Shanakin who had headquarters in Babylon. During this period Assyria was victorious against the Egyptians and became the dominant force in Mesopotamia. Under Ashurbani-pal Nineveh emerged as a cultural centre; here artists produced works of great merit and scribes collected together the literary treasures of Mesopotamian culture. In the kingdom of Judah, Hezekiah's successor Manasseh (687–642 BC) was completely under Assyrian domination. The nation's faith was neglected, and pagan ceremonies again became prevalent. Like Ahaz, Manasseh was forced to worship Assyrian gods as a sign of submission, and his son and successor Amon (642–640 BC) continued his father's policies.

Despite its prominence, Assyria came under increasing threat from the kingdom of Lydia in the north west, the Medes in the east and the Scythians in the north. This weakening of the Assyrian empire brought about a nationalistic revival in Judah. The prophet Jeremiah warned that the southern kingdom would eventually be devastated by foreign powers. The new king, Josiah (640–609 BC), believed he could restore Judah to its former glory through territorial expansion, and religious reform. Josiah banned the symbols of Assyrian domination in the former northern kingdom, destroyed the sanctuary at Bethel established by Jeroboam I and removed many local shrines and their priests. Most importantly, there was found in the Temple a forgotten book – in all likelihood the major portion of the Book of Deuteronomy – which asserted that a single God should be worshipped in a central place by a united people. In a solemn ceremony, the people pledged their allegiance to God: 'And the king stood by the pillar and made a covenant before the LORD, to walk after the LORD and to keep his commandments and his testimonies and his statutes, with all his heart and all his soul, to perform the words of this covenant that were written in this book; and all the people joined in the covenant' (2 Kings 23.3).

While these events took place in Judah, the Babylonians advanced against Assyria and captured all its main cities. Some years after Josiah's reform in 609 BC, the Assyrians made a final attempt to regain the town of Haran. Embroiling himself in this struggle, Josiah tried to halt the Egyptian army which had been summoned by the Assyrians to come to their aid. In the ensuing battle Josiah was mortally wounded, and Judah came under the domination of Egypt. Eventually, however, the Assyrian empire collapsed and the Babylonians succeeded in conquering the Egyptians at Carchemish. At this King Jehoiakim (609–598 BC) who had been put in power by the Egyptians transferred his allegiance to King Nebuchadnezzar II of Babylon. During the reign of Jehoiakim, Jeremiah continued to prophesy disaster: Jerusalem and the Temple itself, he declared, would be destroyed. His contemporary the prophet Habakkuk echoed the prediction that God would use foreign nations as instruments of his wrath. Jehoiakim was undeterred by the message; he believed he could eventually assert his independence from foreign rule.

When Babylon was defeated by Egypt several years later, Jehoiakim decided the time was ripe for rebellion. Nebuchadnezzar, however, quickly responded by invading the country and conquering Jerusalem. In this siege Jehoiakim was killed and replaced by his son Jehoiachin, who was captured. Along with other important citizens he was led into captivity, and the treasuries of the palace and Temple were plundered. A new king, Zedekiah (597–586 BC) was placed on the throne by Nebuchadnezzar in 597 BC. Jeremiah counselled the king to accept Babylonian domination, but he was persuaded to join a rebellion led by Egypt. After a siege of eighteen months, Jerusalem was conquered in 586 BC; all the main buildings were destroyed, and Zedekiah was blinded and exiled to Babylon.

two

Restoration and Destruction of the Kingdom

During the first millennium BC the Israelites watched their country emerge as a powerful state only to see it sink into spiritual and moral decay: these events undermined the vision of Israel as God's Kingdom on earth. Following the Babylonian conquest, they despaired of their fate – the Temple lay in ruins and Jerusalem was demolished. This was God's punishment that the prophets had predicted for their iniquity. Yet despite defeat and exile, the nation arose from the old kingdoms. In the centuries which followed, the Jewish people continued their religious traditions and communal life. Though they had lost their independence, their devotion to God and his law sustained them through suffering and hardship and inspired them to new heights of creativity. In Babylonia the exiles flourished, keeping their religion alive in the synagogues. These institutions were founded so that Jews could meet together for worship and study; no sacrifices were offered since that was the prerogative of the Jerusalem Temple. When in 538 BC King Cyrus of Persia permitted the Jews to return to their former home, the nation underwent a transformation. The Temple was rebuilt and religious reforms were enacted. This return to the land of their fathers led to national restoration and a renaissance of Jewish life which was to last until the first century AD when the Temple was destroyed a second time by the Romans.

Aftermath of the fall of Judah

The anguish of the people facing the tragedy of Babylonian conquest and captivity is reflected in the Book of Lamentations. Here the author bemoans the plight of Jerusalem:

> How lonely sits the city that was full of people!
> How like a widow she has become,
> She that was great among the nations . . .
> The roads to Zion mourn,
>   for none come to the appointed feasts;
> all her gates are desolate,
>   her priests groan;

her maidens have been dragged away,
    and she herself suffers bitterly. (Lamentations 1.1, 4)

In 586 BC Gedaliah, a palace official, was made governor of
Judah with his capital at Mizpah. This appointment, however,
aroused fierce opposition and Gedaliah was assassinated by Ishmael, a member of the former royal family. Fearing Babylonian
vengeance, those who supported this rebellion fled to Egypt taking
the prophet Jeremiah with them against his will. In exile these
rebels believed that the Babylonian invasion had been the fault
of prophets like Jeremiah who had discouraged the people from
worshipping foreign gods. The way to renewed prosperity, they
were convinced, consisted in a return to the religion of Baal. 'But
we will do everything that we have vowed', they declared, 'burn
incense to the queen of heaven and pour out libations to her . . .
since we left off burning incense to the queen of heaven and pouring
out libations to her, we have lacked everything and have been
consumed by the sword and by famine' (Jeremiah 44.17–18). For
Jeremiah such a view was utter blasphemy; it was just such worship that brought about the downfall of Judah. Those exiles who
settled in Babylon appear to have established a relatively prosper-
ous community, keeping their faith alive in the synagogues.
According to Scripture, the Babylonian king, Nebuchadnezzar's
successor Amel-Marduk, released Jehoiachin from prison in
Babylon and offered him a position in the Babylonian court. Yet
despite their affluence, the exiles lamented the loss of their homeland as Psalm 137 records:

By the waters of Babylon, there we sat down and wept,
When we remembered Zion . . .
How shall we sing the LORD's song in a foreign land? (Psalm
    137.1, 4)

The prophet Ezekiel, however, counselled those in Babylon not
to despair. God, he believed, would restore the fallen nation.
Though they were scattered, he would gather them up again: 'I
will rescue them from all places where they have been scattered
on a day of clouds and thick darkness. And I will bring them out
from the peoples, and gather them from the countries, and will
bring them into their own land' (Ezekiel 34.12–13). During the
decades that followed, Babylonia was ruled by a succession of weak
and inept rulers. The Bible records that this was a difficult period
for the Jewish community. The Book of Daniel, for example, relates

how Daniel and his friends were subject to harsh treatment by Belshazzar, the king of Babylon. Such persecution is found also in the Books of Judith and Tobit.

As the Babylonian empire began to disintegrate, the kingdom of Persia grew in strength. In 539 BC Cyrus, king of Persia, conquered Babylon and set about rebuilding the city. Though he himself worshipped the god Marduk, Cyrus believed that all peoples should be free to worship their own gods and live where they wished. As far as the Jews were concerned, the Book of Ezra records Cyrus' pronouncement allowing them to return to their homeland:

> Concerning the house of God at Jerusalem, let the house be rebuilt, the place where sacrifices are offered and burnt offerings are brought . . . let the gold and silver vessels of the house of God which Nebuchadnezzar took out of the temple that is in Jerusalem and brought to Babylon, be restored and brought back to the temple which is in Jerusalem . . . let the governor of the Jews and the elders of the Jews rebuild this house of God on its site. (Ezra 6.3–7)

In the latter part of the Book of Isaiah (which scholars attribute to a second Isaiah), this return is described as leading to a universal redemption for all people, in which Israel would have a special role: 'I will give you as a light to the nations, that my salvation may reach to the ends of the earth' (Isaiah 49.6).

Return and restoration

To implement their policy of repatriation, the Persians appointed Sheshbazzar as governor of Judah. Other returning exiles included Joshua the priest and Zerubbabel, the grandson of Jehoiachin, who supervised the repair and restoration of the Temple. According to the Book of Jeremiah, after Nebuchadnezzar's invasion worshippers continued to make a pilgrimage to the Temple site. These Jews offered their assistance to Zerubbabel but he refused, since he did not regard them as real Jews: they were of uncertain racial origins and their worship was suspect. These Judaean inhabitants and the people of Samaria recognized that the returning exiles were intent on forming a state in which they would have no place. Having their offer of co-operation rejected, they persuaded the Persian officials responsible for the western empire that the plans for restoration were illegal, thereby delaying work on the Temple for ten years or more. This was the start of the enmity between the

Jewish and Samaritan peoples which continued for hundreds of years.

Zerubbabel and Joshua were encouraged in their labours by the prophets Haggai and Zechariah. During the early part of the reign of the Persian king, Darius I, Haggai urged the people to make the rebuilding of the Temple a priority. Once the Temple was restored, he proclaimed, a new era in Jewish history would dawn. Zerubbabel was God's chosen ruler in this task of rebuilding: 'On the day, says the LORD of Hosts, I will take you, O Zerubbabel my servant, the son of Shealtiel . . . and make you like a signet ring; for I have chosen you' (Haggai 2.23). At the same time the prophet Zechariah encouraged the completion of the Temple. He too stressed that God was with Zerubbabel: 'Moreover the word of the LORD came to me saying, "The hands of Zerubbabel have laid the foundation of this house; his hands shall also complete it. Then you will know that the LORD of hosts has sent me to you"' (Zechariah 4.8–9).

In 515 BC the Temple was completed, but little is known about the period from 515 to 444 BC. The Book of Malachi, however, does depict a widespread disregard for Temple worship. The priests appear to have been negligent in their duties, and the faith of Israel seems to have been polluted by magical practices. In addition, social evil had become rampant; according to Malachi, God would eventually judge those who were corrupt. Malachi also complained that Jewish men were marrying women who belonged to the racially mixed population of the country. By the middle of the fifth century BC important steps were taken by Nehemiah and Ezra to reform the life of the Jewish community. At this time Nehemiah was appointed by the Persian king Artaxerxes I as governor of Judah. Previous governors had been more concerned with their own comfort than with the welfare of the people, but Nehemiah was dedicated to the well-being of all. When he arrived from Persia, he discovered that Jews had intermarried with peoples of other races and that the rich were exploiting the poor. To combat such laxity, Nehemiah asserted that the community must purify itself by concentrating Jewish life within the confines of Jerusalem, and he initiated a policy of rebuilding and fortification. Such plans were opposed by Sanballat (the governor of Samaria), Tobiah (a prominent Ammonite), and others who feared that Israelites of mixed stock would be excluded from such plans. Despite this opposition, Nehemiah prevailed and Jerusalem was restored, kindling a new sense of religious identity.

In this policy of reform and renewal, Nehemiah was joined by the priest Ezra. Like Nehemiah, Ezra was a Persian state official who had come to Judah with royal authorization to reorganize religious affairs. Accompanied by other exiles who carried with them substantial financial contributions to the Temple, Ezra was determined to bring the people back to the covenant. For the exiles, the covenantal law had taken on supreme importance, but this was not so in Judah. Traditional worship was frequently neglected. To remedy this situation, Ezra insisted on reading the law to the people, translated by the priests; this was necessary because the law was written in Hebrew but the inhabitants of the land spoke only Aramaic, the official language of the Persian empire. It is not clear exactly what this law was, but probably it was an early version of the Pentateuch as we know it today and included the priestly codes of Leviticus. When the nation heard these words, they were profoundly moved and vowed to observe the religious practices and festivals of their ancestors as recorded in Scripture. The pilgrim festivals (Pesach, Shavuot and Sukkot) in particular provided a reason for the Jews who lived outside the land of Israel to visit Jerusalem regularly and regard it as their spiritual home.

In the years following Ezra's intrusion, the inhabitants of Judah seem to have carried out his reforms, although some scholars believe the Books of Ruth and Jonah were written as propaganda against his xenophobic policies. In contrast the Books of Chronicles seem to support Jewish nationalism. They look back to the reigns of David and Solomon as a golden era and blame the subsequent disasters on the corruption of later kings, particularly on their neglect of Temple worship. These books may be seen against the reforming background of the post-exilic period. The peoples of Samaria on the other hand came to realize that they would not be allowed to worship God in Jerusalem. As a consequence they developed their own beliefs and culture, built their own temple on Mt Gerizim, and eventually established a strong national identity. In 333 BC the Persian king, Darius III Codomannus, was defeated in battle by Alexander the Great from Macedonia. After this victory Alexander progressed towards Egypt, subsequently founded the city of Alexandria on the Nile delta, and died in 323 BC of a fever. After a power struggle among his generals, both Egypt and Judah (by then called Judaea) came under the jurisdiction of the Ptolemaic dynasty which lasted from 320 BC until 198 BC. During this period the Ptolemies were generally tolerant of the Jewish population, and it was at this stage that the Septuagint, the Greek translation of the Torah, was made.

The Seleucids and the rise of Hellenism

Though Ptolemy was victorious in securing Judaea, another of Alexander's generals, Seleucus, was dissatisfied with this outcome. Throughout the third century BC his successors were involved in a series of battles to determine sovereignty over the country. In 198 BC the issue was settled when the Seleucid king, Antiochus III, defeated Scopus, the general of the Egyptian king Ptolemy V. Initially Antiochus III had a positive attitude towards the Jews – he reduced their taxes and made a donation to the Temple. In time he reversed these policies, but in 190 BC he was defeated in a battle against the Romans at Magnesia near Ephesus. In the peace treaty he was forced to hand over his territory in Asia Minor, the richest part of the empire. A year later Antiochus III was killed while robbing a temple to increase his revenue, and was succeeded by his son, Seleucus, who dispatched his chancellor Heliodorus to plunder the Jerusalem Temple.

During the reign of the Seleucids in the second century, two families engaged as rivals in the Judaean Jewish community: the Tobiads and the Oniads. When Seleucus IV was murdered in 175 BC and succeeded by Antiochus IV Epiphanes, Jason, a member of the Oniad family, bribed Antiochus IV to make him high priest in place of his brother Onias. When he was appointed to this position, Jason attempted to Hellenize Jerusalem. This involved the introduction of Greek games in which the athletes competed naked – a sight shocking to traditional sensibilities. Many Jews found these changes abhorrent, and Jason was deposed and replaced by Menelaus, a member of the Tobiad family.

While this internal conflict took place in Judaea, Antiochus IV advanced against Egypt and defeated the Egyptian king, Ptolemy VI; on his return he robbed the Jerusalem Temple. In 168 BC Antiochus IV again invaded Egypt, but this time he encountered the Romans who drove back his onslaught. In Jerusalem it was rumoured that Antiochus IV had been killed, and Jason quickly tried to remove Menelaus. Antiochus IV however acted speedily to crush this rebellion. He conquered Jerusalem and led off some of the people as slaves. In addition he banned circumcision, Sabbath observance and the reading of the Torah. He also decreed that the Temple should be dedicated to the worship of the Greek god Zeus, that pigs should be sacrificed on the altar, and that all people, including non-Jews, should be allowed to worship there. Hellenism, previously encouraged by the Seleucids, thus became official policy.

Antiochus IV underestimated Jewish resistance to his reforms; many Jews were prepared to die rather than violate their traditions. Eventually a guerrilla band led by a priest Mattathias and his five sons engaged in armed revolt. After Mattathias' death, this movement was spearheaded by his son Judas (called 'Maccabee' meaning 'hammer'). Some Jews (the Hasideans) were opposed to armed struggle and retreated to the Judaean desert where they were slaughtered by the Seleucids when they refused to fight in battle on the Sabbath. The event drew other Jews to the side of the rebels, and after a series of military engagements, the oppressive policies of the Seleucids were reversed. Jewish law was reinstituted, and the Temple was restored and rededicated on 14 December 164 BC, an event subsequently commemorated by the festival of Hanukkah. This victory enabled Judas' clan (the Hasmoneans) to establish themselves as the ruling family in Judaea.

Following his campaign against the Seleucids, Judas made a treaty with the Roman republic, but in 160 BC he fell in battle and was succeeded by his brother Jonathan. On the death of the high priest, Jonathan was appointed supreme pontiff even though he lacked hereditary qualification. He was later formally recognized as governor of Judaea. The last surviving brother, Simon, who succeeded Jonathan, asserted formal independence from the Seleucid empire. He expelled the Seleucid garrison from the Jerusalem citadel, captured the fortress of Gazara and compelled the Seleucid monarch to acquiesce. The Maccabean rebellion thus finally triumphed, and Simon took on the hereditary title of ethnarch, a designation which signified the ruler of an *ethnos* (nation). Many scholars believe that the Book of Daniel was written during this period of rebellion as a message of encouragement against the Seleucids, although it ostensibly deals with events belonging to the reign of Jehoiakim in the sixth century BC.

In 135 BC Simon was murdered in a palace intrigue, and his son John Hyrcanus I (134–104 BC) became high priest and ethnarch. During the early part of his reign, the Seleucids besieged Jerusalem and John Hyrcanus I was forced to give up some territory and join the Seleucid king in an unsuccessful campaign against the Parthians. Subsequently John Hyrcanus I conquered large areas in Transjordan and Samaria where he razed the Samaritan temple on Mt Gerizim. He also conquered Idumea and compelled the inhabitants to convert to Judaism. One of his sons, Aristobulus I (104–103 BC) completed the conquest of Galilee, and his son Alexander Jannaeus (102–76 BC) annexed nearly all the Hellenized cities of the coastal region and northern Transjordan.

Judaism under Hellenism and Roman Rule

Although all Jews professed allegiance to the Torah, the Jewish community in Judaea at this time was divided into various sects. According to the first-century AD Jewish historian, Josephus, the three most important groups were the Sadducees, the Pharisees and the Essenes. The Sadducees consisted of a small group of influential individuals including the hereditary priests who controlled Temple worship. Possibly their name derives from King David's priest Zadok. For these Jews there was no reason to interpret and expand the written Law, and they rejected any speculation about a future life. The second group consisted of the Pharisees (their name seems to derive from a Hebrew term *parush*, meaning 'separated'). Their rise appears to date from the Hasideans who broke from the Hasmonean regime in the second century because of its irreligious character. Initially they were not political activists; instead they advocated submission to God's will. Unlike the Sadducees, the Pharisees believed in the resurrection of the body and the world to come. Moreover, they were anxious to make biblical law applicable to contemporary circumstances by offering oral expositions of the text. This procedure, they believed, had been commanded by God to Moses on Mt Sinai when he received the written commandments. In contrast to the Sadducees who were involved in the Temple cult, the Pharisees centred their activities on the synagogue. It was from this sector of society that the scribes emerged as an important force in Jewish life. Although there appear to have been scribes from the time of Jeremiah (such as the prophet's secretary, Baruch), they came to form a recognizable class who copied the law and decided how its prescriptions could be put into effect. Both the Pharisees and the Sadducees were involved in the Great Sanhedrin, the central religious and legislative body of the Judaean community.

The third principal sect were the Essenes who may also have been an offshoot of the Hasideans. Their name possibly derives from the Aramaic word *hasa* (pious). According to the Essenes, the Hellenizers and worldly Sadducees were violators of God's law.

The most important characteristic which differentiates this group from the Pharisees and Sadducees concerned their lifestyle: rejecting the corruption of town life, they congregated in semi-monastic communities. Most scholars believe it was this sect who produced the Dead Sea Scrolls. This literature was the work of a devoted community based near the Dead Sea, who wrote about an ideal Teacher of Righteousness as their leader. The Essenes believed that they alone were members of the new covenant prophesied by Jeremiah. In their community rule (the Manual of Discipline) and war rule, a cataclysmic end of the world is described, to be preceded by a struggle between good and evil in which Israel would emerge victorious.

During the reign of Alexander Jannaeus a number of Pharisees revolted against his Hellenizing influence. It appears that they seized Jerusalem and the royal mint, issuing coins of their own in the name of the Council of Elders; but this rebellion failed, resulting in the loss of many lives. After the death of Alexander Jannaeus, his widow Salome Alexandra (76–67 BC) succeeded him and reversed his religious policies, treating the Pharisees with favour. On her death, her two sons John Hyrcanus II and Aristobulus II struggled for power. A chieftain from Idumea, Antipater, attempted to assist John Hyrcanus II's cause by inviting his allies the Nabateans to march on Jerusalem. But it was left to the Roman leader, Pompey, who had recently annexed Syria, to decide the matter of the Hasmonean succession. Pompey marched into Jerusalem, killed many of its inhabitants, and stepped inside the Holy of Holies in the Temple – an act of blasphemy in the eyes of the Jewish populace. Judaea became a client state of Rome, and John Hyrcanus II was appointed high priest and ethnarch of Judaea and Galilee (territory in the north). In addition he was given the right to intervene in matters relating to the Jewish communities abroad (the Jewish diaspora). After five years, however, he was deprived of his position as ethnarch, and the country was divided into five districts, each under a court of local dignitaries drawn largely from the Sadducees. Antipater was put in charge of Idumea but retained special powers in Jerusalem, such as tax-collecting.

After Pompey's death in 48 BC, John Hyrcanus II and Antipater gave assistance to Julius Caesar in his battle against Egyptian forces. As a reward Caesar enlarged John Hyrcanus II's former state and recognized Antipater as chief minister. Caesar also introduced a number of measures to safeguard the security of Jewish communities outside Judaea: they were allowed liberty of religious observance, freedom to send gifts to the Jerusalem Temple, exemption from military duty and the right to their own jurisdiction. Antipater's son Phasael was made governor of Jerusalem, and his other son Herod became governor of Galilee. When Herod successfully crushed a Galilean revolt, he was censured by the Great Sanhedrin for his brutal behaviour towards those he conquered and was forced to leave Judaea. Nevertheless, the new governor of Syria entrusted him with an important military command, as did Cassius when Caesar was assassinated. After Mark Antony and Octavian had avenged Caesar's death, they confirmed the appointments of Phasael and Herod as tetrarchs (subordinate rulers) of Judaea, despite Jewish resistance. Yet it was not long before the Parthians invaded Roman Asia Minor, Syria and Judaea. John Hyrcanus II was dethroned in favour of his nephew Antigonus; Phasael was killed; and Herod was forced to escape.

After the Parthian victory, Herod set off for Rome to meet Mark Antony, who had secured the eastern provinces from Octavian in the division of the empire. Through Mark Antony's influence the Roman government made a treaty with Herod, establishing him as king of Judaea. By this means the Romans hoped to depose Antigonus, the nominee of the Parthians. With a Roman army Herod conquered Judaea; after a five-month siege Jerusalem fell in 37 BC. Herod unified the country by incorporating Samaria, and replaced the council of elders by an advisory body similar to the privy councils of Hellenistic monarchs. Remembering that the Great Sanhedrin had previously censured him and had also supported the cause of Antigonus against his own, Herod executed forty-five of its seventy-one members, including many Sadducees who supported the Hasmonean dynasty. He did, however, spare the two leaders of the Great Sanhedrin, the Pharisees Hillel and Shammai, who through their schools continued to exert a profound influence on the direction of Pharisaic thought.

Since Herod was from an Idumean family (descendants of the Edomites who were converted to Judaism by the Hasmoneans), he was ineligible for the high priesthood and bestowed this office upon Hananel, a Babylonian Jew who claimed descent from the Zadokite house. According to Herod, Hananel's claims were better than had ever been offered by any Hasmonean ruler. Herod, however, had married a Hasmonean princess, Mariamne, and her mother Alexandra (daughter of John Hyrcanus II) complained to the Egyptian queen Cleopatra about this nomination. As a result Herod was forced to appoint Alexandra's younger son Aristobulus instead;

but he soon died, and Hananel was reinstated. When Antony and Cleopatra were defeated by Octavian's admiral Marcus Agrippa at the battle of Actium in 31 BC, Herod pledged his loyalty to Octavian (later known as Augustus). His declaration was accepted and he received back most of the territory Pompey had taken from Judaea in 63 BC as well as two Greek cities across the Jordan, Hippos and Gadara. Alexandra and her daughter, Herod's wife Mariamne, were put to death along with Costobarus (governor of Idumea) for plotting against Herod.

For the next twenty-seven years Herod acted as Augustus' agent: he initiated games in honour of the victory at Actium, constructed a Greek theatre and amphitheatre in Jerusalem, transformed Samaria into a Graeco-Samaritan city and built the port Caesarea. In addition he created citadels and palaces at such strategic sites as Jericho, Herodium near Jerusalem and Masada on the Dead Sea. The great achievement of his reign was the rebuilding of the Jerusalem Temple on a magnificent scale. All that remains of this Temple are the foundations of the Western Wall which led into the Court of the gentiles. This was open to everyone and served as a meeting place, a market centre and a platform for preachers. Inside the Court of the gentiles was another gateway through which only Jews could enter. This opened into the Court of women, and beyond this was the Court of priests where the Sadducees conducted the sacrifices witnessed by Jewish men over the age of thirteen. The most sacred place in the Temple was the Holy of Holies which was entered only by the high priest on the Day of Atonement.

In the years that followed, Herod managed to obtain two large regions of southern Syria from Augustus. He also intervened with the Romans to stop Greek cities from withholding the privileges to which Jews in the diaspora were entitled. Yet despite such successes, Herod evoked Augustus' displeasure by his executions of those he suspected of intrigue as well as by his attack on his foes, the Nabataeans. To pacify the emperor, Herod ordered that all Jews in Judaea must swear an oath of loyalty to the Roman ruler and to himself. Such a practice was common in Roman client-monarchies, but a number of Pharisees feared that it might involve worship of the emperor's statues and refused to comply. Increasingly these objectors began to indulge in messianic speculation. Previously such eschatological expectation had not been favoured in Pharisaic circles, but those Pharisees were persuaded that the period of messianic redemption was at hand. A few even succeeded in persuading Bagoas (a royal court official) that he was to be the father of the messianic king. Herod regarded such talk as high treason, and he executed Bagoas and others in 5 BC. In the following year a number of Pharisaic scholars instigated demonstrations against the erection of an eagle, a forbidden image, over the main gate of the Temple. The rioters pulled it down, and were put to death for this insurrection. After these final years of bloodthirsty upheavals, Herod himself died in 4 BC.

Rebellion against Rome

After Herod's death, Augustus divided Judaea between three of Herod's sons: Archelaus (4 BC to AD 6) as ethnarch was to rule the central region of Judaea including Samaria; Herod Antipas (4 BC to AD 31) as tetrarch was given Galilee and Peraea; Philip also as tetrarch (4 BC to AD 34) was to reign over the newly acquired lands in southern Syria. Archelaus' rule lasted only ten years; he was deposed and exiled by Augustus after he received complaints from Jews and Samaritans about his high-handedness. Judaea thereby became a small-scale Roman province administered by governors with the title of prefect (later called procurator). When the Romans instituted a census of the population, they provoked Jewish resentment since census-taking was contrary to Jewish law. Under the leadership of Judas the Galilean, a resistance movement (the Zealots) became active. At the same time there appeared a number of messianic aspirants who were regarded with suspicion by the authorities. The Sadducees, however, collaborated with the Romans who continued to appoint high priests from their ranks. Under the prefects, the Sanhedrin was resuscitated in place of Herod's advisory body and played an important role in the administration of the country.

Following his accession in AD 14, the emperor Tiberius relied more and more on the advice of Sejanus (the commander of his bodyguard). Sejanus appears to have been ill-disposed to the Jewish population since two Jews, Hasinai and Hanilai, had set up an autonomous community at Nehardea in Parthian Babylonia; Sejanus feared that such aspirations might spread to Judaea. The fourth prefect of Judaea, Pontius Pilate, experienced a number of difficulties with the Jewish community. They regarded his military standards bearing medallions of the emperor as idolatrous. Following demonstrations in Jerusalem, protesters encamped in front of Pilate's official residence at Caesarea Maritima and then in the stadium. Pilate also caused considerable consternation when he raided a Jewish religious fund to pay for an aqueduct, and again when he set up gilded shields inscribed with both his and the emperor's names in the former palace of Herod.

Under Tiberius' nephew and successor Caligula, the Jews of Alexandria became embroiled in a conflict with the Roman authorities. These Jews had put forward a claim for full citizenship rights, thereby evoking a violent reaction from the gentile Greek community. Mobs broke into synagogues and set up statues of the emperor. The Roman governor of Egypt, Aulus Avillius Flaccus, ordered thirty-eight members of the Jewish council to be flogged in the theatre while Jewish women were forced to eat pork. To calm the situation Agrippa I (the grandson of Herod, who had been appointed king after the death of Philip and the disgrace of Herod Antipas) secured the recall of Avillius Flaccus.

In AD 40 both the Greek and Jewish communities sent delegations to Rome to plead their cases before Caligula. According to an account written by the leader of the Jewish group, the Neoplatonist philosopher Philo from Alexandria, Caligula regarded the Jews' failure to recognize his divinity as lunacy. Meanwhile, at Jamnia on the coast of Judaea, the Greek community erected an altar in honour of Caligula. The Jewish community at Jamnia regarded this act as a deliberate provocation, and destroyed it. As a consequence, the emperor and his advisers decided to revive the policy of Antiochus IV Epiphanes: the Temple and all synagogues were to be transformed into shrines of the imperial cult. Orders were given to the governor of Syria, Publius Petronius, to construct a large statue of Caligula in the guise of Jupiter to be set up in Jerusalem. The governor decided he would need two legions to perform this task, but Agrippa I persuaded him not to carry out his plans on the condition that the Jews would cease trying to stop gentiles from engaging in imperial worship. A short time later Caligula was murdered, and the Jews celebrated this day as a joyful feast.

Claudius, who succeeded Caligula, immediately had to deal with renewed conflict between Jews and Greeks in Alexandria. In his surviving letter to both groups, he urged them to be tolerant of one another; specifically he urged the Jews not to behave with contempt towards the gods of other peoples. In Judaea itself Claudius abolished direct Roman rule and allowed the country the status of a self-governing client kingdom. Agrippa I was permitted to add the Roman province of Judaea to the territories he had already been given when he reigned as king.

But Agrippa I's death in AD 44 ended this period of relative tranquillity as Judaea reverted to the status of a Roman province. Under the governors that followed, various problems became apparent: tensions developed between the rich and the poor; rebels, self-styled prophets and holy men roamed the country; and insurrections occurred in many localities. The procurator Tiberius Julius Alexander had to deal with an extensive famine; Ventidius Cumanus witnessed riots, a massacre at the Temple, and conflict between Samaritans and Galileans; and Antonius Felix was confronted by bands of freedom fighters and miracle workers who preached a message of nationalism and messianic expectation.

Two decades of procurators after the death of Agrippa I marked a period of constant friction between Roman rulers and the Jewish population. Under the procurator Florus fighting took place between Greeks and Jews in Caesarea Maritima. The procurator adopted an anti-Jewish stance and allowed his troops to riot in Jerusalem and execute a number of eminent Jews. After Florus returned to Caesarea, pro-Roman Jews as well as the small Roman legion in Judaea were attacked by Jewish rebels, and sacrifices on behalf of the Roman people and the emperor were stopped. To quell this revolt, the governor of Syria marched with an army to Jerusalem. He began a siege of the Temple, but was met with resistance and retreated to the sea coast.

This success drove out the Roman military presence in Judaea and in its place a provisional government was established. To pacify the country the general Vespasian, acting under the emperor Nero's orders, assembled an army in the north in AD 67. Sepphoris in Galilee refused to join in the revolt, and the Jewish rebels were unable to stand against the Roman legions. Though the fortress of Jotapata held out for forty-seven days, it eventually fell and the Romans slaughtered most of the population. During the winter of AD 67–8 the Zealots overthrew the moderate government in Jerusalem. Those suspected of aiding the Romans were arrested or killed, and anti-Roman groups occupied the city. But in March 67 Vespasian marched against the Jewish population; he subjugated Transjordan, western Judaea, Idumea, Samaria and Jericho. The only parts of the country remaining in Jewish hands were Jerusalem and several Herodian fortresses in other parts of the country. When Nero committed suicide in June 68 the Roman military effort ceased.

During the next year Roman armies in different parts of the empire elevated three generals to the throne; in July 69 the eastern provinces proclaimed Vespasian. Before long Vespasian put his son Titus in charge of the Judaean campaign. During the next year the Roman armies besieged Jerusalem; eventually the Romans captured the city, and Titus ordered that Jerusalem be devastated except for the towers of Herod's palace. For the rest of the year he held celebrations in various cities of the Near East during which Jewish prisoners were thrown to wild animals or were forced to fight with gladiators. In 71 Titus and Vespasian held a triumphal procession in which ritual objects and rebel leaders were exhibited; the surviving Arch of Titus in Rome depicts the *menorah* and other objects that were taken from the Temple. Over the next few years the Romans captured the remaining fortresses including Masada which fell in April 74 when its defenders committed suicide rather than surrender to the Romans.

three
The Messianic Idea

When Judah was destroyed in AD 70, the Israelites were bereft of a homeland. The golden age of past glories had come to an end, and in their despair the nation longed for a kingly figure of the house of David who would bring about the ingathering of the exiles and rebuild Jerusalem. Drawing on messianic conceptions found in Scripture, they foresaw a future redemption when earthly life would be transformed and all peoples would convert to the worship of the true God. Such ideals animated rabbinic speculation about the eschatological unfolding of history. According to a number of scholars, such a process of salvation would be brought about by charity, repentance and the observance of law. Nonetheless, prior to the coming of the Messiah, the world would endure serious tribulations (the birth pangs of the Messiah). These would be followed by the appearance of Elijah, the forerunner of the Messiah. Subsequently a second messianic figure – the Messiah of Joseph – would engage in battle with Gog and Magog (the enemies of the Israelites). Although he would be slain in this war, the King–Messiah – Messiah ben David – would eventually prevail. With his coming the dispersion of Israel would cease and all exiles would return to Zion; during this period of messianic redemption, earthly life would be utterly transformed. Finally, at the end of the messianic age, all human beings would be judged and either rewarded with heavenly life or condemned to eternal punishment. This utopian vision of the future was animated by the Israelite conviction that God would not abandon his people to exile. The promise of messianic redemption and return to Israel served as a means of overcoming the nation's despondency at the loss of the Holy Land and the people's sacred institutions.

Biblical origins

After the collapse of the Second Temple the Israelites yearned for a king or leader of the house of David who would bring about an ideal political existence for the nation as well as the redemption of all people. During this period all human beings would attain an ideal world of truth and harmony – such aspirations were derived

from the earlier biblical concept of a messianic leader of the
Israelites.

The term 'Messiah' is an adaptation of the Hebrew *Ha-Mashiah*
('the Anointed'), a term frequently used in Scripture. Initially in
the Book of Samuel the view was expressed that the Lord had
chosen David and his descendants to reign over Israel to the end
of time (2 Samuel 7; 23.1, 3, 5). In addition it was held that this
figure had been granted dominion over all nations. Thus 2 Samuel
22.50–1 declares:

> For this I will extol thee, O LORD, among the nations,
>   and sing praises to thy name.
> Great triumphs he gives to his king,
>   and shows steadfast love to his anointed,
>   to David, and his descendants for ever.

In this passage David is the anointed in the sense that he was
consecrated for a divine purpose. However, it was not only
Israelites who would become God's emissaries. Second Isaiah, for
example, described Cyrus as the Lord's anointed: 'Thus says the
LORD to his anointed, to Cyrus, whose right hand I have grasped,
to subdue nations before him and ungird the loins of kings, to open
doors before him that gates may not be closed' (Isaiah 45.1). This
early biblical doctrine thus presupposed that David's position
endured throughout his lifetime and would be inherited by a series
of successors (including non-Israelites) who would carry out God's
will. With the fall of the Davidic empire after Solomon's death,
there arose the view that the house of David would eventually rule
over the two divided kingdoms as well as neighbouring peoples. In
the words of Amos:

> In that day I will raise up
>   the booth of David that is fallen
>   and repair its breaches,
>   and raise up its ruins,
>   and rebuild it as in the days of old;
> that they may possess the remnant of Edom
>   and all the nations who are called by my name. (Amos
>   9.11–12)

Again, Hosea proclaimed: 'Afterward the children of Israel shall
return and seek the LORD their God, and David their king; and
they shall come in fear to the LORD and to his goodness in the
latter days' (Hosea 3.5). Eventually Isaiah shifted the emphasis

for the perpetuity of the Davidic dynasty to the nature of the future king: the foundation of his throne would be justice, and he would be endowed with the capacity to exact judgement.

> Of the increase of his government and of peace
>   there will be no end,
> upon the throne of David, and over his kingdom,
>   to establish it, and to uphold it
> with justice and with righteousness
>   from this time forth and for evermore. (Isaiah 9.7)

Such expectations paved the way for the vision of a transformation of earthly life. During the Second Temple period, the idea of eschatological salvation became an animating force in Jewish consciousness. The Book of Tobit, for example, prophesied the rebuilding of Jerusalem, the return of the exiles, and the conversion of the nations to the God of Israel. Similar ideas were expressed in the Book of Ben Sira (Ecclesiasticus) as well as the Book of Daniel which proclaims the messianic figure of the Son of Man:

> I saw in the night visions,
> and behold, with the clouds of heaven
>   there came one like a son of man,
> and he came to the Ancient of Days
>   and was presented before him.
> And to him was given dominion
>   and glory and kingdom,
> that all peoples, nations, and languages
>   should serve him;
> his dominion is an everlasting dominion,
>   which shall not pass away,
> and his kingdom one
>   that shall not be destroyed. (Daniel 7.13–14)

During this period there was intense speculation about the nature of the Messiah. In the Book of Zechariah, for example, two messianic figures – the high priest and the messianic King – are depicted. Later in the Dead Sea sect these two figures also played an important role and were joined by a third personage, the prophet of the last days. These three messianic roles correspond to the three major functions of a future Jewish state where kingship, priesthood and prophecy will exist side by side.

Yet despite such a proliferation of messianic figures, it was the

Davidic Messiah who came to dominate Jewish thought. In the
Sibylline Oracles he is portrayed in utopian terms:

> And then from the sunrise God shall send a king who shall give
> every land relief from the bane of war; some he shall slay and
> to others he shall make faithful vows. Nor shall he do these
> things by his own counsel but in obedience to the good ordi-
> nances of the Mighty God. And again the people of the Mighty
> God shall be laden with excellent wealth, with gold and silver
> and purple adornment. The land shall bear her increase, and
> the sea shall be full of good things. (652–9)

This king–Messiah will put an end to all wars on earth; he will
make a covenant with the righteous and shall slay the wicked in
accordance with God's decree.

Again, the Psalms of Solomon extol the messianic king who will
rebuild the land and draw all nations to Zion.

> He shall gather together a holy people
> whom he shall lead in righteousness.
> And he shall judge the tribes of the people
> that has been sanctified by the LORD his God . . .
> And he shall divide them according to their tribes
> upon the land.
> And neither sojourner nor alien shall sojourn
> with them any more.
> He shall judge peoples and nations
> in the wisdom of his righteousness. Selah.
> The people of the nations shall serve him
> under his yoke:
> He shall glorify the LORD openly in all the earth;
> And he shall purge Jerusalem
> making it holy as of old,
> So that nations shall come from the ends of the earth
> to see his glory. (Ps. Solomon 17)

Such a conception served as the basis for subsequent rabbinic
reflection about messianic redemption, the ingathering of the
exiles, and salvation in the world to come.

The coming of the Messiah

As time passed the rabbis elaborated the themes found in
the Bible and Jewish literature of the Second Temple period. In
the midrashim and the Talmud they formulated an elaborate

eschatological scheme divided into various stages. According to a number of sages, messianic redemption is brought about by charity, repentance and the observance of ceremonial law. Thus R. Jose declared: 'Great is charity, in that it brings the redemption nearer, as it is said (Isaiah 56.1), "Thus saith the LORD, Keep ye justice and do charity; for my salvation is near to come, and my favour to be revealed"' (Baba Bathra 10a). Again R. Jose the Galilean declared: 'Great is repentance, because it brings near redemption, as it is said (Isaiah 59.20), "And a redeemer will come to Zion, and unto them that turn from transgression in Jacob." Why will a redeemer come to Zion? Because of those that turn from transgression in Jacob' (Yoma 86b). Given such conditions, the Messiah would come in power and glory, yet he would be preceded by numerous travails. Such sufferings were referred to in rabbinic literature as 'the birth pangs of the Messiah'. Thus the Talmud states:

> With the footprints of the Messiah, insolence will increase and death reach its height; the vine will yield its fruit but the wine will be costly. There will be none to offer reproof, and the whole empire will be converted to heresy. The meeting-place of scholars will be laid waste and Gablan be made desolate; and the people of the frontier will go about from city to city with none to take pity on them. The wisdom of the scribes will become foolish, and they that shun sin will be despised. The young will insult their elders, and the great will wait upon the insignificant. (Sanhedrin 97a).

Other passages from the school of Akiva describe the prevalence of iniquity as a prelude to the messianic age. Thus R. Nehemiah said: 'In the generation when the son of David comes, impudence will increase and esteem will be perverted; the vine will yield its fruit but the wine will be costly; and the whole empire will be converted to heresy, with none to offer rebuke' (Sanhedrin 97a). Again, R. Judah proclaimed that harlotry and foolhardiness will increase:

> In the generation when the son of David comes, the meeting-place of scholars will be given over to harlotry. Galilee will be laid waste and Gablan be made desolate; and the people of the frontier will go about from city to city with none to take pity on them. The wisdom of the scribes will become foolish, and they that shun sin will be despised. The face of this generation is as

the face of a dog, and truth is lacking, as it is written (Isaiah 59.15): 'And truth shall be lacking, and he that departeth from evil maketh himself a prey.' (Sanhedrin 97a)

According to R. Nehorai, the young will grow increasingly insolent: 'In the generation when the son of David comes, the young will insult their elders, and the elders will wait upon the young: "the daughter riseth up against her mother, the daughter-in-law against her mother-in-law"; and the face of this generation is as the face of a dog; and a son does not feel ashamed before his father' (Sanhedrin 97a).

Finally, R. Simeon ben Yohai depicted the devastation accompanying the coming of the Messiah:

> In the week when the son of David comes, in the first year this verse will be fulfilled: 'I will cause it to rain upon one city, and cause it not to rain upon another city' (Amos 4.7). In the second year the arrows of hunger will be sent forth. In the third a great famine: men, women and children will die; pious men and saints [will be few], and the Law will be forgotten by its students. In the fourth, partial plenty. In the fifth, great plenty, when men will eat, drink and be merry, and the Law will return to its students. In the sixth, voices. In the seventh, wars; and at the end of the seventh year, the son of David will come. (Sanhedrin 97a)

Despite such dire predictions, the rabbis believed that the prophet Elijah would return prior to the coming of the Messiah to resolve all earthly problems. An illustration of this belief is found in the Talmud where the Aramaic word *Teku* is used whenever a religious question cannot be resolved. Literally the word means 'let it remain undecided', but the term was interpreted as a phrase meaning: 'The Tishbite (Elijah) will resolve difficulties and problems'. In addition, Elijah's role in the messianic age would be to certify the ritual cleanliness of families that suffered from mixed marriages or forbidden unions, and grant permission to hitherto excluded peoples to marry Jews. Further, Elijah's task was to bring back to the Jewish people those who had been wrongfully excluded from the community. This is the meaning of the classic passage in the tractate *Eduyyoth* in the Talmud which describes his mission:

> R. Joshua said: I have received as a tradition from Rabban Johanan ben Zakkai, who heard from his teacher, and his teacher from his teacher, as a *halakhah* given to Moses from

Sinai, that Elijah will come not to declare unclean or clean (families in general), to remove afar or bring nigh (in general), but to remove afar those (families) that were removed afar by force. The family of Beth-Zerepha was in the land beyond Jordan, and the sons of Zion removed it afar by force. And yet another (family) was there, and the sons of Zion brought it nigh by force. The like of these Elijah will come to declare unclean or clean, to remove afar or to bring nigh. R. Judah (ben Bathyra) says: To bring nigh but not to remove afar. R. Ishmael says: To bring agreement where there is a matter for dispute. And the Sages say: Neither to remove afar nor to bring nigh, but to make peace with the world, as it is written (Malachi 3.23–4), 'Behold I will send you Elijah the prophet . . . And he shall turn the heart of the fathers to the children, and the heart of the children to their fathers.' (*Eduyyoth* 8.7)

As the forerunner of the Messiah, Elijah will announce from the top of Mt Carmel his coming: it will be the king–Messiah of Israel who will bring about the end of history and the advent of God's Kingdom on earth.

Messiah ben Joseph and Messiah ben David

In their depictions of the Messiah, the rabbis formulated the doctrine of a second Messiah, the son of Joseph, who would precede the king–Messiah, the Messiah ben David. According to legend this Messiah would engage in battle with Gog and Magog, the enemies of Israel, and be slain; only after this would the Messiah ben David arrive in his glory. As a hero, the Messiah ben Joseph will be mourned by the people. Thus the Talmud declares:

And the land shall mourn, every family apart; the family of the house of David apart, and their wives apart (Zechariah 12.12) . . . What is the cause of this mourning? R. Dosa and our teachers differ on the point. One said, The cause is the slaying of Messiah ben Joseph, and another said, The cause is the slaying of the evil inclination. It is well with him who said the cause is the slaying of Messiah ben Joseph, for that agrees with the verse (Zechariah 12.10), 'And they shall look upon him who they have pierced, and they shall mourn for him as one mourneth for his only son.' (Sukkah 52a)

In this final struggle against Israel's enemies, God himself would act on Israel's behalf. Thus in the midrash, the rabbis argue that

> There are four shinings forth: the first was in Egypt, as it is written (Psalm 80.2), 'Give ear, O Shepherd of Israel, thou that leadest Joseph like a flock, thou that art enthroned upon the cherubim, shine forth'; the second was at the time of the giving of the Law, as it is written (Deuteronomy 33.2), 'He shone forth from Mount Paran'; the third will take place in the days of Gog and Magog, as it is written (Psalm 94.1), 'Thou God to whom vengeance belongeth, shine forth'; the fourth will be in the days of the Messiah (ben David) as it is written (Psalm 50.2), 'Out of Zion, the perfection of beauty, shall God shine forth.' (Siphre, Deut. 343)

Regarding this war the rabbis speculated that God had already revealed the defeat of Gog and Magog to Moses. Thus R. Nehemiah maintained that in Numbers 11.26, Eldad and Medad prophesied concerning this battle,

> as it is written (Ezekiel 38.17), 'Thus saith the LORD God: Art thou he of whom I spoke in old time by my servants the prophets of Israel, that prophesied in those days (for many) years that I would bring thee against them?' and so on. Read not *shanim* (years) but *shnayim* (two). And which two prophets prophesied the same thing at the same time? Eldad and Medad, of course. (Sanhedrin 17a)

According to Simeon ben Yohai, the war with Gog and Magog was one of the worst misfortunes to beset humanity:

> Viciousness in a man's own household is worse than the war with Gog and Magog, for it is said (Psalm 3.1), 'A Psalm of David, when he fled from Absalom his son', and next it is written (Psalm 3.2), 'LORD how many are mine adversaries become! Many are they that rise up against me.' Now in regard to the war with Gog and Magog it is written (Psalm 2.1), 'Why are the nations in an uproar? And why do the peoples mutter in vain?', but it is not written, 'How many are mine adversaries become!' (Berakoth 7b)

Yet after Israel is delivered from this terrible struggle, the king–Messiah will come to bring about the actual messianic Kingdom.

During the early rabbinic period numerous legends emerged about the names and personality of this glorious figure. In their speculations about the nature of the Messiah ben David, a number of scholars applied various titles to him. R. Jose the Galilean for example stated: 'The Messiah's name is called Peace, for it is written (Isaiah 9.6), "Everlasting Father, Prince (called) Peace"' (Klausner, p. 462). Another name of the Messiah was *Hadrach*, as Rabbi Judah explained, 'In the land of Hadrach and in Damascus shall be his resting place, for the LORD's is the eye of man and all the tribes of Israel (Zechariah 9.11). This (the name *Hadrach*) is the Messiah, who will be *Had* ("sharp") toward the nations of the world, but *Rach* ("soft") toward Israel' (Siphre, Deut. 1). Again in the Talmud the Messiah is depicted as having several titles: 'The School of Shila said: His name is Shiloh . . . The School of R. Yannai said: His name is Yinnon . . . The School of R. Haninah maintained: His name is Haninah' (Sanhedrin 98b). In such cases these schools chose a name resembling their name or particular head. Other names had symbolic significance; thus for instance the Messiah is called the 'Comforter' on the basis of Lamentations 1.16: 'Because the comforter is far from me, even he that should refresh my soul' (Sanhedrin 98b).

Turning to the nature of the Messiah ben David, the early sages focused on his exalted and moral character. According to one Baraitha, he already existed in paradise: 'Nine persons entered into paradise during their lifetime: Enoch son of Jared, Elijah, the Messiah, Eliezer the servant of Abraham, Hiram king of Tyre, Ebedmelech the Ethiopian, Jabez son of R. Judah the patriarch, Bithiah daughter of Pharaoh, and Serah daughter of Asher' (Derekh Erets Zuta, end of ch. 1). Of his characteristics R. Tanhum emphasized his spiritual integrity:

> Bar Kappara expounded in Sepphoris: Why is it written (Ruth 3.17) 'These six of barley gave he to me'? . . . He (Boaz) symbolically intimated to her (Ruth) that six sons were destined to come forth from her, who should each be blessed with six blessings: David, Messiah, Daniel, Hananiah, Mishael, and Azariah . . . (Concerning the Messiah) it is written (Isaiah 11.2): 'And the spirit of the LORD shall rest upon him, the spirit of wisdom and understanding, the spirit of counsel and might, the spirit of knowledge and the fear of the LORD.' (Sanhedrin 93ab)

With the coming of the Messiah ben David, the dispersion of Israel will cease; all exiles will return from the four corners of the earth to the Holy Land. Thus Simeon ben Yohai declared:

Come and see how beloved is Israel before the Holy One, blessed is he; for wherever they went into exile the Shekinah (God's presence) was with them. They went into exile in Egypt, and the Shekinah was with them, as it is written (1 Samuel 2.27), 'Did I indeed reveal myself unto the house of thy father when they were in Egypt?' They went into exile in Babylonia, and the Shekinah was with them, as it is written (Isaiah 43.14), 'For your sake I was sent to Babylonia.' Likewise, when they shall be redeemed in the future, the Shekinah will be with them, as it is written (Deuteronomy 30.3), 'Then the LORD thy God will return with thy captivity.' It does not say 'will bring back thy captivity' but 'will return with thy captivity' – teaching that the Holy One, blessed is he, returns with them from the places of exile. (Megillah 29a)

Here God is described as accompanying his chosen people in exile, sharing their sufferings. Yet with the messianic redemption, the exiles will return to Zion in triumph with God at their head. Clouds of glory shall be spread over them, and they will come singing with joy on their lips.

The messianic age and heaven

In rabbinic literature there was frequent speculation regarding the Days of the Messiah (also referred to as 'The World to Come'). Thus one Baraitha discusses how the land will be divided:

And the division in the world to come will not be like the division in this world. In this world, should a man possess a cornfield he does not possess an orchard; should he possess an orchard he does not possess a cornfield. But in the world to come, there will be no single individual who will not possess land in mountain, lowland and valley; for it is said (Ezekiel 48.31), 'the gate of Reuben, one; the gate of Judah, one; the gate of Levi, one' (that is, all the tribes will have equal possessions). (Baba Bathra 122a)

In their descriptions of the messianic age, the rabbis stressed that the Days of the Messiah will be totally unlike the present world. Regarding the fruitfulness of the harvest, for example, they maintained that this era 'is not like this world. In this world there is the trouble of harvesting and treading (grapes); but in the world to come a man will bring one grape on a wagon or in a ship, put it in the corner of his house, and use its contents as if it had been a large wine cask . . . There will be no grape that will not contain thirty kegs of wine' (Klausner, p. 410).

Speculating on the length of this epoch, the rabbis differed as to its duration. Rabbi Eliezer, for example, said: 'The Days of the Messiah will be forty years; for it is written in one place (Deuteronomy 8.3), "And he afflicted thee, and suffered thee to hunger, and fed thee with manna"; and in another place it is written (Psalm 90.15), "Make us glad according to the days wherein thou hast afflicted us according to the years wherein we have seen evil."' R. Dosa said: 'Four hundred years; for it is written in one place (Genesis 15.13), "And they shall serve them, and they shall afflict them four hundred years"; and in another place it is written (Psalm 90.15), "Make us glad according to the days wherein thou hast afflicted us."' R. Jose the Galilean said: 'Three hundred and sixty-five years, according to the number of days in the solar year, as it is written (Isaiah 63.4), "For the day of vengeance was in my heart, and my year of redemption has come"' (Sanhedrin 99a).

According to another Baraitha: 'It was taught in the school of Elijah: The world will endure six thousand years: two thousand in chaos, two thousand under the Law, and two thousand during the messianic age; but because of our many iniquities time has been lost from the last period (that is, four thousand years have already passed, yet the Messiah has not yet arrived)' (Sanhedrin 97ab). Again, another passage relates:

Rab Hanan bar Tahlifa sent this word to Rab Joseph: I met a man who had a scroll written in the Assyrian character and in the holy language. I said to him, 'Where did you get this?' He said to me, 'I hired myself as a mercenary in the Persian (Roman) army, and I found it among the secret archives of Persia (Rome).' In it is written: 'Four thousand two hundred and ninety-one years after its creation, the world will be orphaned. As to the years which follow, some of them will witness the wars of the dragons, some the wars of Gog and Magog, and the rest will be the messianic age, and the Holy One, blessed be he, will not renew his world until after seven thousand years.' (Sanhedrin 97b)

Other traditions however assert that such reckoning is fruitless. Thus the Talmud records: 'Seven things are hidden from men. These are the day of death, the day of consolation, the depth of judgement, no man knows what is in the mind of his friend; no man knows which of his business ventures will be profitable, or when the kingdom of the house of David will be restored or when the sinful kingdom will fall' (Pesahim 54b).

Despite such disagreements about the length of this period, there was a general acceptance among the sages that at the end of the Days of the Messiah, all would be changed. At the close of this era, a final judgement would come upon all humankind. Those who are judged righteous will enter into heaven (Gan Eden) which is portrayed in various ways in rabbinic literature. One of the earliest descriptions portrays its nature:

> The Gan Eden at the east measures 800,000 years (at ten miles per day or 3650 miles per year). There are five chambers for various classes of the righteous. The first is built of cedar, with a ceiling of transparent crystal. This is the habitation of non-Jews who become true and devoted converts to Judaism. They are headed by Obadiah the prophet and Onkelos the proselyte, who teach them the Law. The second is built of cedar, with a ceiling of fine silver. This is the habitation of the penitents, headed by Manasseh, king of Israel, who teaches them the Law.

> The third chamber is built of silver and gold, ornamented with pearls. It is very spacious, and contains the best of heaven and of earth, with spices, fragrance, and sweet odours. In the centre of this chamber stands the Tree of Life, 500 years high. Under its shadow rest Abraham, Isaac, and Jacob, the tribes, those of the Egyptian exodus, and those who died in the wilderness, headed by Moses and Aaron. There are also David and Solomon, crowned, and Chileab, as if living, attending on his father, David. Every generation of Israel is represented except that of Absalom and his confederates. Moses teaches them the Law, and Aaron gives instruction to the priests.

> The Tree of Life is like a ladder on which the souls of the righteous may ascend and descend. In a conclave above are seated the Patriarchs, the Ten Martyrs, and those who sacrificed their lives for the cause of his sacred Name. These souls descend daily to the Gan Eden to join their families and tribes, where they lounge on soft cathedras studded with jewels. Everyone, according to his excellence, is received in audience to praise and thank the ever-living God; and all enjoy the brilliant light of the Shekinah. The flaming sword, changing from intense heat to icy cold, and from ice to glowing coals, guards the entrance against living

mortals. The size of the sword is ten years. The souls on entering paradise are bathed in the 248 rivulets of balsam and attar.

The fourth chamber is made of olive-wood and is inhabited by those who have suffered for the sake of their religion. Olives typify bitterness in taste and brilliancy in light (olive oil), symbolizing persecution and its reward. The fifth chamber is built of precious stones, gold and silver, surrounded by myrrh and aloes. In front of the chamber runs the river Gihon, on whose banks are planted shrubs affording perfume and aromatic incense. There are couches of gold and silver and fine drapery. This chamber is inhabited by the Messiah of David, Elijah, and the Messiah of Ephraim (Joseph). In the centre are a canopy made of the cedars of Lebanon, in the style of the tabernacle, with posts and vessels of silver; and a settee of Lebanon wood with pillars of silver and a seat of gold, the covering thereof of purple. (Cohn-Sherbok 1991, pp. 22–3)

Punishment for the wicked

As with heaven, we also find extensive and detailed descriptions of hell in Jewish literature. In the Talmud R. Joshua b. Levi deduces the divisions of hell from biblical quotations: *she'ol, abaddon, be'er shahat, bor sha'on, tit ha-yawen, zel mawet* and *erez ha-tahtit.* This Talmudic concept of the sevenfold structure of hell is greatly elaborated in midrashic literature. According to one source it requires 300 years to traverse the height or width or the depth of each division, and it would take 6300 years to go over a tract of land equal in extent to the seven divisions. Each of these seven divisions of hell is in turn divided into seven subdivisions and in each compartment there are seven rivers of fire, and seven of hail. The width of each is 1000 ells, its depth 1000, and its length 300; they flow from each other and are supervised by the angels of destruction. Besides, in each compartment there are 7000 caves, and in each cave there are 7000 crevices, and in every crevice there are 7000 scorpions. Every scorpion has 300 rings, and in every ring 7000 pouches of venom from which flow seven rivers of deadly poison. If a man handles it, he immediately bursts, every limb is torn from his body, his bowels are cleft, and he falls upon his face.

Confinement to hell is the result of disobeying God's Torah as is illustrated by the midrash concerning the evening visit of the soul to hell before it is implanted in an individual. There it sees the angels of destruction smiting with fiery scourges; the sinners all the while are crying out, but no mercy is shown to them. The angel guides the soul and then asks: 'Do you know who these are?' Unable to respond, the soul listens as the angel continues: 'Those who are consumed with fire were created like you. When they were put into the world, they did not observe God's Torah and his commandments. Therefore they have come to this disgrace which you see them suffer. Know your destiny is also to depart from the world. Be just, therefore, and not wicked, that you may gain the future world.'

The soul was not alone in being able to see hell; a number of biblical personages entered into its midst. Moses, for example, was guided through hell by an angel, and his journey there gives us the most complete picture of its torments:

> When Moses and the angel of hell entered hell together, they saw men being tortured by the angels of destruction. Some sinners were suspended by their hair and their breasts by chains of fire. Such punishments were inflicted on the basis of the sins that were committed: those who hung by their eyes had looked lustfully upon their neighbours' wives and possessions; those who hung by their ears had listened to empty and vain speech and did not listen to the Torah; those who hung by their tongues had spoken foolishly and slanderously; those who hung by their hands had robbed and murdered their neighbours. The women who hung by their hair and breasts had uncovered them in the presence of young men in order to seduce them. (Cohn-Sherbok 1991, p. 24)

In another place, called Alukah, Moses saw sinners suspended by their feet with their heads downward, and their bodies covered with long black worms. These sinners were punished in this way because they swore falsely, profaned the Sabbath and the holy days, despised the sages, called their neighbours by unseemly nicknames, wronged the orphan and the widow, and bore false witness.

In another section Moses saw sinners prone on their faces with 2000 scorpions lashing, stinging, and tormenting them. Each of these scorpions had 70,000 heads, each head 70,000 mouths, each mouth 70,000 stings, and each 70,000 pouches of poison and venom. So great was the pain they inflicted that the eyes of the sinners melted in their sockets. These sinners were punished in this way because they had robbed other Jews, were arrogant in the community, put their neighbours to shame in public, delivered their fellow Jews into the hands of the gentiles, denied the Torah, and maintained that God is not the creator of the world.

In another place, called Tit ha-Yawen, sinners stood in mud up to their navels while angels of destruction lashed them with fiery chains, and broke their teeth with fiery stones. These sinners were punished in this way because they had eaten forbidden food, lent their money at usury, had written the name of God on amulets of gentiles, used false weights, stolen money from fellow Jews, eaten on the Day of Atonement, and drunk blood. Finally, after seeing these tortures, Moses observed how sinners were burnt in the section of hell called Abaddon. There one half of their bodies was immersed in fire and the other half in snow while worms bred in their own flesh crawled over them and the angels of destruction beat them incessantly. By stealth these sinners took snow and put it in their armpits to relieve the pain inflicted by the scorching fire. These sinners were punished because they had committed incest, murder, idolatry, called themselves gods, and cursed their parents and teachers.

This eschatological scheme, which was formulated over the centuries by innumerable rabbis, should not be seen as a flight of fancy. Rather it was a serious attempt to explain God's ways. Israel was God's chosen people. The nation had been driven from their homeland, but the Messiah would come to deliver them from exile and redeem the world. The period of messianic redemption would unfold in numerous stages, culminating in a final judgement with reward for the righteous and punishment for the wicked; in this way the vindication of the righteous was assured in the hereafter.

four

Early Messianic Expectations

The destruction of the Temple and the city of Jerusalem in the first century AD intensified Jewish longing for the coming of the Messiah who would bring about the restoration of the kingdom. In this milieu, a Jewish sect emerged during the years following Herod's death, which believed that Jesus, a carpenter from Galilee, would usher in the era of messianic redemption. Attracting adherents from among the most marginalized sectors of Jewish society, Jesus soon aroused hostility and was put to death during the reign of Pontius Pilate. Nonetheless, his disciples believed he had risen from the dead and would return to reign in glory. Although mainstream Judaism rejected such claims, the Jewish community continued to long for divine deliverance, and in 132 a messianic revolt was led by Simon bar Kochba. This rebellion was inspired by the conviction that God would empower the Jews to throw off Roman oppression. When this rebellion was crushed, Jews put forward the year of messianic deliverance until the fifth century. In about 448 a messianic figure named Moses appeared in Crete, declaring he would lead the Jews across the sea to Judaea. After his plan failed, Jews continued to engage in messianic speculation and their reflections are recorded in a number of midrashic works of the next few centuries. In the ninth century the scholar Saadia Gaon calculated the date of final redemption on the basis of biblical texts. During these centuries of heightened messianic awareness, a number of pseudo-Messiahs (Abu Isa al-Ispahani, Serene, and Yudghan) appeared on the scene, and the traveller Eldad Ha-Dani brought reports of the ten lost tribes which further stimulated Jewish longing for a return to Zion.

Jesus the Christ

From the Gospels of the New Testament as well as information from Jewish Greek and Roman sources, it appears that a Jewish sect of Christians emerged during the years of unrest following Herod's death in 4 BC. In consonance with messianic expectations of this period, these believers expected Jesus as the Messiah to bring about the fulfilment of human history. According to the

Christian Scriptures, Jesus of Nazareth spent most of his life in Galilee where he acted as a healer, exorcist and itinerant preacher who proclaimed the imminent arrival of the Kingdom of God. After a brief association with John the Baptist (whom Jesus hailed as Elijah who was to announce the advent of the messianic age), he attracted disciples from among the most marginalized sectors of society but soon aroused suspicion and hostility. In about AD 30 he was put to death during the reign of Pontius Pilate. Afterwards his followers believed he had risen from the dead, appeared to them, and promised to return to usher in the period of messianic rule.

There has been considerable debate about Jesus' relationships with the Sadducees, Pharisees, Essenes, scribes, priests and Roman officials. It is unclear, for example, if Jesus intended to violate Jewish law, whether the titles he used (such as 'Son of God' and 'Son of man') simply reflect his own messianic consciousness or point to an acknowledgement of his divine nature. None the less, there is no doubt that Jesus inspired a considerable number of Jewish followers. According to the Acts of the Apostles, Jews who accepted Jesus as their Saviour in the 30s and 40s continued to pray at the Temple, observed Jewish laws, and considered themselves members of the Jewish people.

In the spreading of the gospel, Paul, a diaspora Jew from Tarsus in Asia Minor, played a pivotal role. His letters to scattered Christian communities provide first-hand evidence of the growth of this new religion. In his Epistle to the Galatians, Paul describes himself as a Pharisee who had persecuted Christians until he had a revelation from God in which he was transformed into an apostle:

> For you have heard of my former life in Judaism, how I persecuted the church of God violently and tried to destroy it; and I advanced in Judaism beyond many of my own age among my people, so extremely zealous was I for the traditions of my fathers. But when he who had set me apart before I was born, and had called me through his grace, was pleased to reveal his Son to me, in order that I might preach him among the Gentiles ... (Galatians 1.13–16)

Subsequently Paul travelled around Asia Minor and Greece as a Christian missionary.

It is likely that Paul's thought is largely a fusion of elements of Pharisaic and Hellenistic Judaism. According to Paul, the new era was at hand, but he distinguished between the period before the coming of Christ and the time afterwards in terms of two states of being. The first, fleshly, state is the realm of death, bondage and the rule of sin; the second, the spiritual state, is a condition of eternal life, freedom and the right relationship to God. The crucifixion and resurrection represent the inbreaking of the *eschaton*, and even though the day of final judgement has not yet arrived, those who accept Christ are redeemed from the burden of evil, death and sin. Jesus was sent to conquer death, and as God's Son, he humbled himself so that all could come to the Father. Central to this theology is the distinction between 'works' and 'faith'. Faith, Paul believed, is a gift – a sign of divine grace. Salvation cannot be earned by observing the Law but 'he who through faith is righteous shall live' (Galatians 3.11).

In his epistles, Paul differentiates the new life in Christ from licentiousness as well as from the belief that all things are permitted to those who believe. On the basis of this belief, Paul stressed the importance of love: just as God's act in Christ was motivated by love, so love is the supreme spiritual gift. A second theme in Paul's letters is his rejection of the demands of the Mosaic Law: it is unnecessary, he argued, for Christians to be circumcised and to follow Jewish food regulations. Underlying these attitudes was Paul's conception of an apocalyptic history of salvation. Through Adam's transgression, sin and death entered the world. Abraham's trust in God illustrates that faith is more important than law. Mosaic legislation was binding only for a limited period; it cannot by itself bestow justification. The more one attempts to observe legal prescriptions, the greater one is conscious of sin. Thus God made Christ available to overcome humanity's evil propensity. In this context, Paul interprets Abraham's two sons, Ishmael and Isaac, allegorically: Ishmael symbolizes the old covenant; Isaac represents the new dispensation. Now that Christ has come, it is not simply the Jews who are Israel; instead all those whom God has called through Christ are the true Israel.

The next stage in the development of Christianity took place in the decades following Paul's death. As time passed traditions about Jesus circulated and eventually formed the basis of the Synoptic Gospels and Acts which were written down during approximately the last quarter of the first century A D. Each Gospel was composed with different religious intentions and concerns. Mark appears to be the earliest of the Gospels and portrays Jesus as a divinely appointed figure whose task was to bring about God's Kingdom on earth. In the Gospel of Matthew Jesus is presented as a lawgiver instructing the people in the principles of moral living. The Gospel of Luke and the Acts of the Apostles depict Jesus as the fulfilment of the Old Testament and portray the subsequent transference of the Church to the gentiles of the Graeco-Roman world. In the Gospel of John, Jesus is described as the divine Logos who is 'the way, the truth, and the life'. Not surprisingly the message of the New Testament was firmly rejected by mainstream Judaism. Rejecting the Christian claim that Jesus is the Messiah who has come to redeem the world, the Jewish community responded to the challenge of Christianity by anathematizing its followers.

The Mishnaic and Talmudic Period

Despite the devastating victory of the Romans in the first century, Jewish revolts continued into the second century. When the emperor Trajan invaded the east up to the Persian coast, uprisings among Babylonian Jews took place. Moreover, riots occurred in many parts of the Roman diaspora; according to the fourth-century writer Eusebius, Jews were massacred in these rebellions:

> In Alexandria and the rest of the east, and in Cyrene as well ... [the Jews] rushed into a faction fight against their Greek fellow citizens ... against them the emperor sent Marcius Turbo with land and sea forces, including a contingent of cavalry. He pursued the war against them relentlessly in a long series of battles, destroying many thousands of Jews. (Cohn-Sherbok 1988, p. 57)

Between 114 and 117 Jewish centres in Alexandria, Cyrenaica, Egypt and Cyprus were decimated. After Trajan's death his successor Hadrian abandoned the effort to extend the empire eastwards, leaving the Jewish diaspora in Babylonia free from Roman domination.

During this period messianic speculation became a dominant feature of Jewish life: the rabbis of the latter half of the first and those of the early half of the second century believed that the Israelite nation would be redeemed from the yoke of Roman oppression and that the people would be restored to political independence. Thus the scholars of the time immediately after the destruction of the second Temple discussed the day and month of the Messiah's coming. Rabbi Joshua for example declared: 'In Nisan (the 14th day) were they (the children of Israel) redeemed, in Nisan will they again be redeemed.' This view was based on

Exodus 12.42: 'It was a night of watching by the LORD, to bring them out of the land of Egypt; so this same night is a night of watching kept to the LORD by all the people of Israel throughout their generations.' Rabbi Eliezer however maintained that the redemption would take place in Tishri (New Year's day) on the basis of a combination of Psalm 81.4–5 ('For it is a statute for Israel, an ordinance of the God of Jacob. He made it a decree in Joseph, when he went out over the land of Egypt') and Isaiah 27.13 ('And in that day a great trumpet will be blown, and those who were lost in the land of Assyria and those who were driven out to the land of Egypt will come and worship the LORD on the holy mountain at Jerusalem') (Rosh Hashanah 11b).

Other sages were preoccupied with the period of messianic travail prior to the coming of the Messiah. Thus Rabbi Eliezer ben Hyrcanus argued that this era would last forty years. According to one Baraitha such a conviction was based on Psalm 95.10, 'For forty years I loathed that generation'. According to another Baraitha, it was based on a combination of Deuteronomy 8.3 ('And he humbled you and let you hunger and fed you with manna' forty years in the wilderness), and Psalm 90.15 (Sanhedrin 99a). Other scholars held different views about the duration of this period: Jose the Galilean, sixty years, and Rabbi Eleazar ben Azariah, seventy years. Yet despite such disagreement, Jews who lived during the first and the early half of the second centuries believed they were living at the close of the fifth millennium, the last epoch before the thousand years of peace which would be ushered in by the Messiah.

In such a milieu a messianic revolt was led in 132 by Simon Bar Kochba (also called Bar Kosiba) which was aided by Rabbi Akiva and other scholars from Jamnia and touched off by Hadrian's programme of Hellenization. This Jewish revolt was inspired by the conviction that God would empower the Jews to regain control of their country and rebuild the Temple. Although the rebels fought a valiant battle against their oppressors, the Romans crushed the uprising. Hundreds of thousands of Jews were killed, and Judaea was almost completely devastated. In 135 the rebellion came to an end with the fall of Bethar, south-west of Jerusalem. According to tradition, this event occurred on the 9th of Av, the same day as the destruction of the first and second Temples. During the course of the campaign Bar Kochba was killed in battle, and Rabbi Akiva was eventually flayed alive.

Following the collapse of this revolt, the date of the coming of the Messiah was put forward; it was estimated it would occur

400 years after the destruction of Judah; this figure was naturally assumed since it corresponded with the period of the Egyptian exile. Hence R. Dosa maintained that the Messiah would come in the fifth century; this calculation was based on a comparison of Psalm 90.15 with Genesis 15.13 ('Then the LORD said to Abraham, "Know of a surety that your descendants will be sojourners in a land that is not theirs, and will be slaves there, and they will be oppressed for four hundred years"') (Sanhedrin 99a). A similar view was expressed by Judah ha-Nasi who argued that the coming of the Messiah would occur 365 years after the destruction of Jerusalem – this number corresponds to the days of the solar year and is based on Isaiah 63.4, 'For the day of vengeance was in my heart, and my year of redemption has come' (that is, one year for every day in the solar year) (Sanhedrin 99a). Similarly, Rabbi Hanina believed the Messiah would arrive 400 years after the fall of Jerusalem. 'If 400 years after the destruction a man says to you "Buy my field, which is worth one thousand dinars, for one dinar", do not buy it,' he declared (Ab. Zar. 9b).

In connection with this messianic date, there is a legend about a mysterious scroll found in the archives of Rome. Concerning this discovery Rabbi Hanan ben Tahilpa sent word to Rabbi Joseph:

I happened upon a man who had in his possession a scroll written both in Assyrian and Hebrew script. I asked him where he got it, and he told me that he had hired himself out as a servant in the Roman army, and that he had found this scroll in the archives of Rome. In it is written: 4291 years after creation the present order of the world will come to an end. The Wars of the Serpents will then take place, and the Wars of Gog and Magog, following which the messianic age will set in. (Sanhedrin 97b)

A similar calculation was allegedly revealed to Rabbi Judah by Elijah: 'The world will endure no less than 85 jubilees (4250 years), and in the last jubilee the son of David will come' (Sanhedrin 97b).

As the fifth century approached, messianic expectations were heightened. With the collapse of the Roman empire, the Jewish nation believed it was living in the final days before the advent of the messianic age. In this milieu a pseudo-Messiah appeared in about 448 among the Jews in Crete. According to tradition he declared that his name was Moses and promised the Jews on the island that he would bring them to Judaea without ships. He fixed a date for this march to take place, and ordered them to jump into the sea. In consequence a number drowned. This tragedy, as well as the failure of the Messiah to appear as predicted, produced a lessening of messianic expectations, yet the hope of messianic redemption continued to remain a central feature of rabbinic speculation in the centuries that followed.

Midrashic apocalypses

During the sixth and seventh centuries the rabbis continued to engage in messianic speculation, producing a number of works such as *The Signs of the Messiah*, and the *Agada of the Messiah*. Such literature may have been precipitated by the crises in Babylon during the reign of Kavadh which led to the revolt of the exilarch Mar Zuta II at the beginning of the sixth century. Alternatively they may have emerged when the Persians conquered Syria and Palestine a century later. In any event the return of the Byzantines under Heraclius in 629 brought about Jewish persecution which lasted until the rise of Islam. The victories of the Arabs and the collapse of the Persian and Byzantine empires fuelled the flames of messianic expectation: as the followers of Muhammad embarked on their campaigns, the Jewish community expressed their hopes for redemption in a variety of writings.

The first among these works was the *Pirke de Rabbi Eliezer*, a pseudepigraphon of Palestinian origin which was edited in the eighth century. In Chapter 28 the author explains that in Abraham's vision of the 'covenant between the pieces' in Genesis 15, God disclosed the events that would befall his descendants. On the basis of Genesis 15.9 ('Bring me a heifer three years old, a she-goat three years old, a ram three years old, a turtledove, and a young pigeon'), four empires would rule over the Jewish nation: the heifer was identified with Rome; the she-goat with Greece; the ram with Persia; the ox with Ishmael (the Arabs), and the pigeon with Israel. According to another view five empires would rule over the Israelites, based on Genesis 15.12: 'And as the sun was going down, a deep sleep fell upon Abram, and lo, a dread (Rome), and great (Persia) darkness (Greece) fell (Babylon) upon him (Ishmael).' The implication is that the Messiah will appear after the emergence of Islam.

The text also specifies the date of the advent of the Messiah. Thus Rabbi Joshua declared:

Abraham took his sword and divided them, each one into two parts, as it is said, 'And he took him all these and he divided them in the midst' [Genesis 15.10]. Were it not for the fact that he divided them, the world would not have been able to exist, but because he divided them he weakened their strength, and he brought each part against its corresponding part, as it is said, 'And he laid each half over against the other.' [Here Joshua is referring to the division of the Roman empire which occurred after the death of Theodosius in 395; thus the Western empire came to an end in 476.] And the young pigeon, he left alive, as it is said, 'But the bird he divided not', hence thou mayest learn that there was not any other bird there except a young pigeon (Israel). The bird of prey came down upon them to scatter them and to destroy them. The bird of prey is naught else but David, the son of Jesse, who is compared to a speckled bird of prey, as it is said, 'Is mine heritage unto me as a speckled bird of prey?' [Jeremiah 12.9]. When the sun was about to rise in the east, Abraham sat down and waved his scarf over them, so that the bird of prey could not prevail over them until the raven came.

In this passage the writer explains why the Messiah did not emerge in the fifth century as expected; instead he will tarry until after the conquests of the Arabs (Mid. R. Ber. 50.5).

Rabbi Eleazar ben Azariah commenting on this passage explained that, 'from this incident thou mayest learn that the rule of the four kingdoms (Persia, Greece, Rome and Arab) will last only one day according to the day of the Holy One, blessed be he' (one day = 1000 years). Assuming that according to Jewish chronology the rebuilding of the Temple took place in 352, the end of the last kingdom would be *c*. 648. A differing view was expressed by Rabbi Eleazar ben Arak who stated:

Verily, it is so according to thy word, as it is said, 'He hath made me desolate and faint all the day', except for two thirds of an hour (of God). Know that it is so. Come and see, for when the sun turns to set in the west, during two thirds of an hour its power is weakened, and it has no light; likewise, whilst the evening is not yet come, the light of Israel shall arise, as it is said, 'And it shall come to pass that at evening time there shall be light' [Zechariah 14.7].

Since two thirds of God's hour would be about 28 years, the deliverance of Israel would take place in 620 (rather than 648).

Another prediction was put forward in Chapter 30 by Rabbi Ishmael:

> In the future the children of Ishmael will do fifteen things in the land (of Israel), in the latter days, and they are . . . and they will build a building in the Holy Place; and two brothers will arise over them, princes at the end; and in their days the branch of the son of David will arise, as it is said, 'And in the days of those kings shall the God of heaven set up a kingdom which will never be destroyed.'

The building referred to here is the Mosque of Omar, and in all likelihood the brothers are Moawiya (who was appointed governor of Syria and Palestine in 639 and in 661 was declared caliph in Jerusalem) and Ziyad (who became ruler of Basra and the eastern provinces in 665). The author thus would have expected the Messiah to appear in the latter half of the seventh century.

Another work of this period, the *Book of Elijah*, contains a similar prognostication about the messianic age. Here the angel Michael appears showing Elijah the regions of heaven and reveals the end of human history. The Messiah, he explains, will come in the reign of the last king of Persia. In the text the rabbis then debate his identity: one calls him Armilius; another Cyrus. Simeon ben Yohai, however, states that his name is Kersra – Chosroes II who conquered Jerusalem in 614. Again, another apocalypse, *The Chapters of the Messiah*, indicates that the conquests of the Arabs will be followed by messianic redemption. In the next century, the *Revelations of Simeon ben Yohai* expresses the view that the Muslims are God's instrument in bringing about Rome's destruction, and places the advent of the messianic age immediately after the collapse of the Omayyad dynasty. In this work Rabbi Simeon ben Yohai is portrayed in his cave considering Numbers 24.21: 'And he looked on the Kenite'. Complaining to God, he cries: 'Is it not enough what the kingdom of Edom has done unto us? Must thou now send upon us also the kingdom of Ishmael?' In response, the angel Metatron states: 'Fear not, man, the LORD, blessed be he, brings this kingdom of Ishmael upon you only to deliver you from this wicked one.' When Rabbi Simeon demands proof of this claim, the angel appeals to Scripture: 'Go, get a watchman, let him announce what he sees. When he sees riders, horsemen in pairs, riders on asses, riders on camels, let him listen diligently, very diligently' (Isaiah 21.6–7). Here the riders on camels (the Arabs) precede the rider on the ass (the Messiah). The angel then traces the history of Islam from Muhammad through the Omayyad caliphs.

Following the death of Merwan II, the angel proclaims that a cruel king will rule for three months, and then the wicked king (Byzantium) will rule over Israel for nine months. Then the Messiah ben Joseph will appear, restore the Jews to Jerusalem and rebuild the Temple. However, the cruel king Armilius will arise, wage war against the Messiah, and force Israel into the wilderness for forty-five days where the Messiah will die. Then the Messiah ben David will arrive; although the Jews will initially reject him, they will eventually accept his messiahship. He will then slay Armilius, and assemble all Israel in Jerusalem, which will be cleansed of all sinners and the uncircumcised. Heavenly Jerusalem will then descend, and Israel will dwell in peace for two thousand years to be followed by final judgement.

Another source from this period is the *Midrash of the Ten Kings*, which lists the kings who will reign over the world prior to the advent of the Messiah: (1) God, (2) Nimrod, (3) Joseph, (4) Solomon, (5) Ahab, (6) Nebuchadnezzar, (7) Cyrus, and (8) Alexander. The midrash then relates the destruction of the Temple, the establishment of the academy at Jamnia, the Bar Kochba rebellion, and the Hadrianic persecutions. This is followed by prophecies revealed to Rabbi Simeon ben Yohai. Here the Messiah is predicted during the reign of the two brothers (in the latter half of the seventh century); however, if the Jews are not worthy of his deliverance, then his arrival will be postponed until the fall of the Omayyad dynasty. Near the end of this work, it is asserted that the ninth king will be the Messiah ben David and the tenth will be God himself.

The Prayer of Rabbi Simeon ben Yohai is based on the *Revelations of Simeon ben Yohai*. However, where the *Revelations* implies that after the death of Merwan II (750) the Messiah will come, this text continues the history to the time of the Crusades. A similar date of the Messiah's coming is also implied by the *Alphabet of Rabbi Akiva*, a treatise on the mystical significance of the Hebrew letters: 'Eight hundred years after the destruction of the Second Temple the Kedarenes will decrease in number . . . at the end of 295 years, according to the calendar of the gentiles [dating from the Hegira, AD 622], this kingdom will vanish from the earth . . . at the end of 304 years according to their calendar the Son of David will come, God willing.' Thus the Messiah was expected in the tenth century. Another apocalyptic work, *The Story of Daniel*, also predicts his coming at this time. Finally *The Book of Zerubbabel* predicts that the Messiah will come 990 years after the destruction of the Temple (1060).

Pre-Crusade speculations

In addition to midrashic sources, the scholar Saadia Gaon (882–942) engaged in messianic speculation. In the eighth chapter of his *Emunot ve-Deot*, his commentary on the Book of Daniel, and his *Sefer ha-Galui* he discussed the nature of messianic predictions and the final redemption. In the *Emunot* he attempted to reconcile the various figures given to Daniel. Regarding Daniel 12.6–7 ('"How long shall it be till the end of these wonders?" The man clothed in linen, who was above the waters of the stream, raised his right hand and his left hand toward heaven; and I heard him swear by him who lives for ever that it would be for a time, two times, and half a time'), Saadia argues that here 'time and a half' refers to 1335 years (the days are in this instance to be reckoned as years). The expression 'times' refers to the two periods when the kingdom of Israel existed. The first period consisted of 480 years up to the creation of the first Temple; the second period lasted 410 years until its destruction – this totals 890 years, half of which is 445 years. Thus 'times and a half' = 1335 years.

The second figure is given in Daniel 12.11: 'And from the time that the continual burnt offering is taken away, and the abomination that makes desolate is set up, there shall be a thousand two hundred and ninety days.' According to Saadia, this refers to an event which occurred during the period of the second Temple – 45 years after the first prophecy in Daniel – thereby producing the number 1335. A third prophecy is found in Daniel 8.14: 'And he said to him, "For two thousand and three hundred evenings and mornings; then the sanctuary shall be restored to its rightful state."' This number 2300 is to be divided by two since both nights and days are included, producing 1150. This date refers to an occurrence which took place 185 years after the first prophecy to Daniel, again producing 1335. Arguably Saadia believed the period began in the third year of the reign of Cyrus when Jews were allowed to return – this would have been 367 BC. On this calculation the Messiah would arrive in AD 978. A Karaite contemporary of Saadia, Salmon ben Yeroham, came to the same conclusion in his commentary on Daniel, and in the next century the Karaite scholar and commentator Japheth Ha-Levi mentioned that it was common among the rabbis to count the 1335 day–years from the third year of the reign of Cyrus.

As the year 978 approached, expectations mounted throughout the Jewish world. In the Rhineland the community sent an inquiry to the School of Jerusalem in 960 asking for a verification of the report of the coming of the Messiah. The reply expressed dismay: 'As regards your question about the coming of the Messiah, you do not even deserve a reply. For do you not believe in the words of our sages and their signs (which they specified for the identification of the true Messiah), and these have not as yet come to pass.' Other evidence that Jews in Germany were enthusiastically awaiting the Messiah's coming at this time is implied in Benjamin or Tudela's (twelfth-century) *Itinerary*, which contains an insertion of an earlier account:

> If we were not afraid that the appointed time has not yet been reached, we should have gathered together, but we dare not do so until the time for song has arrived, when the messengers will come and say continually: 'The Lord be exalted'. Meanwhile they send missives to one another, saying: 'Be ye strong in the law of Moses, and do ye, mourners for Zion, and ye, mourners for Jerusalem, entreat the Lord, and may the supplications of those that wear the garments of mourning be received through their merits.'

At the same time Hasdai Ibn Shaprut (*c.* 915–70) inquired of Joseph, king of the Khazars, about the time of the messianic deliverance:

> Again I would ask of my master the King, to let me know whether there is among you any tradition concerning the time of the end, for which we have been waiting these many years, during which time we have been going from one captivity to another, and from one exile to another. For one must be very strong, indeed, to refrain from inquiring about it. How can I be silent about the destruction of the Temple in our glory, and about the remnant escaped from the sword, which has passed through fire and water? We who were many are now few, and are fallen from our high estate and dwell in exile. We have no retort to those who say to us daily, 'Every people has a kingdom, but you have none.'

In response the king stated:

You ask furthermore concerning the end of wonders. Our eyes are turned to the LORD our God, and to the wise men of Israel in the academies of Jerusalem and Babylon, for we are very far from Zion, but we have heard that because of the sins of the people, the calculations have gone astray and we know nothing ... We have nothing but the prophecy of Daniel. May the God of Israel hasten the redemption and gather our exiled and scattered people in our lifetime and in yours, and in the lifetime of the house of Israel, who love his name. (Silver, pp. 53–4)

Among the Karaites of this period Japheth Ha-Levi noted that it was commonly believed that the Messiah would arrive after 2300 years, beginning with the Exodus which, according to Karaite chronology, occurred in 1332 BC. Thus the Messiah was foreseen as coming in AD 968. Thus believing himself to be living in this messianic milieu, the Karaite Sahl ben Mazliah Ha-Kohen (tenth century) wrote in *Sefer Tokahot*: 'And behold the days of the visitation of the nations are at hand, and the time of the salvation of Israel is also at hand. May God hasten that day and deliver us from the two women (the rabbinic academies of Sura and Pumbeditha) and cause the Messiah ben David to rule over us.' With pride he pointed to the Karaite communities established in Jerusalem, who were praying continuously for the coming of the Messiah.

Pseudo-Messiahs

From 600 to 1000 several messianic figures excited Jewish aspirations for the return to Zion. The first was Abu Isa al-Ispahani. According to the Karaite scholar al-Kirkisani, he lived during the reign of Caliph Abd al-Malik ibn Marwan who reigned from 685 to 705. However, the Arabic historian al-Shahrastani placed him during the reigns of the Omayyad caliphs Marwan ibn Muhammad (744–50) and al-Mansur (745–75). In any event Abu Isa declared he was a prophet and the herald of the Messiah. When he led a revolt against the Muslims, he was joined by many Persian Jews. After several years, the revolt was suppressed: his army was conquered near the ancient city of Rhagae, and Abu Isa was killed. His followers, however, did not believe he had died; instead they were convinced he disappeared into a cave. Another tradition relates that he placed his followers in a circle which he drew with a myrtle branch enabling them to remain beyond the reach of the enemy. Only Abu Isa rode out of this circle to inflict a blow on the Muslims; subsequently he went beyond the desert to prophesy among the 'Sons of Moses'.

The sect founded by Abu Isa was known as the Isunians (or Isfahanians) who continued to exist until the time of al-Kirkisani (tenth century). According to his followers, Abu Isa was an illiterate tailor who composed his books through prophetic inspiration. In his view five prophets preceded the coming of the Messiah. On the basis of Psalm 119.164 ('Seven times a day do I praise thee'), Abu Isa believed himself to be the last harbinger of messianic redemption, and he ordained seven daily prayers for his disciples, although he did not reject the recitation of the *Shema* and the *Amidah* or the observance of the holy days as practised by the rabbis. Yet in his revolt against various rabbinic doctrines and practices, he was a forerunner of the Karaites. As for Abu Isa's view of other faiths, tradition relates that he was tolerant of both Christianity and Islam. In this regard al-Kirkisani states that he

> acknowledged the prophecy of Jesus, the son of Mary, and the prophecy of the Master of the Mohammedans, contending that each of these two was sent to his own people. He advocated the study of the Gospels and of the Koran, as well as the knowledge of their interpretation, and he maintained that the Mohammedans and Christians were both guided in their faith by what they possessed, just as the Jews were guided in their faith by what they possessed. (Silver, pp. 55–6)

A second pseudo-Messiah of this period was Serene from Shirin who announced himself the Messiah in about 720 and promised to liberate Jerusalem from the Arabs. According to Isador Pacensis writing in 750, he gained a large following of Spanish and French Jews who abandoned their homes and possessions and set out to meet him. Acting in accordance with his self-designated role as the Messiah, Serene rejected many Talmudic laws, including those dealing with forms of prayer, forbidden foods, marriage contracts, and marriages between close relations. Eventually he was captured and brought before the caliph, Yazid II. In response to cross-examination, he denied that he had been serious about his messianic pretensions; his aim was to mislead and mock his followers. Rather than punish Serene, the caliph handed him over to the Jewish community. According to the responsum of Natronai Gaon, Serene and his followers were guilty of violating rabbinic law (just as the disciples of Abu Isa had been).

Another eighth-century messianic figure was Yudghan of

Hamadan (also known as al-Rai) who was a follower of Abu Isa: he claimed to be a prophet of his disciples (the Yudghanites) who regarded him as the Messiah. According to al-Kirkisani in his book *Gardens and Parks*, the Yudghanites 'prohibit meat and intoxicating drinks, observe many prayers and fasts, and assert that the Sabbath and holidays are at present no longer obligatory'. The Muslim historian al-Shahrastani further stated in his book *Religions and Sects* that Yudghan believed the Torah contains an allegorical and a literal interpretation different from that held by the rabbis. Again, the Karaite exegete Japheth ben Ali stated that the Yudghanites view the holidays as symbols and maintain that after the destruction of the Temple many laws were no longer binding.

In the second half of the ninth century the traveller Eldad Ha-Dani brought reports of the ten lost tribes whose restoration was part of the scheme of messianic redemption. Although he did not regard himself as the Messiah, his accounts heightened messianic expectations. Professing himself to be a member of the tribe of Dan, he claimed that the tribes of Dan, Naphtali, Gad and Asher formed an independent kingdom in Havilah, the land of gold (near Ethiopia), under their king Addiel. These tribes, he stated, were constantly at war with their neighbours. Eldad also referred to the 'Sons of Moses' who lived nearby but were cut off from the world by an impassable river of rolling stones and sand which stops only on the Sabbath when it is surrounded by fire or covered by a cloud. In his account Eldad recounted how he and a companion of the tribe of Asher set out on a journey, were shipwrecked and captured by cannibals. His companion was eaten, but he was eventually rescued by a Jew of the tribe of Issachar. In this report, he also described the ten tribes, their location, and independent existence. By providing such information, Eldad intensified the messianic hopes of Jews of the ninth century who were longing for a return to Jerusalem.

five

Medieval Speculation

During the time of the Crusades Jewish aspirations for the coming of the Messiah intensified. Initially the date of the First Crusade (1096) was viewed as the year of the messianic deliverance. When the massacres of this year occurred, the Jewish community envisaged this tragedy as the birth pangs of the Messiah. In later years the same longing for redemption and return to Zion was expressed by Jews who continued to suffer at the hands of Christians. In the next two centuries a number of Jewish writers attempted to determine the date of deliverance on the basis of verses in the Book of Daniel – prominent among these scholars was Solomon ibn Gabirol, Rashi, Judah Halevi, and Abraham bar Hiyya. During this period several would-be Messiahs appeared in the Jewish world. Previously such figures came from Asia Minor, Babylonia and Persia, but with the shift of Jewry to Mediterranean countries pseudo-Messiahs also emerged in western Europe. The most important false Messiah of this period was David Alroy who, even after his death, was viewed by his followers as the Redeemer of Israel. In the following centuries messianic calculators continued to speculate about the year of deliverance and return of the exiles to the Holy Land on the basis of scriptural texts. Frequently they relied on kabbalistic forms of exegesis in their computations. Notable among such writers were Nahmanides, Isaac ben Judah Halevi, Levi ben Gershon, and Bahya ben Asher. Mystical works of this era such as the *Zohar* also contained speculations about the advent of the Messiah. In the thirteenth century another messianic figure, Abraham Abulafia, appeared on the scene; although he attracted a wide circle of followers, he also evoked considerable hostility from such scholars as Solomon ben Abraham Adret of Barcelona.

The Crusades

At the end of the eleventh century, Crusaders devastated Jewish communities between the Rhine and the Moselle. Cities particularly affected included Metz, Speyer, Worms, Mainz, Cologne and Trier. During this onslaught approximately 4000

Jews were killed, and the horror of these massacres is recorded in numerous *selihot* (potential prayers), *kinnot* (lamentations), and memoirs.

Paradoxically the date of the First Crusade (1096) was generally fixed upon as the year of deliverance. Thus the chronicler of the First Crusade, Solomon ben Simeon (twelfth century) emphasized the widespread acceptance of this calculation:

> And it came to pass in the year 4856, the 1028th year of our exile, in the eleventh year of the 256th cycle (1096), when we had hoped for salvation and comfort, according to the prophecy of Jeremiah: 'Sing (the Hebrew equivalent of which is 256 according to *gematria* [numerical mystical calculation]) with gladness for Jacob and shout at the head of the nation' [31.7]. But it was turned into sorrow and groaning, weeping and lamentation.

Again, Eliezer ben Nathan (twelfth century) in his report of Jewish persecution during this year stressed that many Jews regarded the first year of the 256 cycle (1096) as the year of redemption. Thus he wrote in his *selihah*:

> Time and time again our soul waited
> But the end was long delayed and the wound was not healed;
> In the season of 'Sing' (256 in *gematria*) we hoped that
>   redemption would come.
> But we hoped for peace, and there was none; for a time of
>   healing and behold dismay!

The widespread acceptance of 1096 as the date of the coming of the Messiah is also supported by the midrashic commentary of Tobiah ben Eliezer, written in 1097. Commenting on Exodus 3.20 ('So I will stretch out my hand and smite Egypt with all the wonders which I will do in it; after that he will let you go'), he stated:

> And in the year 4857, that is to say, the year 1029 since the destruction of the second Temple, which is also the twelfth year in the 256th cycle, I, Tobiah, son of R. Eliezer, looked searchingly into our divine books and considered the length of our exile, how 'their power is gone, and there is none remaining, bond or free' (Deuteronomy 32.36), and how all the ends have passed and redemption is now dependent upon repentance alone, as it is written, 'If you return, O Israel, says the LORD,

to me you should return' (Jeremiah 4.1); and again 'If you return, I will restore you, and you shall stand before me' (Jeremiah 15.19). We are now looking to the Rock of our salvation, trusting that even as in the days of Egypt he will now show us wonders.

In another text of this period, Benjamin ben Zerah (eleventh century) (who possibly witnessed the First Crusade) recounted taunts delivered by the enemies of Israel concerning Jewish messianic longing such as: 'Ye have calculated the times of redemption and they are now past, and the hope of salvation is over and gone.'

After the tragedy of 1096 the Jewish community began to hope that this calamity constituted the 'birth pangs of the Messiah'. Thus Samuel ben Judah (twelfth century) in his dirge for the Sabbath before Shavuot (which mentions the year 1096) prayed that Jewish suffering might inaugurate the beginning of the messianic age:

> Bring nigh the end of the wonders,
> Deliver thy people from hardship
> Thou, our Redeemer, Lord of Hosts.
> Be thou not quiet, Lord!

Another writer of this time, David ben Meshullam, concluded his lament about the martyrs of the Crusades with a plea for redemption:

> O living God! Accredit thou to us the merit of their blameless lives (the martyrs) and put an end to our suffering.

Again, David ben Samuel Halevi (twelfth century) prayed in his *piyyut* (liturgical prayer):

> Our soul languishes for thy salvation. When wilt thou comfort us?
> Do it for the sake of thy holy name. Not for our sake, O Lord, not for our sake.

The same longing for redemption is found in the writings of the chroniclers of the Second Crusade (1145–7) and the Third Crusade (1189–90) as well as other disasters of the twelfth century. Thus Isaac ben Shalom concluded his *piyyut* about the massacre of the German communities on the 12th Nisan 1147 with a prayer for salvation:

Have pity upon thy scattered ones, O Holy One,
And with thy gracious spirit uphold us.
Arise, our help, deliver us.

Another Jewish scholar, Ephraim ben Jacob of Bonn (1133–
c. 1196), who witnessed the horrors of the Second and Third Crusades, longed for deliverance after the destruction of the Jewish
community of Blois in 1171. 'How long shall I hope for redemption
at the hands of the sons of David and the prophet Elijah?', he
asked. Likewise Hillel ben Jacob, in his *selihah* on those who were
killed in Blois, prayed:

Accept, I pray thee, my prayer, O God on high!
Hasten deliverance, and rescue thy poor people.
Establish thy city and thy dwelling place as of old in beauty
So that God may dwell in Zion.

Another poet of this period, Menahem ben Jacob, who
recounted the tragedy of Boppard in 1179 (where Jews were falsely
accused of killing a Christian woman, thrown into the river, and
drowned) similarly pleaded:

And if we be unworthy of redemption,
Remember thy servants Hananiah, Mishael and Azariah
who would not defile themselves.

The Crusades thus gave rise to widespread longing for messianic
redemption. Faced with destruction and massacre, the Jewish
community eagerly awaited the Redeemer who would come to
relieve them of their miseries and usher in God's Kingdom on
earth.

Messianic calculations

During the eleventh and twelfth centuries a number of Jewish
writers attempted to calculate the date of messianic redemption.
Solomon ibn Gabirol (eleventh century) for example is referred to
in Abraham Ibn Ezra's (twelfth century) commentary on Daniel
11.30 as having determined the end on the basis of astrological
computations. Although Ibn Gabirol's own messianic predictions
have been lost, his poetry abounds in messianic reflections. Thus
in one *piyyut* he depicted a dialogue between God and Israel in
which Israel laments: 'Thy end is long drawn, and my gloom has
lasted long. How long will the exile last? When will the appointed

season arrive? When wilt thou resolve what is hidden and sealed?'
The answer is given: 'Hope on, hapless one, yet a little while
longer!' In another *piyyut* the same consolation is expressed:
'Hearken now, hapless and pilloried one, hope and wait for me,
for very soon will I send my angel to prepare my way' (Davidson-
Zangwill, p. 22).

Another eleventh-century scholar, Rashi (1040–1105) argued
that Daniel 8.14 ('For two thousand and three hundred evenings
and mornings; then the sanctuary shall be restored to its rightful
state'), and Daniel 12.11 ('And from the time that the continual
burnt offering is taken away, and the abomination that makes
desolate is set up, there shall be a thousand two hundred and
ninety days'), point to 1352 as the year of redemption. According
to *gamatria*, the words 'evening' and 'morning' in Daniel 8.14 =
574; to this should be added the number 2300 mentioned in the
same verse. This produces 2874. The *terminus a quo* is the
beginning of Egyptian captivity. The Jews were in Egypt for 210
years; 480 years elapsed from their deliverance to the establishment of the Temple; the Temple existed for 410 years; the
Babylonian captivity lasted for 70 years; and the second Temple
stood for 420 years. This produces a total of 1590 years from
Egyptian captivity to the destruction of the second Temple, and
Daniel 12.11–12 states that 1290 years must elapse from the
time that the continual burnt offering is taken away until deliverance. Rashi maintains that the offering ceased six years before
the destruction (in the 1584th year since the Egyptian captivity).
Adding 1584 to 1290 makes 2874. The Temple was destroyed
in AD 68; the Messiah will arrive 1290 years after the cessation
of the burnt offering – this took place six years before the
destruction (AD 62). Rashi thus believes the messianic age would
begin in 1352.

A contemporary of Rashi, Judah Halevi (11th–12th century)
encouraged Jewry not to become impatient about the coming of
the Messiah. In one of his poems he wrote: 'Let thy heart be strong,
awaiting thine appointed season (of redemption). Why do you
calculate the end of the captivity and grow disturbed? . . . Thou
hast done well to wait for thy Redeemer. Do not, therefore, be
impatient; thou wilt behold the glory of my work' (Davidson-
Zangwill, p. 25). None the less, Halevi himself engaged in messianic calculation. In one of his poems he related that he had a
dream in which he beheld the fall of Ishmael: 'In the year 1130 all
thy pride (Ishmael) will be shattered. Thou wilt be abashed and

ashamed of the things which thou didst devise' (*Poems* I, pp. 57–8). Here he asserts that Ishmael is the fourth kingdom mentioned in Daniel whose destruction would bring about God's deliverance: 'Art thou the miry clay in the feet of iron which came at the end and wast exalted?' (*Poems* II, p. 151). Fixing upon this date, Halevi was following a tradition among Jews in Muslim lands that the Messiah would arrive 500 years after the rise of Islam: in the previous century it was commonly believed the Messiah would come 400 years after the Hegira (in 1022). The Karaite commentator of the eleventh century, Jacob ben Reuben, for example, declared his belief that 'it is likely that the redemption will occur at the end of 400 years of the rule of the little horn (Islam)' (*Poems* II, p. 151). When this hope evaporated the period was put forward to 100 years.

In the same century Abraham bar Hiyya (d. 1136) also speculated about the coming of the Messiah. In his *Megillat ha-Megalleh*, he defended such calculation: it was sanctioned by the Torah and practised by rabbinic scholars. According to bar Hiyya, the world was created for the sake of Israel, thus every cycle in the creation narrative has symbolic significance in the nation's history. The creation week signifies that the world will endure 6000 years to be followed by a millennial Sabbath – such reckoning is based on Psalm 90.4: 'For a thousand years in thy sight are but as yesterday when it is past, or as a watch in the night.'

According to bar Hiyya a day in God's sight is in fact 857 1/7 years since a watch in the night = 1/3 of the night (4 hours). Thus a day = 6/7 of 1000 years (857 1/7 years). Each day is again divided into seven parts, and each part (122 years) = 1 generation. On this basis bar Hiyya formulated a number of alternative dates of divine deliverance. Firstly the flood, he argued, occurred at the close of the second day (1714 AM); the Torah was given towards the end of the third day (2448 AM). From such calculations it is evident that the next three days will last another 2448 years: thus the total calculation is 4896 (AD 1136). This is the year of messianic redemption. Alternatively, as a second calculation, it is possible to reckon that the third day ended at the conquest of Canaan (2495 AM) – this would place the year of the advent of the Messiah at 4990 AM (2495 × 2 = 4990 AM or AD 1230).

As a third calculation, it is possible to interpret Deuteronomy 28.63 ('And as the LORD took delight in doing you good and multiplying you, so the LORD will take delight in bringing ruin upon you and destroying you; and you shall be plucked off the land which you are entering to take possession of it') as indicating that the period of suffering will be as long as the time of rejoicing. The period of rejoicing which began with the giving of the Torah (2448 AM) ended with the destruction (3828 AM) = 1380 years. The period of suffering will last an equal time until 5208 AM – this year, AD 1148, would therefore be the year of redemption.

A fourth calculation was based on the assumption that the Torah was given in 2448 AM at the close of the third day. The remaining four days would thus last 3552 years (approximately 890 years per day). The first Temple was destroyed at the end of the fourth day (3338 AM = 890 years after the giving of the Torah). The fifth and sixth days will last 1780 years (890 × 2). At the close of the sixth day the Messiah will come (1780 + 3338 = 5118 AM or AD 1358). Thus the Messiah will come at this time. This latter calculation is further supported by astrological evidence. According to bar Hiyya, the history of Israel from the time of Exodus to his own day illustrates the relative positions of the conjunction of the two highest planets, Saturn and Jupiter. The conjunction of these two planets in the sign of Pisces in the watery trigon occurred in 2365 AM. This presaged the redemption from Egypt and the giving of the Torah. This same conjunction will not take place again until after 2859 years (or in 5224 AM = AD 1464). Messianic redemption will occur in the last of the twelve major conjunctions between 1226 and 1464; specifically it will take place in the thirteenth year of the seventh minor conjunction within this trigon (AD 1358).

False Messiahs

During the last quarter of the eleventh and the entire twelfth century a number of pseudo-Messiahs appeared in the Jewish world. In 1096 the arrival of the Crusaders engendered considerable excitement among Jews in the Byzantine empire. As a result the French Jewish community sent a messenger to Constantinople to obtain information about the coming of the Messiah. In Khazaria seventeen communities marched into the desert to meet the ten lost tribes. In Salonika it was asserted that Elijah had arrived; according to several reports someone had received the staff of Elijah and another had been cured of blindness. As a result, many

Jews fasted, prayed and did penance. At this time a proselyte, Obadiah, travelled to northern Palestine where he met the Karaite Solomon Ha-Kohen who announced that he was the Messiah and would soon deliver Israel. In Mesopotamia another messianic figure, ben Chadd, appeared but was later arrested by the caliph of Baghdad.

The appearance in 1172 of a false messianic forerunner in Yemen was described by Maimonides (1135–1204) in his *Iggeret Teman*:

> In Yemen there arose a man who said that he was the messenger of the Messiah, preparing the way for his coming. He also announced that the Messiah would appear in Yemen. Many Jews and Arabs followed him. He traversed the country and misled the people, urging them to follow him and to go to meet the Messiah. Our brothers of Yemen wrote to me a long letter informing me about the manner of the man and the innovations which he introduced in the prayers, and what he told them, and reporting also the miracles which he performed, and they solicited my opinion about the matter. I understood from what they wrote that that poor man was ignorant although God-fearing, and that all that men reported concerning his performances was absolutely false.
>
> I feared me for the safety of the Jews living there, and so I composed for them three dissertations . . . on the subject of the king–Messiah, and how to know him, and the signs which will usher him in. And I urged upon them to warn that man lest he be lost and lest he also bring destruction upon the (Jewish) communities. The upshot of the matter was that at the end of the year the man was caught and all of his followers deserted him.
>
> An Arab king questioned him, and he replied that he had spoken the truth and that he had obeyed the word of God. The king asked him for a sign. He replied, 'Cut off my head and I will return to life again.' The king said that there could be no greater sign than that, and if his word came true, he and all the world would believe that he spoke the truth . . . The king commanded and they cut off his head, and the poor man was killed. May his death atone for him and for all Israel. The Jews in many communities were heavily fined. To this day there are ignorant men who believe that he will arise from his grave and appear.

Maimonides in his *Iggeret Teman* also refers to other messianic figures of the eleventh century. 'And similarly', he wrote, 'there arose a man in the West in the city of Fez 44 years ago (1127) and said that he was the herald announcing that the Messiah would appear that year. His word did not come true, and because of him persecutions befell Israel. A man who witnessed it all told me about it.' Again, he continued, 'And ten years before this event there arose in Cordoba, Spain, a man who boasted that he was the Messiah, and because of him Israel came very near destruction.' Another messianic figure appeared in 1087: 'And thirty years before this time (1087) there arose a man in France who announced that he was the Messiah, and performed signs, according to their opinion, and the French killed him, and many other Jews were slain with him.'

The most important pseudo-Messiah of this period was David Alroy. Born in Amadiya, his name was originally Menahem ben Solomon. According to tradition he was educated at the Baghdad academy, learned in mysticism, and skilled in sorcery. The movement to recognize his messiahship appears to have originated among mountain Jews of the north-east Caucasus before 1121, and gathered strength in the ferment that resulted from the struggle between Christianity and Islam following the First Crusade. The suffering and massacres of this period persuaded many Jews that they were living in the time of the birth pangs of the Messiah. The central figure of this messianic circle was Alroy's father Solomon, who claimed to be Elijah.

The leaders of this messianic sect sought to announce Alroy's coming by addressing a letter to 'all Jews dwelling near-by or far off and in all the surrounding countries'. In their proclamation, they stated: 'The time has come in which the Almighty will gather together his people Israel from every country to Jerusalem the holy city.' To prepare for this event, they stressed the importance of penitential preparation through fasting and prayer. After opponents of this group protested about such exhortations, the movement was suppressed and Alroy re-established his centre in Amadiya. There he besought other Jews from the vicinity as well as those living in Azerbaijan, Persia, and the Mosul region to join his entourage.

A contemporary, Benjamin of Tudela, described this messianic movement in his itinerary:

> He (David Alroy) took it into his head to revolt against the king of Persia, and to gather around him the Jews who lived in the

mountains of Chaftan, in order to war against the gentiles and to capture Jerusalem. He showed miraculous signs to the Jews, and declared that God sent him to capture Jerusalem and to lead them forth from among the nations, and the people believed in him and proclaimed him the Messiah.

Tradition relates that two impostors forged a letter from Alroy in which he promised to transport Jews of Baghdad to Jerusalem by night on the wings of angels. When this event failed to materialize, his pretensions were ridiculed. Eventually he was murdered, possibly by his father-in-law who was bribed by the governor of Amadiya. Nonetheless a number of his followers (the Menahemites) continued to believe in him after his death.

Messianism in the thirteenth and fourteenth centuries

Despite the disappointments of the eleventh and twelfth centuries, messianic speculation continued to preoccupy Jewish thinkers. The hope of deliverance from suffering and persecution encouraged theologians to engage in messianic computation. Under the influence of mystical thought, these writers increasingly relied on kabbalistic exegesis to determine the date of the coming of the Messiah. Prominent among writers of the thirteenth century was Nahmanides; in his *Book of Redemption*, he attempted to harmonize dates in the Book of Daniel and deduce from them the year of the Messiah's arrival. According to Nahmanides, Daniel 12.11 ('And from the time that the continual burnt offering is taken away, and the abomination that makes desolate is set up, there shall be a thousand two hundred and ninety days') implies that 1290 years after the destruction of the Temple the Messiah ben Joseph will appear. To substantiate this claim, Nahmanides utilized several *gematriot*: Genesis 15.13 ('They will be oppressed for 400 years') = 1293; Deuteronomy 4.30 ('When you are in tribulation, and all these things come upon you in the latter days') = 1291. In both cases the number of years between the destruction and the redemption is approximately 1290.

Again referring to Daniel 12.11, he asserted that the burnt offering was taken away on the day of destruction; 45 years later the Messiah ben David will arrive. This accounts for the figure of 1335 in the following verse: 'Blessed is he who waits and comes to the thousand three hundred and thirty-five days', Daniel 12.12. This figure, 1335 years, helps to explain the numbers in Daniel 8.14:

'For two thousand and three hundred evenings and mornings; then the sanctuary shall be restored to its rightful state.' Here 2300 refers to the number of years which will elapse from David's reign to the termination of the exile: David's reign (40 years) + the duration of the first Temple (40 years) + the Babylonian captivity (70 years) + the duration of the second Temple (420 years) + the duration of the last exile (1335) = 2275 (approximately 2300 years).

These verses in Daniel thus demonstrate that the duration of the last exile will last 1335 years; at this point in time the Messiah ben David will arrive. In what year will this take place? In his public disputation with Pablo Christiani in 1263, Nahmanides declared: 'It is now 1195 years since the destruction, or 95 years less than the messianic figure of Daniel (1195 + 95 = 1290). We believe that the Messiah will come that year.' This means that the Messiah ben Joseph would arrive in 1358 (1263 + 95 = 1358). Forty-five years later, 1403, the Messiah ben David will appear (1263 + 95 + 45 = 1403).

Another calculator of the thirteenth century, Isaac ben Judah Halevi, in his commentary on the Pentateuch, quoted the author of the biblical commentary *Gan* as indicating that Deuteronomy 28.63 ('And as the LORD took delight in doing you good and multiplying you, so the LORD will take delight in bringing ruin upon you and destroying you') contains a messianic prediction. This verse is to be combined with Daniel 12.11 ('And from the time that the continual burnt offering is taken away . . . there shall be a thousand two hundred and ninety days'). These verses, he believed, imply that the exile will endure as long as the period of rejoicing. The period of rejoicing lasted from the sojourn in Egypt to the destruction of the first Temple (1290 years); thus the exile will last 1290 years. The number 1335 in the following verse in Daniel (Daniel 12.12) refers to the complete conquest of the world by the Messiah, which will take place 45 years after his appearance.

It is, however, impossible to determine with certainty when this period commences and ends. 'We do not know when the period of 1290 years begins', Halevi writes, 'or we would know exactly when it will end . . . it may begin with the taking away of the continual burnt offering in the days of Hyrcan and Aristobulus . . . or it may begin with the reign of Herod, who was not fit to be king over Israel, or perhaps at an even later date, i.e. with the expulsion. At the time of the end when the Messiah will come . . . it shall become clear when the period actually began.'

In the fourteenth century Levi ben Gershon also found evidence of messianic redemption in the final chapter of the Book of Daniel. On the basis of Daniel 12.11, he argued that 1290 years will elapse from the destruction to the redemption: since the destruction took place in 3828 AM, messianic deliverance will occur in 5118 AM (AD 1358). The number 1335 in the following verse (Daniel 12.12), 45 years later, refers to the end of the messianic wars against Gog and Magog (AD 1403).

Another scholar of this period, Bahya ben Asher (d. 1340), offered messianic calculations in his commentary on the Torah where he points out that the Bible gives three numbers for the duration of the Egyptian exile: 210; 400; and 430 years. The duration of the present exile will also have three figures: 1150 (Daniel 8.14) (2300 mornings and evenings = 1150 days); 1290 (Daniel 12.11); and 1335 (Daniel 12.12). Thus, if Israel is unworthy to be redeemed after 1150 years (AD 1218), the redemption will take place after 1290 years (AD 1358). Again, if Israel continues to be unworthy, messianic redemption will not take place until after 1335 years (AD 1403). To this calculation, Bahya added another based on the view that the seven days of creation and rest indicate the seven millennia of the earth's existence and the final destruction. The first day, he contends, symbolizes the fifth millennium (the period of exile); the sixth day is symbolic of the sixth millennium when the Messiah will come. In his commentary written in 1291, he declares that his generation is in the 51st year of that millennium. According to Bahya, the Messiah will arrive after the end of the first tenth of the millennium (in 5118 AM or AD 1358). The figure 1335 in Daniel 12.12 – 45 day–years later – refers to the close of the period of the wars which the Messiah's coming will bring about (AD 1403).

In addition to these calculations, a number of mystical texts from this period contain speculations about the date of redemption. The *Zohar*, for example, gives a number of messianic dates based on mystical computations. One calculation is based on the mystic value of God's name (*yod, he, vav, he*). When Israel went into exile, the last letters of this name were separated. The letter *he* symbolizes 5000 years; the *vav* 6000 years. When the fifth millennium will end and the sixth begin, these letters will be joined – this will take place in the 60th year of the sixth millennium (AD 5060 = 1300). Thus 1300 AD is the date of messianic redemption. Another calculation, based on the mystic numerical value of the letter *vav* (6), sets the date as AD 1306. The *vav* in the name Jacob in the verse

'I will remember my covenant with Jacob' (Leviticus 26.42) is the key to this computation. The act of remembrance will occur in the 60th year of the 6th millennium (AD 1300). In the 66th year of the sixth millennium the Messiah will arrive. Yet another calculation is based on the 12 tribes who represent 1200 years. Twelve hundred years after the destruction of the Temple (AD 1268), the night will darken on Israel. This darkness will last for 66 years (AD 1334). At the end of this period, the Messiah will appear and engage in warfare. Sixty-six years later (AD 1400), the letters of God's name will appear inscribed in the lower and higher perfection; 132 years later (AD 1532), the resurrection will take place in Palestine; 144 years later (AD 1676), the dead in other lands will also be resurrected.

Abraham Abulafia

The most important messianic figure of this period was Abraham Abulafia (thirteenth century) who announced himself as the Messiah at the end of the century. When a child, his parents moved from Saragossa to Tudela in Navarre. His father died when he was eighteen, and Abulafia subsequently travelled to Palestine where he searched for the mystical river Sambatyon where the ten tribes were believed to reside. Returning by way of Greece, he spent some time in Capua where he studied Maimonides' *Guide of the Perplexed* under Hillel ben Samuel of Verona. In addition he was introduced to the kabbalah by Baruch Togarmi, who wrote a commentary on the *Sepher Yetzirah*. In 1271 he studied Maimonides' work in Barcelona, became convinced that he attained prophetic inspiration, and proclaimed his mystical doctrine to a small circle of followers. In 1273 he wandered through Italy, Sicily, and Greece, and also wrote a number of mystical essays combining kabbalistic ideas and Maimonides' philosophy. In 1277 he lived in Patras in Greece where he wrote a series of mystical tracts; three years later he attracted a large circle of disciples in Capua.

In 1280 Abulafia went to Rome in an effort to persuade Pope Nicholas III to improve the condition of the Jewish people. On his arrival, the Pope sentenced him to death by burning. However, because of the Pope's death, the decree was not carried out, and after a month in prison Abulafia was released and went to Sicily. In Messina he wrote *Or ha-Sekhel* about the mysteries of God's name, and the autobiographical text *Ozar Eden Ganuz*. Here he announced the onset of the messianic era in 1290; many were persuaded by this prediction and prepared to emigrate to Palestine. Nonetheless, his teachings aroused great hostility, and his opponents approached the scholar Solomon ben Abraham Adret of Barcelona, accusing Abulafia of claiming to be the Messiah. In response Adret called him a scoundrel: Abulafia was forced to flee to the island of Comino where he wrote polemical treatises in which he defended himself and his views.

Abulafia's mystical ideas were based on the doctrine of the ten *Sephirot* (divine emanations), and utilized the methods of *zeruf* (combination of letters), *gematria* (numerical value of Hebrew words), and *notarikon* (letters of a word as abbreviations of sentences). Believing prophetic kabbalah enabled human beings to have prophetic powers and commune with the Deity, he argued that human reason can thereby become subject to the rule of God's universal reason. This process he called the 'Way of Divine Name'. Believing he had such knowledge of the mystery of the alphabet and numbers, he was persuaded that he could attain the heights of revelation. 'But when I reached to the Names and untied the seal bands', he stated, 'the Lord of all revealed himself to me and made known to me his secret, and informed me concerning the end of the exile and the beginning of the redemption through the blood avenger.' By understanding the mystery of letters, vowels, numerals, and God's name, it became possible for him to exercise miraculous powers. According to Abulafia, Israel suffers in exile, because it has forgotten God's true name; only by means of such knowledge (which Abulafia possessed) will the redemption take place. Hence Abulafia's messianic role was determined by such esoteric mystical comprehension of the divine mysteries. In all likelihood the rumours of his messiahship contributed to the emigration of Jews, headed by Rabbi Meir of Rothenburg, for Palestine in 1286.

Several of Abulafia's disciples continued his prophecies and predictions after his death. In Avila, one of his followers, Abraham of Avila, declared that the Messiah would arrive on the last day of the fourth month in the year 1295. Such a prediction persuaded the community there to await the appointed day with anticipation; yet when this event failed to occur, those residents who had assembled in the synagogues were profoundly discouraged. Attentive to this affair, Adret stressed that proper precautions should be taken when confronted by a messianic pretender. In all cases, the prophecies of a would-be Messiah must be investigated, and his character, conduct and motives must be scrutinized with care.

six

Messianism in the Early Modern Period

During the fourteenth and fifteenth centuries the Jewish community continued to long for the Messiah who would return the Jewish people to their homeland despite his failure to appear in 1348 and 1403. These centuries witnessed the production of messianic treatises and such scholars as Simeon ben Zemah Duran and Isaac Abrabanel speculated about the year of his arrival. The tradition of messianic calculation was practised in the sixteenth century by such scholars as Abraham Halevi, Mordecai ben Judah Dato, Isaac Luria, Naphtali Herz ben Jacob Elhanan, Gedalia ibn Yahya and David ben Solomon ibn Abi Zimra. During this century several false Messiahs, such as David Reuveni and Solomon Molko, appeared, claiming to inaugurate a new age. Undaunted by the failure of these would-be Messiahs to lead the Jewish nation to the Holy Land and bring about messianic deliverance, messianic calculators of the seventeenth century persisted in their investigations. Prominent among the messianic speculators of this century was Manasseh ben Israel who believed that the hour of deliverance was near. The Cossack Rebellion which began in 1648 AD and devastated Polish Jewry heightened the belief that the coming of the Messiah was close at hand. In 1665 the arrival of the self-proclaimed messianic king, Shabbatai Tzevi, was announced by his disciple Nathan of Gaza. Throughout the world, Jewry was electrified. Yet when Shabbatai converted to Islam rather than face death, his apostasy evoked widespread despair. None the less, a number of his followers continued to adhere to his claim of messiahship, and a schismatic group of his disciples (*Doenmeh*) broke away from mainstream Judaism. In the eighteenth century the Shabbatean movement was led by Jacob Frank, who became the leader of a dissident sect (Frankists) which continued to subscribe to a version of the Shabbatean kabbalistic tradition.

Messianic computations in the fourteenth and fifteenth centuries

The failure of the Messiah to appear in 1348 and 1403 was a terrible shock to the Jewish community, discouraging further calculations. Instead of a divine deliverance, the fourteenth century brought further terrible tragedies to the Jewish population. Nonetheless there did appear a few rabbinic treatises on messianic deliverance in the latter part of the fourteenth and fifteenth centuries. *The Book on the Alphabet*, for example, is a mystic treatise on the Hebrew alphabet in which the author calculates that the Messiah will appear in 1430 on the basis of *gematria* and *notarikon*. In another mystical treatise of this period, *Sefer ha-Pelia'ah we-ha-Kanah*, composed in the fifteenth century by a Sephardi kabbalist, the date 1490 is given as the year of redemption on the basis of kabbalistic calculations.

Outstanding scholars of this period such as Simeon ben Zemah Duran (14th–15th century) also predicted the coming of the Messiah. In his commentary on the Book of Job, he determines that the year of messianic redemption will take place in 1850. This calculation is based on an allegorical reading of Job 40.41. To buttress this conclusion he also cited Ezekiel 4.4ff. His interpretation of this passage gives rise to the number 2450 years. Duran appears to think that 150 years elapsed from the expulsion of some of the tribes of the northern kingdom under Tiglath-Pileser to the final expulsion under Sennacherib; this accounts for the discrepancy in the two revelations in Daniel 12.7 and 8.14. Duran argues that the first text gives the figure 2450, and the second 2300. If one assumes Duran's starting point to have been the final destruction of the kingdom of Israel – which according to the old chronology was *c.* 450 BC – then the redemption will take place 2300 years later = AD 1850. Duran further maintains that the figure in Daniel 12.11 (1290) refers to the conquest of Jerusalem by the Muslims. According to Duran, the end of Islamic rule will take place 1290 years after the rise of Muhammad 622 + 1290 = AD 1912. The beginning of the end would be 60 years earlier (*c.* AD 1850).

During the fourteenth century the pseudo-Messiah Moses Botarel appeared. A scholar and kabbalist, he announced himself to be the Messiah in 1393 after widespread persecution in Spain, which was generally perceived in the Jewish community as the birth pangs of the messianic epoch. As Abraham of Granada explained in his *Berit Menuha*:

> And this is an indication of the approach of redemption. When it is near, the sufferings of the exile will increase, and many of the faithful ones will stumble when they see the terrible confusion of the exile and the great sufferings, and many will leave the faith

in order to escape the sword of the destroyer . . . but blessed is
the man who will cling to his faith and walk in the right path.
Perhaps he will be saved from the tribulations which are called
the pangs of the Messiah.

Not only was Botarel accepted as the Messiah by the general population, but scholars such as Hasdai Crescas appear to have believed
in his claims as well.

The events of the next century led to intense messianic
speculation. The expulsion of Jewry from Spain in 1492, from
Portugal in 1498, and from Germanic provinces in the last
decades of the fifteenth century increased Jewish longing for a
return to the Promised Land. The most outstanding messianic
writer of this period was Isaac Abrabanel (15th–16th century):
Wells of Salvation is a treatise on the Book of Daniel in which he
attempts to determine the date of deliverance. In the first section
he explains that the prohibition against calculating the advent
of the Messiah applies only to those who use astrological calculations, but not to those who interpret Scripture correctly. 'Our
life is so hard', he writes, 'and our fortunes so unhappy that we
are constrained to inquire after the hour of our release and
redemption. Furthermore, the end is not far off, and it is now
proper to reveal it.' In the next section he asserts that the fourth
kingdom mentioned in Daniel is Rome, and that the vision of
the chariot in Ezekiel is messianic in character: the 'four living
creatures and the four wheels' refer to the four kingdoms. He
then explains the motivation of messianic prophecies. They were
made, he argues, to proclaim the power of God and to bring
human beings to repentance. Salvation is the reward for the
righteous, and the prophet therefore announces that ultimate
redemption will be vouchsafed to those who trust in God whereas
those who sin will be punished.

After these preliminary observations, Abrabanel proceeds to
write a running commentary on the Book of Daniel itself. Here
he discusses Nebuchadnezzar's dream and Daniel's interpretation.
The land of gold, he asserts, is Babylon; the breast and arms of
silver are Persia; the belly and thighs of brass, Greece; the legs of
iron, Rome; the feet (part iron and part clay) refer to Christianity
and Islam which divided the Roman world. The fifth kingdom is
Israel, and the one who shatters the feet of iron is the Messiah.
This discussion is followed by Abrabanel's exegesis of the dream
in Daniel 7: the first beast, which is likened to a lion, is Babylon;

the second beast, likened to a bear, is Persia; the third beast, likened to a leopard, is Greece; the fourth beast is Rome. The fifth beast, he maintains, will be destroyed because of the teaching of the papacy. Then the Messiah will come after a period of great suffering and Israel will endure forever.

The duration of the fourth kingdom will be for 'a time and times and half a time' (Daniel 7.25). A 'time', he believes, is the period of the duration of the first Temple (410 years): three and a half times = 1435 years. This figure, dating from the year of the destruction (AD 68), = 1503. This date, AD 1503, is thus the time when the Messiah will arrive (or the preliminary events – the destruction of Rome and the punishment of the gentiles – will take place). Such a calculation is further supported by an account of Daniel's second vision in Daniel 8. The ram Daniel saw is Persia; the two horns of the ram are Persia and Media (or Darius the Mede and Cyrus the Persian); the he-goat which smote the ram is Greece; and the conspicuous horn which was between his eyes was Alexander. The four horns are the four parts into which Alexander's empire was divided. The little horn which came out of one is Antiochus Epiphanes. The host in whose hands the continual offering was given over because of the people's sins is Titus. The two holy ones are the angels Michael and Gabriel. The 2300 evenings and mornings – the duration of the exile – are 2300 years which are to be counted from the division of the kingdom which occurred in 2965 AM. Adding 2300 + 2965 = 5265 AM or 1504 (c. AD 1503).

Abrabanel's second book, the *Salvation of His Anointed*, is polemical in character; its purpose was to refute Jewish apostates who attempted in public disputations to prove that the Messiah had already come. The Talmud appears to contain messianic calculations that point to a previous date; in addition, there are some rabbis who seem to have believed the Messiah will never come. In this work Abrabanel attempts to demonstrate that these texts do not in fact deny the ultimate appearance of the Messiah nor do the talmudic dates suggest that the Messiah has already come. In a final treatise, *Announcing Salvation*, Abrabanel attempted to refute those who construed the messianic prophecies in the Bible as applying to the first restoration; in addition, he sought to contradict the belief that the coming of the Messiah is not based on Scripture.

Sixteenth-century calculators

Messianic calculation continued into the sixteenth century with the writings of the Spanish exile and kabbalist Abraham Halevi (early sixteenth century) who predicted that the messianic age would dawn in 1530. His tract on the Book of Daniel (completed in 1508 in Seres, Greece) was published in Constantinople in 1510. At the beginning of this work, he confesses that his calculations are the result of logical deduction and are therefore subject to error. None the less he believed the messianic period began with the conquest of Constantinople by the Turks in 1453; this victory will be followed by the fall of Rome. The authority he adduces for this claim is the Targum of Jonathan ben Uzziel on Lamentations 4.21 and Obadiah 1.20: 'The exiles in Halah who are of the people of Israel shall possess Phoenicia as far as Zarephath; and the exiles of Jerusalem who are in Sepharad shall possess the cities of the Negeb' (i.e. Palestine). According to Halevi, Jews are now living in the final hour of exile. The basis of this calculation is found in Daniel 12.11 where the figure 1290 is mentioned. According to Halevi this period should not be reckoned from the destruction (3828 AM), but from 4000 AM. Thus the Messiah may be expected in 5290 AM (4000 + 1290) or AD 1530.

A second figure of this period was Solomon Molko (sixteenth century), the Marrano kabbalist, mystic and pseudo-Messiah. Using *gematria* he concluded that the messianic year would take place in 5300 AM or AD 1540. At the end of his messianic work, *Sepher ha-Mefoar*, he stated: 'I have no permission to reveal that which is hidden, but our deliverance is near at hand and will be revealed to all soon in our own days.' Again, in a letter to his friends he paraphrased Proverbs 3.2–18 as prophetic of the history of Israel, and argued that the present time is the period of divine love in which the Lord is about to fulfil his promise of deliverance as stated in Jeremiah 31.3 ('I have loved you with an everlasting love; therefore I have continued my faithfulness to you').

The Italian rabbi and kabbalist Mordecai ben Judah Dato (sixteenth century) believed the Messiah would arrive in 1575. In the words of his contemporary Azariah dei Rossi: 'And more particularly do we know that a famed kabbalist and scholar, Mordecai Dato, wrote a special book named after his brother, *Migdal David*, in which he convincingly proved that the great hope of Israel for the beginning of redemption and the building of the Temple will be fulfilled in the year 1575.' It appears that this date was regarded by many scholars as the year of messianic redemption. Thus dei Rossi stated: 'I am aware of a whole group of the "sons of prophets" who are waiting for the year 1575 as the day of God, in which God will lead forth his people in joy to everlasting salvation.' Such a view was based on the figure 1335 in Daniel 12.12, which was counted from the year 4000 AM (4000 + 1335 = 5335 AM or AD 1575).

It appears that the kabbalist Isaac Luria (sixteenth century) also expected the Messiah to appear in AD 1575. According to the narrative of Solomon Shelemiel ben Hayyim written in 1609:

> At one time near to the hour of his death, we stood with our master Luria by the tomb of Shemaya and Abtalion in Giscala, which is three miles distant from Safed, and he said to us that Shemaya and Abtalion had told him that we should pray that the Messiah ben Joseph should not die. But we did not understand and we did not inquire further . . . It was not long before our master was summoned on high. It was then that we understood that he spoke of himself, and that he was the first Messiah ben Joseph, whose sole mission on earth was to bring about the redemption and fill the whole earth with the messianic kingdom.

On another occasion, Luria asked his followers whether they would accompany him to Jerusalem on the Sabbath. When they hesitated, he declared: 'Woe unto us that we have not proved worthy to be redeemed. Had you promptly and unanimously replied that you were ready to go, Israel would have then and there been redeemed. For the hour had come, but you were not ready.'

At the end of the sixteenth century Naphtali Herz ben Jacob Elhanan, who was a German kabbalist and disciple of Luria, compiled a mystical treatise in which he asserted that Isaac Luria was the Messiah ben Joseph. If Luria had lived two years longer, he stated, he would have inaugurated the messianic era. But because the age was unworthy, he died after two years' sojourn in Palestine. The year 1475 was a time of grace – since that year God raises up a righteous person in every generation who could become the Messiah if the nation merits redemption.

Another figure of this period, Gedalia ibn Yahya (sixteenth century), suggested 1598 as the year of the Messiah:

> But I, though young, have bethought me to tell you in connection with this matter (the messianic calculation) what occurred

to me, and I swear to you that my words are true. On the night of the seventh day of Passover in the year 1555, being unable to sleep, I began to reflect on how long it will be to the end of the wonders. After a long time I fell asleep, but in the morning, behold, there was an olive leaf in my mouth. The verse 'I see him, but not now' (Numbers 24.17) came to my mind. I found that the numerical value of the entire verse is 5358. Actually the value of the verse is 5312, which is equal to the *gematria* of the letters *he, shin, yod, bet,* suggesting the verse 'he has turned back my wrath from the people of Israel' (Numbers 25.11). Add to this figure the number of letters in Numbers 24.17 from the words 'a star shall come forth' to the end of the verse = 46 and you have the year 5358, or 1598 AD.

Again, David ben Solomon ibn Abi Zimra (15th–16th century) argued on the basis of *gematria* that the final redemption will occur 600 years before the close of the sixth millennium (5400 AM or AD 1640). According to ibn Abi Zimra, this occurrence will take place in the first century of the fifth millennium (AD 1540–1640). Even though the sins of the people may delay the arrival of the Messiah, he will arrive during this time. A later date was advanced by Samuel ben Judah Velerio (second half of the sixteenth century) who wrote a commentary on the Book of Daniel in which he argues that the time of exile will be 1800 years. (In Daniel 7.25 'time' = 400 years; 'times' = 800 years; 'half a time' = 600 years $[\frac{400+800}{2}]$ = 400 + 800 + 600 = 1800). The second Temple was destroyed in 3828 AM; the end of the present exile will thus take place in 5628 AM (3828 + 1800) or AD 1868. An even later year was given by Joseph ben David ibn Yahya (15th–16th century) who wrote a commentary on Daniel. The prophecy in Daniel 8.14, he maintains, which contains the figure 2300, was given during the reign of Cyrus in 3391 AM; messianic redemption will take place 2300 years later in 5691 AM (or AD 1931).

Pseudo-Messiahs

At the beginning of the sixteenth century the German Jew Asher Lämmlein appeared in Isphia near Venice, proclaiming that the Messiah would appear in 1502. In his chronicle *Tzemah David*, David Gans (1541–1613) described Lämmlein's claim:

In the year 1502 Rabbi Lämmlein announced the advent of the Messiah, and throughout the dispersion of Israel his words were credited. Even among the gentiles the news spread, and many believed him. My grandfather Seligman Ganz smashed his oven in which he baked the *matzot*, being firmly convinced that the next year he would bake his *matzot* in the Holy Land. And I heard from my old teacher, Rabbi Eliezer Trivash, of Frankfurt, that the matter was not without basis, but that he (Lämmlein) had shown signs and proofs, but that perhaps because of our sins was the coming of the Messiah delayed.

During this period David Reuveni also aroused messianic expectations, claiming to be the son of a King Solomon and the brother of a King Joseph who ruled over the lost tribes of Reuben, Gad and half Manasseh in the desert of Habor; simultaneously he also claimed descent from the tribe of Judah, tracing his origins to King David. In 1523 he arrived in Venice, declaring that he was the commander-in-chief of his brother's army. There he requested Venetian Jews to assist him with a mission to the Pope. In February of the next year he arrived in Rome riding on a white horse and was greeted by the humanist Cardinal Egidio da Viterbo. Later he was received by Pope Clement VII to whom he proposed an alliance between his state and Christendom against the Muslims. To this end he recommended that the Pope give letters to the Holy Roman emperor Charles V, Francis I of France, as well as a letter to the mythical 'Prester John' in Ethiopia. Although the Pope sought an anti-Turkish alliance, he delayed about a year before he gave Reuveni a letter for the king of Portugal and another for the Ethiopian king. In the meantime, Reuveni gained support from a number of Jews who sent him money as well as a silk banner embroidered with the Ten Commandments.

From 1525 to 1527 Reuveni sojourned in Portugal where King John II received him as an official ambassador. The Marrano community viewed him as the Messiah, and he declared to the representative of the sultan of Fez that the time had come for Jews to liberate the Holy Land from the Muslims. In addition, he established contact with Jews in North Africa. Despite such a reception, his claims brought about considerable unrest and suspicion at court. Summoned by the king, he was accused of attempting to persuade Marranos to return to Judaism. When Diego Pires (Solomon Molko) proclaimed he was a Jew, Reuveni was ordered to leave Portugal, much to the despair of the Marrano community. On his departure he encouraged these Jews to remain faithful – he had come to declare their imminent deliverance. Eventually he was arrested, but later released on the instructions of the emperor Charles V.

For a brief time he was shipwrecked off the coast of Provence, then imprisoned for two years, and finally released at the request of the king of France on the payment of a ransom by the Avignon and Carpentras communities. In 1530 he returned to Venice after visiting several places in Italy; there he attempted to have consultations with the city governors to bring his plans to the attention of the emperor. Again, he evoked messianic longing among the Jewish population. At the suggestion of Frederick, Marquis of Mantua, he was encouraged to settle in Mantua. However, Reuveni's enemies among the Jews charged that Reuveni had forged a number of letters that he had previously lost on his travels. In response, Frederick warned the Pope and Charles V when Reuveni and Solomon Molko appeared before the emperor in 1532. There they were imprisoned. Molko was burned at the stake, and Reuveni was taken to Spain in chains where he was charged with seducing new Christians back to the Jewish faith and put to death.

A third messianic figure of this period was Solomon Molko (sixteenth century). Born in Lisbon of Marrano parents, he was originally called Diego Pires. At the age of twenty-one he became secretary to the king's council and a recorder at the court of appeals. After meeting David Reuveni when he arrived in Portugal in 1525, he asked to be circumcised. When Reuveni refused to perform this act, he circumcised himself and adopted a Hebrew name. When Reuveni was forced to leave Portugal because he was suspected of his involvement in Molko's conversion, he suggested to Molko that he flee as well. Although the details of Molko's departure are unclear, Reuveni later asserted that he had sent Molko on a secret diplomatic mission to Turkey; Molko himself claimed that he received a divine communication which dictated his departure.

After travelling to various lands he settled in Salonika for some time where he studied kabbalah and gathered followers who urged him to publish a collection of his sermons about messianic redemption. When Rome was sacked in 1527, he believed he saw the signs of the impending deliverance; he returned to Italy in 1529 where he preached about messianic redemption. When an informer revealed that he was a Marrano who had reverted to Judaism, he fled to Pesaro and later to

Rome. By this time he was persuaded he was the Messiah. To fulfil the talmudic legend about the suffering of the Messiah, he dressed as a beggar and sat for thirty days, fasting among the sick on a bridge over the Tiber near the pope's palace.

Eventually Pope Clement VII granted him protection and he preached extensively. At the end of 1530 he left Rome for Venice where he met with Reuveni. When he attempted to mediate in a dispute between Jacob Mantino, the pope's physician, and Elijah Halfon, a kabbalist and physician, Molko aroused the hatred of Mantino and fled to Rome. None the less Mantino followed him and spread rumours about his activities. Molko was accused by an inquisitional court of judaizing and condemned to be burned at the stake. When the pope intervened on his behalf, he was saved and another burned in his place. In 1532 Molko travelled to northern Italy where he again met Reuveni, and together they went on a mission to emperor Charles V. According to Rabbi Joselmann of Rosheim, Molko came in order to rouse the emperor to enlist the Jews to fight against the Turks. However, instead the emperor brought Molko to Mantua where he was burned at the stake in 1532 for refusing to convert to Christianity. After his death many of his disciples refused to believe he had died, remaining faithful to his messianic vision.

Seventeenth-century messianic expectations

In the seventeenth century, Hayyim Vital (16th–17th century), the disciple and successor to Isaac Luria, announced himself as the Messiah ben Joseph. Although he set no specific year for the advent of the messianic age, he stated that the Messiah would certainly come during his lifetime. Thus he wrote:

> In the year 1553 a man from Persia, whose name was Rabbi Shaltiel Alshaikh, who sees visions in his waking state, a wise and pious man, who fasts daily, told me that he was continually being informed (by visions) that the redemption of Israel depends upon me (Vital) through my causing Israel to repent, and they also informed him concerning my excellence; and unto this very year (1610) he is still writing me letters about his visions regarding myself and the redemption which is depended upon me.

At about the same time he also recounted that a certain Rabbi Sagura visited a magician and fortune-teller to inquire about the redemption, and was told that Israel's lack of repentance delayed the coming of the Messiah. However, if the Jewish people listened to Hayyim Vital, good fortune would come to them; on the other hand much suffering would befall them if they did not hearken to his words.

Another figure of this period, Isaiah Horowitz (16th–17th century) emphasized that the study of the *Zohar* was imperative. 'Those who study kabbalah', he wrote, 'are tenfold more exalted than those who study the Bible and Mishnah.' This mystical work was hidden purposely; it would not be revealed until the end of time. Previously it was with the angels for their erudition, but with the approach of the messianic era it was revealed to human beings so that they might engage in its study and the merit accruing from this activity would hasten the coming of the Messiah. Referring to the messianic calculations in *Midrash ha-Neelam* where the biblical phrase, 'In this year of jubilee each of you shall return to his property', is adduced to demonstrate the year of the Messiah's arrival, Horowitz asserted this would occur in 1648. Yom-Tob Lipmann Heller (16th–17th century) in his commentary on Avot also appears to adopt this date as the year of messianic deliverance, as did many other scholars of this period.

Prominent among the messianic speculators of the seventeenth century was Manasseh ben Israel who was convinced that the hour of redemption was near, awaiting the complete dispersion of Israel throughout the world. On the basis of this belief he petitioned Oliver Cromwell to readmit the Jews into England. Thus in his *Vindiciae Judaeorum*, he wrote: 'For I conceived that our universal dispersion was a necessary circumstance to be fulfilled before all that shall be accomplished which the Lord hath promised to the people of the Jews, concerning their restoration and their returning again into their own land.'

His belief that the messianic epoch was near at hand was based on several assumptions. First, the present tribulations of Israel were so great that they could be nothing other than the sufferings prophesied in Scripture prior to the coming of the Messiah. 'Oh, how we have seen these things in the banishment of England, France and Spain!' he wrote. The Inquisition, frequent martyrdoms, and universal persecution are the fulfilment of the prophet's warnings. Yet, he stated, 'if the Lord fulfil his words in calamities, he will fulfil it also in felicities'. A second factor was Israel's faithfulness during such persecution. Such constancy demonstrates that God has prepared a reward for his chosen people. Even now, he asserted, there is an indication of God's favour in the attainments of certain prominent Jews. A third conviction undergirding Manasseh's messianic beliefs was his opinion that Israel must be dispersed throughout the world before the Jewish people can be redeemed. Such a view was based on Daniel 12.7: 'When the shattering of the power of the holy people comes to an end all these things would be accomplished.'

Finally, Manasseh argued that the prophecy of the two legs of the image of Nebuchadnezzer in Daniel, which will be overthrown by the fifth monarchy, refers to the Ottoman Empire. In his *Piedra Gloriosa o de la Estatua de Nebuchadnesar*, he summed up this interpretation:

Whereby one sees in this prophecy five propositions diffusely expressed, namely:

I. That by those four figures of beasts the four monarchies are signified, as it says in verse 17: these beasts are four, four monarchies, this being described with all the circumstances and typified by the statue of Nebuchadnesar.

II. That the fourth monarchy will be divided into two nations, of different laws, this division being made by the little Mohammedan horn, and they are the two legs of the statue.

III. That this Roman empire will be divided into ten kingdoms, which are the ten horns derived from that beast and the ten toes of the statue.

IV. That after the termination and destruction of these kingdoms there will follow the monarchy of Israel, as it is the holy people and the stone which turns into a mountain, filling up the whole world.

V. That this monarchy of Israel will be temporal and terrestrial, as it says 'under the heaven', all that which the Lord revealed to Nebuchadnesar, in a general way as to a heathen, he explained again with more diffusion and latitude and other circumstances perfectly to Daniel, revealing to him at the same time the duration of the fourth monarchy, although in such enigmatic terms that he alone understood them and kept them in his heart, as he affirms himself in the last words of this chapter.

In response to the Christian Paul Felgenhauer of Bohemia's claim that the coming of the Messiah was imminent, Manasseh pointed out that a condition of the messianic age is Israel's supremacy over all people. In a reply to Felgenhauer, he wrote:

> That good news brought by you, O most respected Sir, to the people of Israel in these recent times of affliction was the more welcome to my mind since, after the sorrows of so many ages and the long deferring of our hopes, I have not ceased to desire the same most ardently . . . So then, O worthy messenger of good things, is the arrival of our God at hand, who pities us, and will he send in a short time to us the desire of so many ages, the Messiah at our head? . . . As for what you say about the third sign of the coming of the Messiah, concerning this prediction of a kingdom of Israel throughout the world, that not only appears probable to me but we see something of the kind already coming to light and producing its effect.

The Shabbatean Movement

Messianic expectations increased as the year 1648 – the *annus mirabilis* of the *Zohar* – approached. Throughout the Jewish world, pious Jews waited in expectation of divine deliverance. In Palestine the rabbis sent an encyclical prayer to be recited evening and morning throughout the diaspora asking for the restoration of the Davidic kingdom and for the remission of the birth pangs of the Messiah. Another pastoral letter was sent from Palestine to the diaspora encouraging all people to act peacefully and with good will in preparation for the coming of the Messiah. In addition, various pamphlets on the correct practice of repentance were widely circulated.

In the midst of such messianic longing, the *Zohar* was zealously studied; according to tradition, such a preoccupation would hasten the advent of the messianic age. Thus Hayyim Vital wrote in the introduction to his *Etz Hayyim* that it is a religious duty and a joy to God to have the kabbalah widely known: through such study the Messiah would come. Similarly Abraham Azulai (d. 1643) wrote: 'This book (the *Zohar*) will be revealed in the days of king Messiah in order to give support to the Shekinah, and all those who will be favoured by this revelation will also merit redemption. Verily this service (the study of the *Zohar*) which is all too rare in our day is more important than all "the rams of Nebaioth" which were sacrificed in the days when the Temple existed.'

In this milieu following the Cossack Rebellion which decimated Polish Jews, the arrival of a self-proclaimed messianic king Shabbatai Tzevi (1626–76) brought about a transformation of Jewish life and thought. Born in Smyrna into a wealthy family, Shabbatai received a traditional Jewish education and later engaged in study of the *Zohar*. After leaving Smyrna in the 1650s he spent ten years in various cities in Greece as well as in Constantinople and Jerusalem. Eventually he became part of a kabbalistic group in Cairo and travelled to Gaza where he encountered Nathan Benjamin Levi who believed Shabbatai was the Messiah. In 1665 his messiahship was proclaimed and Nathan sent letters to Jews in the diaspora asking them to repent and recognize Shabbatai Tzevi as their redeemer. Shabbatai, he announced, would take the sultan's crown, bring back the ten lost tribes and inaugurate the period of messianic redemption.

After a brief sojourn in Jerusalem, Shabbatai went to Smyrna where he encountered strong opposition on the part of some local rabbis. In response he denounced the disbelievers and declared that he was the Anointed of the God of Jacob. This action evoked a hysterical response – a number of Jews fell into trances and had visions of him on a royal throne crowned as king of Israel. In 1666 he journeyed to Constantinople, but on the order of the grand vizier he was arrested and put into prison. Within a short time the prison quarters became a messianic court; pilgrims from all over the world made their way to Constantinople to join in messianic rituals and ascetic activities. In addition hymns were written in his honour and new festivals were introduced. According to Nathan, who remained in Gaza, the alteration in Shabbatai's moods from illumination to withdrawal symbolized his soul's struggle with demonic powers: at times he was imprisoned by the powers of evil, but at other moments he prevailed against them.

The same year Shabbatai spent three days with the Polish kabbalist, Nehemiah ha-Kohen, who later denounced him to the Turkish authorities. Shabbatai was brought to court and given the choice between conversion and death. In the face of this alternative, he converted to Islam and took on the name Mehemmet Effendi. Such an act of apostasy scandalized most of his followers, but he defended himself by asserting that he had become a Muslim in obeisance to God's commands. Many of his followers accepted this explanation and refused to give up their belief. Some thought it was not Shabbatai who had become a Muslim, but rather a phantom who had taken on his appearance; the Messiah himself had ascended to heaven. Others cited biblical and rabbinic sources to justify Shabbatai's action. Nathan explained that the messianic task involved taking on the humiliation of being portrayed as a traitor to his people. Furthermore, he argued on the basis of Lurianic kabbalah, that there were two kinds of divine light – a creative light and another light opposed to the existence of anything other than the *Ayn Sof* (the Infinite). While creative light formed structures of creation in empty space during creation, the other light became the power of evil after the divine contraction at the time of creation. According to Nathan, the soul of the Messiah had been struggling against the power of evil from the beginning; his purpose was to allow divine light to penetrate this domain and bring about cosmic repair. In order to do this, the soul of the Messiah was not obliged to keep the law, but was free to descend into the abyss to liberate divine sparks which had become trapped there and in this way conquer evil. In this light Shabbatai's conversion to Islam was explicable.

After Shabbatai's act of apostasy, Nathan visited him in the Balkans and then travelled to Rome where he performed secret rites to bring about the end of the papacy. Shabbatai remained in Adrianople and Constantinople, where he lived as both Muslim and Jew. In 1672 he was deported to Albania where he disclosed his own kabbalistic teaching to his supporters. After he died in 1676, Nathan declared that Shabbatai had ascended into the supernal world. Eventually a number of groups continued in their belief that Shabbatai was the Messiah, including a sect, the Dissident (*Doenmeh*), which professed Islam publicly but nevertheless adhered to their own traditions. Marrying among themselves, they eventually evolved into antinomian sub-groups which violated Jewish sexual laws and asserted the divinity of Shabbatai and their leader, Baruchiah Russo (d. 1720). In Italy several Shabbatean groups also emerged and propagated their views.

In the eighteenth century the most important Shabbatean sect was led by Jacob Frank (1726–91) who was influenced by the *Doenmeh* in Turkey. Believing himself to be the incarnation of Shabbatai, Frank announced that he was the second person of the Trinity and gathered together a circle of disciples who indulged in licentious orgies. In the 1750s disputations took place between traditional Jews and Frankists; subsequently Frank expressed his willingness to become a Christian but he wished to maintain his own group. This request was refused by church leaders, yet Frank and his disciples were baptized. The clergy, however, became aware that Frank's trinitarian beliefs were not consonant with Christian doctrine, and he was imprisoned in 1760 for thirteen years; Frank then settled in Germany where he continued to subscribe to a variant of the Shabbatean kabbalistic tradition.

seven

Religious and Spiritual Zionism

With the conversion of Shabbatai Tzevi in the seventeenth century, the Jewish preoccupation with messianic calculation diminished. Many Jews became disillusioned with centuries of messianic anticipation and disappointment: the longing for the Messiah who would lead the Jewish people to the Holy Land and bring about the end of history seemed a distant hope. Instead eighteenth- and early nineteenth-century Jewry hailed the breaking down of the ghetto walls and the elimination of social barriers between Jews and Christians. In this milieu the belief in the Kingdom of God inaugurated by the Messiah–king receded in importance; in its place the clarion call for liberty, equality and fraternity signified the dawning of a golden age for the Jewish people. Yet despite the fact that the Enlightenment moulded the consciousness of most modern Jews, there were a number of religious figures who continued to subscribe to the traditional belief in the advent of the messianic era. Prominent among such figures was Yehuda hai Alkalai (18th–19th century) who argued that Jewish settlers should establish Jewish colonies in Palestine in anticipation of the coming of the Messiah. According to Alkalai the advent of the Messiah is not simply a divine act – it requires human labour and dedication. A similar view was adopted by Zwi Hirsch Kalischer (18th–19th century) who maintained that the messianic era will not take place immediately. Rather, the redemption of the Jewish people will occur gradually through the ingathering of the Jewish nation in their ancestral home. Like these two figures Ahad Ha-Am (19th–20th century) was also concerned with the spiritual redemption of the Jewish people, but his thought is devoid of traditional ideas of messianic deliverance. None the less, he emphasized that the Jewish state should embody the religious and spiritual ideals of the Jewish heritage. Another seminal early Zionist was Aharon David Gordon (19th–20th century) who advocated a mystical conception of the interaction between human beings and nature. For Gordon manual labour is central to personal and national salvation. Finally, Abraham Isaac Kook (19th–20th century) attempted to harmonize messianic aspirations with the efforts of modern secular Zionists. According to Kook, the divine spark is evident in the work of secular pioneers who sacrificed themselves to the land of Israel. In their different ways these five religious and spiritual champions of Zionism attempted to reconcile the Jewish tradition with the quest to rebuild modern Jewish life in the Holy Land.

Yehuda hai Alkalai: the Messiah and modern Zionism

In the nineteenth century within religious Orthodoxy there emerged a new trend, the advocacy of an active approach to Jewish Messianism. Rather than adopt a passive attitude towards the problem of redemption, these writers maintained that the Jewish nation must engage in the creation of a homeland in anticipation of the advent of the Messiah. Pre-eminent among such religious Zionists was Yehuda hai Alkalai, born in 1798 in Sarajevo to Rabbi Sholomo Alkalai, the spiritual leader of the local Jewish community. During his youth he lived in Palestine where he was influenced by kabbalistic thought. In 1825 he served as a rabbi in Semlin in Serbia; in 1834 he published a booklet entitled *Shema Yisrael* in which he advocated the establishment of Jewish colonies in Palestine, a view at variance with the traditional Jewish belief that the Messiah would come through an act of divine deliverance. When in 1840 the Jews of Damascus were charged with the blood libel, Alkalai became convinced that the Jewish people could be secure only in their own land. Henceforth he published a series of books and pamphlets explaining his plan of self-redemption.

In his *Minhat Yehuda* he argued on the basis of Scripture that the Messiah will not miraculously materialize; rather, he will be preceded by various preparatory events. In this light the Holy Land needs to be populated by Jewry in preparation for messianic deliverance: 'This new redemption will', he wrote,

> be different; our land is waste and desolate, and we shall have to build houses, dig wells, and plant vines and olive trees. We are, therefore, commanded not to attempt to go at once and all together in the Holy Land ... the Lord desires that we be redeemed in dignity; we cannot, therefore, migrate in a mass, for we should then have to live like Bedouins, scattered in tents all over the fields of the Holy Land. Redemption must come slowly. The land must, by degrees, be built up and prepared. ('The Third Redemption', in Hertzberg, p. 105)

For Alkalai, redemption is not simply a divine affair – it is also a human concern requiring labour and persistence.

This demystification of traditional messianic eschatology extends to Alkalai's advocacy of Hebrew as a language of communication. Traditionally Hebrew was viewed as a sacred language; it was not to be profaned by daily use. Alkalai, however, recognized the practical importance of having a single language for ordinary life in Palestine. He wrote:

> I wish to attest to the pain I have always felt at the error of our ancestors, that they allowed our Holy Tongue to be so forgotten. Because of this our people was divided into seventy peoples; our one language was replaced by the seventy languages of the lands of exile. If the Almighty should indeed show us his miraculous favour and gather us into our land, we would not be able to speak to each other and such a divided community could not succeed. (Hertzberg, p. 106)

It would be a mistake, he continues, to think that God will send an angel to teach his people all seventy languages. Instead the Jewish people must ensure that Hebrew is studied so that it can be used for ordinary life: 'We must redouble our efforts to maintain Hebrew and to strengthen its position. It must be the basis of our educational work' (Hertzberg, p. 106).

How can this process of redemption be accomplished? Alkalai stresses the importance of convening an assembly of those dedicated to the realization of this goal. Thus he asserts that the redemption must begin with efforts by Jews themselves. They must 'organize and unite, choose leaders, and leave the lands of exile. Since no community can exist without a governing body, the very first new ordinance must be the appointment of the elders of each district, men of piety and wisdom, to oversee all the affairs of the community' (Hertzberg, p. 106).

Reinterpreting the concept of the Messiah ben Joseph, he argues that this assembly of elders is in fact what is meant by the promise of the Messiah, the son of Joseph. For Alkalai, the process of deliverance follows a different sequence from what is depicted in traditional sources. The organization of an international Jewish body is, he believes, the first step to the redemption because out of this organization will emerge a fully authorized assembly of elders, and from the elders, the Messiah, son of Joseph, will appear. The vision of this first messianic figure should thus be understood as a process involving the emergence of a political leadership among the Jewish nation that would prepare the way for divine deliverance.

According to Alkalai, it is not impossible for Jews to carry out this project. The sultan, he maintains, would not object to such an aim since he knows that his Jewish subjects are loyal. What is required is that the Jewish people create a company along the lines of fire insurance or railroad companies. This body should then appeal to the sultan to give back the ancestral home to the Jewish people for an annual rent. 'Once the name of Israel is again applied to our land', he declared, 'all Jews will be inspired to help this company with all the means at their disposal. Though this venture will begin modestly, its future will be very great' (Hertzberg, p. 107).

Zwi Hirsch Kalischer: divine redemption and resettlement

Another early pioneer of religious Zionism was Zwi Hirsch Kalischer, the rabbi of Toun in the province of Posen. An early defender of Orthodoxy against the advances made by Reform Judaism, he championed the commandments prescribing faith in the Messiah and devotion to the Holy Land. In 1836 he expressed his commitment to Jewish settlement in Palestine in a letter to the head of the Berlin branch of the Rothschild family. 'The beginning of the redemption', he wrote, 'will come through natural causes by human effort and by the will of the governments to gather the scattered of Israel into the Holy Land' (Hertzberg, pp. 109–10).

Such a conviction did not actively engage Kalischer until 1860 when a society was organized in Frankfurt on the Oder to encourage Jewish settlement in Palestine. After joining this group, he published a Zionist work, *Derishat Zion*, which appeared in 1862. In this treatise he advocated the return of Jews to their native soil. The redemption of Israel, he argued, will not take place miraculously: 'The Almighty, blessed be his Name, will not suddenly descend from on high and command his people to go forth. Neither will he send the Messiah from heaven in a twinkling of an eye, to sound the great trumpet for the scattered of Israel and gather them into Jerusalem. He will not surround the holy city with a wall of fire or cause the holy Temple to descend from heaven' (see Avineri, p. 53). Instead the redemption of Israel will take place slowly, through awakening support from philanthropists and gaining the consent of other nations to the gathering of the Jewish people into the Holy Land.

This view, Kalischer maintained, is inherent in Scripture. Thus the prophet Isaiah declared:

> In days to come Jacob shall take root, Israel shall blossom and put forth shoots, and fill the whole world with fruit . . . In that day from the river Euphrates to the Brook of Egypt the Lord will thresh out the grain, and you will be gathered one by one, O people of Israel. And in that day a great trumpet will be blown, and those who were lost in the land of Assyria and those who were driven out to the land of Egypt will come and worship the LORD on the holy mountain at Jerusalem. (Isaiah 27.6, 12–13)

According to Kalischer, this passage implies that not all of Israel would return from exile at once, but instead would be gathered by degrees. This concept of redemption, he continues, is also contained in Isaiah 11.10: 'In that day the root of Jesse shall stand as an ensign to the peoples; him shall the nations seek, and his dwellings shall be glorious.' Here, he asserts, both a first and a second gathering are intended. The first ingathering will be to work the land, after which the nation will blossom forth to a glorious extent.

The coming of the Messiah must therefore be preceded by the creation of a Jewish homeland. It is not enough to wait for miracles; instead Jews must act to bring about this event. Quoting from a medieval devotional book, he asserted:

> When many Jews, pious and learned in the Torah, will volunteer to go to the Land of Israel and settle in Jerusalem, motivated by a desire to serve, by purity of spirit, and by love of holiness; when they will come, by ones and twos, from all four corners of the world; and when many will settle there and their prayers will increase at the holy mountain in Jerusalem, the Creator will then heed them and hasten the day of redemption. ('Seeking Zion', in Hertzberg, pp. 112–13)

Kalischer was aware that there were many Jews who would refuse to support those who are poor in the Holy Land. Such an attitude, he believed, is an argument put forward by Satan since the people of Palestine have risked their lives to become pioneers. 'In this country', he writes, 'which is strange to them, how could they go about finding a business or occupation, when they had never in their lives done anything of this kind? Their eyes can only turn to their philanthropic brethren, of whom they ask only enough to keep body and soul together, so that they can dwell in that Land which is God's portion on earth' (Hertzberg, p. 113).

For Kalischer practical steps must be taken to fulfil this dream of resettlement. What is required is that an organization be created to encourage emigration, and to purchase and cultivate farms and vineyards. Such a programme would be a ray of deliverance to those who are now languishing in Palestine due to poverty and famine; this situation would be utterly changed if those able to contribute to this effort were inspired by the vision of a Jewish homeland. An advantage of this scheme would be to bring to fruition those religious commandments that attach to working the soil of the Holy Land. Even those Jews who supervised the labourers would be aiding in the working of the land and would therefore have the same status as if they had personally fulfilled these commandments. But beyond all this, Kalischer was convinced that Jewish farming would be a spur to messianic redemption. The policy of active participation in the cultivation of the soil would not divert the people from the task of divine service; rather such labour would add dignity to God's Torah. By working the land, Jews would be dedicating themselves to bringing about the advent of the messianic age.

In addition, such a policy would raise the dignity of the Jewish people among the nations, for then the foreign peoples would say of the children of Israel that they have the will to redeem the land of their ancestors. In conclusion, Kalischer declared:

> Let us take to heart the examples of the Italians, Poles, and Hungarians, who laid down their lives and possessions in the struggle for national independence, while we, the children of Israel, who have the most glorious and the holiest of lands as our inheritance, are spiritless and silent. We should be ashamed of ourselves! All the other peoples have striven only for the sake of their own national honour; how much more should we exert ourselves, for our duty is to labour not only for the glory of our ancestors but for the glory of God who chose Zion. (Hertzberg, p. 114)

Because Kalischer was financially independent, he was able to engage in a variety of activities to bring about the fulfilment of this vision. In 1866 he was instrumental in persuading a group to purchase land for colonization on the outskirts of Jaffa. Eventually he influenced the Alliance Israélite Universelle – the organization founded in France in 1860 to protect Jewish rights throughout the world – to establish an agricultural school in Jaffa in 1870. Nonetheless Orthodox critics of his views denounced what they believed was a departure from tradition. Even in Jerusalem pietists

who benefited from collections of alms for the poor in the Holy
Land attacked his plans. According to these zealous upholders of
tradition, the creation of agricultural settlements where Jews would
engage in tilling the soil would lead the people away from the study
of the Torah and provoke heretical attitudes contrary to the Jewish
faith.

Ahad Ha-Am: the Jewish state and spiritual values

Like Alkalai and Kalischer, Asher Zvi Ginsberg (later known as
Ahad Ha-Am) was concerned with the spiritual redemption of the
Jewish people, although his thought is devoid of traditional Jewish
ideas of messianic deliverance. Born in Skvira in the Russian
Ukraine on 18 August 1856, he initially received a traditional Jewish education. In 1868 his family moved to an estate which his
wealthy father leased; there he studied the works of medieval Jewish philosophers and writers of the Enlightenment. At the age of
twenty he pursued French and German literature and philosophy,
and later unsuccessfully attempted to continue his study in various
European capitals. In 1886 he moved to Odessa where he began
to publish articles dealing with contemporary Jewish life.

His first essay, 'Wrong Way', which appeared in 1889, set the
stage for his role within the Hovevei Zion movement. In this work
he advocated the return to Zion, but remained critical of a number
of aspects of the movement's platform. In a later essay, 'The Jewish
State and the Jewish Problem', written after his return from the
First Zionist Congress, he discussed Max Nordeau's opening statement to the Congress. According to Nordeau, the major problem
facing East European Jewry is economic misery, whereas Western
Jewry is confronted by the failure of the Emancipation to provide
a firm base for Jewish identity in modern society. According to
Nordeau, these dilemmas point to the need for the creation of a
Jewish state in Palestine.

For Ahad Ha-Am, however, the matter is more complicated.
Assuming that the Zionist movement attains this goal, what would
occur when the Jewish state absorbs the first wave of immigrants?
Will the Jewish problem be solved? Clearly not all Jews throughout
the world (numbering 10,000,000) will be able to settle in Palestine.
What would be the result if only a small section of the world Jewish
population emigrated? Ahad Ha-Am argues that the economic
problems facing East European Jewry would not be solved for
those who remained behind. The Jewish state could only contribute

to cultural and spiritual regeneration. Thus the central dilemma faced by Zionism is how the spiritual perplexities of Jews in the diaspora could be resolved by the creation of a Jewish homeland.

According to Ahad Ha-Am, Zionism is able to solve the problems of Western Jewry more readily than to ameliorate the condition of Jews in Eastern Europe. The Jew in the West is separated from Jewish culture and simultaneously alienated from the society in which he resides. The existence of a Jewish state would enable him to solve the problems of national identity, compensating him for his lack of integration into the culture of the country in which he lives:

> If a Jewish state were re-established [in Palestine], a state arranged and organized exactly after the pattern of other states, then he [the Western Jew] could live a full, complete life among his own people, and find at home all that he now sees outside, dangled before his eyes, but out of reach. Of course, not all the Jews will be able to take wing and go to their state; but the very existence of the Jewish state will raise the prestige of those who remain in exile, and their fellow citizens will no more despise them and keep them at arm's length as though they were ignoble slaves, dependent entirely on the hospitality of others. (Ha'am, pp. 74–5)

It is this ideal which is able to cure the Jew in the West of his social unease, the consciousness of his inferiority in lands where he is an alien.

In Eastern Europe, however, such a solution is inadequate. With the disappearance of ghetto life, Judaism lost its hold on the Jewish population. In the past, Jews were able to sustain their traditions through common experience. The passing of this closed society led to the disintegration of the Jewish heritage. For Ahad Ha-Am, it is impossible for Eastern European Jews to return to the traditional religious symbolism of the ghetto. What is required is the establishment of a new Jewish social identity in Israel:

> Judaism needs at present but little. It needs not an independent state, but only the creation in its native land of conditions favourable to its development: a good-sized settlement of Jews working without hindrance in every branch of culture, from agriculture and handicrafts to science and literature. This Jewish settlement, which will be a gradual growth, will become in course of time the centre of the nation, wherein its spirit will

find pure expression and develop in all its aspects up to the highest degree of perfection of which it is capable. Then from the centre the spirit of Judaism will go forth to the great circumference, to all the communities of the diaspora, and will breathe new life into them and preserve their unity; and when our national culture in Palestine has attained that level, we may be confident that it will produce men in the country who will be able, on a favourable opportunity, to establish a state which will be truly a Jewish state, and not merely a state of Jews. (Ha'am, pp. 78–9)

Israel is thus to be a state infused with Jewish values, and not simply a homeland for the Jewish people; it must embody the religious and cultural ideals of the Jewish past. According to Ahad Ha-Am, the strength of Judaism resided in the prophetic emphasis on spiritual values; a Jewish state devoid of such an orientation will lose the support of diaspora Jewry. A secular state is not viable, he argues, because 'a political ideal which does not rest on the national culture is apt to seduce us from our loyalty to spiritual greatness, and to beget in us a tendency to find the path of glory in the attainment of material power and political dominion, thus breaking the thread that unites us with the past, and undermining our historical basis' (Ha'am, p. 80).

Without spiritual ideals, political power may become an end in itself. To clarify this point, he uses the example of Judaea under Herod the Great:

History teaches us that in the days of the Herodian house Palestine was indeed a Jewish state, but the national culture was despised and persecuted, and the ruling house did everything in its power to implant Roman culture in the country, and frittered away the national resources in the building of heathen temples and amphitheatres, and so forth. Such a Jewish state would spell death and utter degradation for our people. Such a Jewish state . . . would not be able to give us a feeling of national glory; and the national culture, in which we might have sought and found our glory, would not be implanted in our state and would not be the principle of its life. (Ha'am, pp. 80–1)

After visiting Jewish settlements in Palestine, Ahad Ha-Am wrote an essay, 'Truth from the Land of Israel', filled with his impression of the country. Deploring land speculation, he called on the Hovevei Zion to intervene in this odious practice. In addition, he focuses on the dilemmas faced by Zionism because of the existence of the sizeable Arab population. This people, he maintains, must be confronted by those wishing to settle in the land. As early as 1891 he recognized that the Arab Palestinians might press for the creation of a national movement. It is a mistake to believe that Palestine is devoid of a native population. He writes, 'We tend to believe abroad that Palestine is nowadays almost completely deserted, a non-cultivated wilderness, and anyone can come there and buy as much land as his heart desires. But in reality this is not the case. It is difficult to find anywhere in the country Arab land which lies fallow' (Avineri, p. 122).

What is required is a sense of realism. Jews should not regard themselves as superior to their Arab neighbours. Instead they should perceive that the Arabs are fiercely proud and determined:

> We tend to believe abroad that all Arabs are desert barbarians, an asinine people who do not see or understand what is going on around them. This is a cardinal mistake . . . The Arabs, and especially the city dwellers, understand very well what we want and what we do in the country; but they behave as if they do not notice it because at present they do not see any danger for themselves or their future in what we are doing and are therefore trying to turn to their benefit these new guests . . . But when the day will come in which the life of our people in the land of Israel will develop to such a degree that they will push aside the local population by little or much, then it will not easily give up its place. (Avineri, p. 123)

In order to flourish in the land of their ancestors Ahad Ha-Am insists that the Jewish people act with love and respect to those Arabs in their midst.

Although Ahad Ha-Am's vision of the return to the Holy Land was not filled with messianic longing, his idealization of the spiritual, religious and cultural dimensions of Judaism and their embodiment in a Jewish state was rooted in Jewish messianism. For Ahad Ha-Am, it would not be a divinely appointed Messiah who would bring about the realization of God's Kingdom on earth. Rather this would be the task of the Jewish people themselves. Through the creation of a Jewish state, the spiritual values of the faith are to materialize in the Holy Land.

Aharon David Gordon: Man and Nature

Like other modern religious and spiritual writers, Aharon David
Gordon was anxious to confront the problem of Jewish regeneration in the Holy Land. In formulating his conception of Jewish
life in Palestine, he grounded his outlook in a mystical conception
of the interaction of human beings and nature. Born in a village
in the province of Podolia, Gordon spent his youth in a farming
village on an estate which his father managed for the family of
Baron Horace Günzburg. After his marriage, he served as an
official from 1880 to 1923 on a large tract of land the Günzburgs
leased for farming. At the age of forty-seven, he emigrated to Palestine where he worked as a labourer in the vineyards and wineries
of Petah Tikva. Later he worked in Galilee; his final days were
spent in Degania, one of the earliest kibbutzim.

According to Gordon, manual labour is central to both personal
and national salvation. In an essay, 'Some Observations', published in 1910, he outlines two alternatives facing the Jewish community in Palestine. The first is 'the practical way of the world
wise . . . the continuation of exile life, with all its shortsighted
practical wisdom'. For Gordon exile is not simply geographical
dislocation: it involves psychological and existential alienation,
combining dependence on others and estrangement from creative
life. The second alternative calls for a renaissance of Jewish life:
the way of manual labour. This latter option, he believes, will
renew the national energies of the Jewish people:

> We have as yet no national assets because our people have not
> paid the price for them. A people can acquire a land only by its
> own effort, by realizing the potentialities of its body and soul,
> by unfolding and revealing its inner self. This is a two-sided
> transaction, but the people comes first – the people comes before
> the land. But a parasitical people is not a living people. Our
> people can be brought to life only if each one of us recreates
> himself through labour and a life close to nature. ('Some Ques-
> tions', in Hertzberg, p. 376)

Gordon's understanding of Jewish life in the diaspora was
related to his theories of anthropology and psychology. To Gordon
a person can become fully human only through contact with
nature. Physical labour is thus essential for personal growth and
fulfilment. In this light Jewish existence in the diaspora is a distorted mode of living, not only because the Jewish nation lost its

homeland, but also because it lacked the land in which Jews could realize their full human potential through physical work. In Gordon's view, a Jewish national renaissance will not take place simply through migration: it must involve a return to the self through the cultivation of the land. A fundamental distinction must hence be drawn between a transference of exiles to the Holy Land, and a radical reconstruction of Jewish life through agricultural employment.

Such a radical analysis calls for the total transformation of Jewish life. The way of national rebirth, he writes,

> embraces every detail of our individual lives. Every one of us is required to refashion himself so that the *Galut* (diaspora) Jew within him becomes a truly emancipated Jew; so that the unnatural, defective, splintered person within him may be changed into a natural, wholesome human being who is true to himself; so that his *Galut* life, which has been fashioned by alien and extraneous influences, hampering his natural growth and self-realization, may give way to one that allows him to develop freely, to his fullest stature in all dimensions. (Hertzberg, p. 376)

Such a process of rehabilitation must take place if Jewish exile is to cease, even if Palestine becomes populated with Jewish emigrants.

According to Gordon, traditional Jewish life in the diaspora was richer than modern existence in the post-Emancipation world. Prior to the Emancipation Jews sought to ameliorate their position without abandoning Torah Judaism. Yet today material prosperity has overshadowed all other values. To counteract this corrosive attitude, the 'religion of nature' must become the dominant ideology in Palestine. In an essay entitled 'Labour' Gordon insists that the Jewish people is linked to its homeland; if it is divorced from agricultural labour, it becomes disfigured and emasculated. In their advocacy of a Jewish state, modern Zionist writers have overlooked the fundamental requirements for a vibrant national life. He writes:

> A people that was completely divorced from nature, that during two thousand years was imprisoned within walls, that became inured to all forms of life except to a life of labour, cannot become once again a living, natural, working people without bending all its willpower toward that end. We lack the fundamental element: we lack labour (not labour done because of

necessity, but labour to which man is organically and naturally linked), labour by which a people becomes rooted in its soil and its culture. (Avineri, p. 155)

The absence of physical work is, he believes, an essential defect in the Jewish character. Such a condition was created by the exile, and its perpetuation has contributed to the continuation of exile; paradoxically the denigration of labour enabled Jews to accommodate to a diaspora existence. If, however, the Jewish people had been more concerned with land, they would have sought to return to their former landed existence. Now that the Jews have a country of their own, Gordon is fearful of the resurgence of this contempt for natural work:

> Now let us assume that somewhere we already have settled a goodly number of Jews. Will this attitude of ours change there of itself? Will a transformation of our soul take place without a radical cure? Will not our Jewish people at all times prefer trading, speculation, especially business in which others will labour while they will manage the enterprise? (Avineri, p. 155)

What is required is a cultural revolution. The Holy Land must be cultivated; buildings constructed; and roads built.

> Each piece of work, each deed, each act is an element of culture. Herein is the foundation of culture, the stuff of which it is made. Arrangement, method, shape, the way in which a thing is done – these are forms of culture. What a man does, what he feels, thinks, lives, while he is at work, and while he is not working, the conditions arising from these relations – these mould themselves into the spirit of culture. From these, higher culture draws nourishment – science, art, beliefs and opinions, poetry, ethics, religion. (Avineri, p. 156)

Authentic Zionism must bring to Palestine the foundations of manual labour from which such a higher culture can emerge. The task of modern Zionism is thus to foster a sense of dedication to ordinary toil. '(We have) to work with our very own hands at all things which make up life (in Palestine), to labour with our own hands at all kinds of works, at all kinds of crafts and trades from the most skilled, the cleanliest and the easiest to the coarsest, the most despised, the most difficult. We must feel all that the worker feels, think what he thinks, live the life he lives, in ways that are our ways. Then we can consider that we have our own culture, for then we shall have life' (Avineri, p. 156).

What is lacking in contemporary Zionism, he argues, is a recognition of the essential link between man and nature. This is the cosmic element of national identity. Jews who have been uprooted must learn to know the soil and prepare it for the transplantation of the Jewish nation. It is necessary to study climatic conditions and everything required to grow agricultural produce: 'We who have been torn away from nature, who have lost the savour of natural living – if we desire life, we must establish a new relationship with nature, we must open a new account with it' (Avineri, p. 157). This quest to bring about a radical transformation in Jewish consciousness was motivated by a utopian vision of Jewish life in Palestine. Although Gordon's thinking lacked the religious framework of Orthodox Jewish Zionists, it had quasi-religious connotations reminiscent of previous writers who longed for the redemption of the Jewish nation.

Abraham Isaac Kook: Jewish pioneers and divine deliverance

Following in the footsteps of such religious Zionists as Alkalai and Kalischer, Abraham Isaac Kook – the first Ashkenazi chief rabbi of Palestine after the British mandate – formulated a vision of messianic redemption integrating the creation of a Jewish state. Such a conception was influenced by stirrings within the religious wing of the Hovevei Zion movement. Leaders like Shmuel Mohiliver, Yitzhak Yaakov Reines, and Yehiel Michal Pines paved the way for Kook's religious espousal of Jewish nationalism. In Kook's writings there is the first attempt systematically to combine the centrality of the Holy Land within the religious tradition with the Zionist attempt to resettle the Jewish people in their homeland.

Born in Greiva, Latvia, in 1865, Kook received a traditional Jewish education and in 1895 became rabbi of Bausk. In 1904 he emigrated to Palestine where he served as a rabbi of Jaffa. During this period he wrote prolifically and became an important communal leader. In 1914 Kook visited Europe, but was stranded in Switzerland at the outbreak of World War I. From 1916 to 1919 he served as a rabbi in London, and eventually returned to Palestine to serve as chief rabbi of the Ashkenazi Jews in Jerusalem. Two years later he was elected Ashkenazi head of the new rabbinic court of appeals (in effect the Ashkenazi chief rabbi of Palestine), and served in this post until his death in 1935.

Unlike secularists who advocated practical efforts to secure a

Jewish state, Kook embarked on the task of reinterpreting the Jewish religious tradition to transform religious messianic anticipation into the basis for collaboration with the aspirations of modern Zionism. According to Kook, the centrality of Israel is a fundamental dimension of Jewish life and a crucial element of Jewish religious consciousness. Yet the fervent belief in messianic deliverance has not been accompanied by an active policy of resettlement. This disjunction between religious aspirations for the return from exile and the desire of most Jews to live in the diaspora highlights the confusion in Jewish thinking about the role of Israel in Jewish life. There is thus a contradiction between the messianic belief in a return to Zion and the accommodating attitude to exile of most Jews throughout history.

For Kook, this contradiction at the heart of Jewish existence must be confronted and resolved. The land of Israel, he argues, 'is not something apart from the soul of the Jewish people; it is no mere national possession, serving as a means . . . of survival. Eretz ['land of'] Israel is part of the very essence of our nationhood' ('The Land of Israel', in Hertzberg, p. 419). The fact that Jews have been cut off from their homeland is a major difficulty. Kook maintains that a Jewish person in the diaspora is able to observe all commandments of the Law and live as a devout Jew. Yet because he lives outside the Jewish homeland, an essential dimension of Jewishness is missing from his life. Life in the diaspora involves one in unholiness whereas by settling in Palestine it is possible to live a spiritually unsullied life. Return to Zion is thus imperative for an authentic Jewish existence:

> A Jew cannot be as devoted and true to his own ideas, sentiments, and imagination in the diaspora as he can in Eretz Israel. Revelations of the Holy, of whatever degree, are relatively pure in Eretz Israel; outside it, they are mixed with dross and much impurity . . . In the Holy Land man's imagination is lucid and clear, clean and pure, capable of receiving the revelations of divine truth and of expressing in life the sublime meaning of the ideal of prophecy and to be illuminated by the radiance of the Holy Spirit. In gentile lands the imagination is dim, clouded with darkness and shadowed with unholiness, and it cannot serve as the vessel for the outpouring of the divine light. (Hertzberg, pp. 420–1)

If such a conviction had animated religious consciousness in the diaspora, the history of the Jewish people would have been utterly different: accommodation to exile would have been seen as a betrayal of religious principles. But now that Zionism has emerged as an active force in Jewish life, it is possible to reconsider the nature of Jewish identity. According to Kook, peoplehood, the Torah and the land of Israel are inseparably linked. It is a profound error to maintain, as did nineteenth-century reformers, that Judaism can be separated from the land of its birth. On the contrary, the return to Zion is a vital dimension of the Jewish faith. What is of consequence is not an idealized concept of a heavenly Jerusalem, but the actual manifestation of Jewish existence on earth. For this reason Kook argues that 'a valid strengthening of Judaism in the diaspora can come only from a deepened attachment to Eretz Israel. The hope for the return to the Holy Land is the continuing source of the distinctive nature of Judaism' (Hertzberg, p. 419).

For Kook this attachment to the land must serve as the foundation of Jewish life in the modern world. Although the secular pioneers who came to Palestine were motivated by ideological convictions alien to traditional Judaism, their actions are paradoxically part of God's plan of redemption. In the cosmic scheme of the divine will, seemingly atheistic and secular actions are absorbed into the unfolding of God's plan for his chosen people. Therefore these pioneers unintentionally contributed to the advent of the Messiah. Without consciously recognizing the significance of their work, they served God's purpose. Thus Kook maintains:

> Many of the adherents of the present national revival maintain that they are secularists. If a Jewish secular nationalism were really imaginable, then we would, indeed, be in danger of falling so low as to be beyond redemption. But Jewish nationalism is a form of self-delusion: the spirit of Israel is so closely linked to the spirit of God that a Jewish nationalist, no matter how secularist his intention may be, must, despite himself, affirm the divine. An individual can sever the tie that binds him to life eternal, but the house of Israel as a whole cannot. All of its most cherished national possessions – its land, language, history and customs – are vessels of the spirit of the Lord. ('Lights for Rebirth', in Hertzberg, p. 430)

Such observations led Kook to insist that the divine spark is evident in the work of secular Zionists who sacrificed themselves for the land of Israel. Such pioneers were not godless blasphemers, but servants of the Lord. Unaware of their divine mission, they actively engaged in bringing about God's Kingdom on earth.

Religious Zionism must grasp the underlying meaning of these efforts to redeem the land, and attempt to educate secularists about the true nature of their work. 'Our quarrel with them', he writes, 'must be directed only to the specific task of demonstrating their error and of proving to them that all their efforts to fragmentize the higher unity of Israel is foredoomed to failure. Once this truth is established, our opponents will ultimately have to realize that they were wasting their efforts. The values they attempted to banish were none the less present, if only in an attenuated and distorted form' ('The Rebirth of Israel', in Hertzberg, p. 426).

In Kook's view the redemption of Israel is part of a universal process involving all humanity. The salvation of the Jewish nation is not simply an event of particular importance – it provides the basis for the restoration of the entire world (*tikun olam*). Through the rebirth of the Jewish nation in this previous homeland, all humanity will be redeemed. This is the universal meaning of the return to Zion:

> All the civilizations of the world will be renewed by the renascence of our spirit. All quarrels will be resolved, and our revival will cause all life to be luminous with the joy of fresh birth. All religions will don new and precious raiment, casting off whatever is soiled, abominable, and unclean; they will unite in imbibing of the dew of the holy lights, that were made ready for all mankind at the beginning of time in the well of Israel. The active power of Abraham's blessing to all the peoples of the world will become manifest and it will serve as the basis of our renewed creativity in Eretz Israel. ('The War', in Hertzberg, p. 423)

This redemptive vision of a global transformation of human life is directly related to the aspiration of earlier Jewish writers who awaited the return of the Messiah to bring about the end of history. For Kook, however, the rebuilding of a Jewish state – even by secular, atheistic pioneers – is an essential ingredient for this process of universal salvation and divine deliverance.

eight

Secular Zionism

In contrast with such figures as Alkalai, Kalischer, and Kook, modern secular Zionists have been preoccupied with the problem of anti-Semitism rather than messianic deliverance. Moses Hess (nineteenth century), for example, argued that anti-Jewish sentiment is unavoidable; no reform of Judaism can eliminate Jew-hatred from Western society. According to Hess, the only solution to the Jewish problem is the creation of a Jewish state which will enable world Jewry to undergo a renaissance and serve as a spiritual centre for all of humanity. Similarly Leon Pinsker (nineteenth century) contended that Judeophobia is inextricably part of Western society – the only remedy for anti-Semitism is for Jewry to reconstitute themselves as a separate people in their own land. Echoing such sentiments Theodor Herzl (19th–20th century) espoused the creation of a Jewish homeland and undertook political steps to bring about its realization. Among Jewish activists who joined this quest to deliver the Jewish nation from their wanderings was Ber Borochov (19th–20th century) who attempted to integrate Jewish nationalism with Marxist ideology. For Borochov, the national struggle will liberate Jewry from its dependence on non-Jewish economic structures and enable Jews to be integrated with the universal revolutionary movement. Another major thinker of this period was Vladimir Jabotinsky (19th–20th century) who stressed the importance of armed struggle in the quest for national autonomy. Although these various figures departed radically from traditional patterns of thought about Jewish redemption, like their religious and spiritual counterparts they foresaw the need for a Jewish state in contemporary society. Their desire for a return to Israel was a modern expression of a deep longing within the Jewish soul.

Moses Hess: national consciousness and universalism

Modern secular Zionism begins with the writings of Moses Hess. Born in Bonn, Germany, he published his first philosophical work, *The Holy History of Mankind, by a young Spinozist*, in 1837. By 1840 he had settled in Paris where he was active in socialist circles; from

1842 to 1843 he served as the Paris correspondent of the *Rheinische Zeitung*, edited by Karl Marx. In 1862 he published *Rome and Jerusalem*, a systematic defence of Jewish nationalism. In this work he explains that after twenty years of estrangement from Judaism, he has returned to his people:

> Once again I am sharing in its festivals of joy and days of sorrow, in its hopes and memories. I am taking part in the spiritual and intellectual struggles of our day, both within the house of Israel and between our people and the gentile world. The Jews have lived and laboured among the nations for almost two thousand years, but none the less they cannot become rooted organically within them. A sentiment which I believed I had suppressed beyond recall is alive once again. It is the thought of my nationality, which is inseparably connected with my ancestral heritage, with the Holy Land and the eternal city, the birthplace of the belief in the divine unity of life and of the hope for the ultimate brotherhood of all men. ('Rome and Jerusalem', in Hertzberg, p. 119)

Anti-Jewish sentiment, he believes, is unavoidable. Progressive Jews think they can escape from Judeophobia by recoiling from any Jewish national expression, yet the hatred of Jews is inescapable. No reform of the religion is radical enough to avoid such sentiments, and even conversion to Christianity cannot relieve the Jew of this disability. 'Jewish noses', he writes, 'cannot be reformed, and the black, wavy hair of the Jews will not be changed into blond by conversion or straightened out by constant combing' (Hertzberg, p. 121). For Hess, Jews will always remain strangers among the nations: nothing can alter this state of affairs. The only solution to the problem of Jew-hatred is for the Jewish people to come to terms with their national identity.

According to Hess, the restoration of Jewish nationalism will not deprive the world of the benefits promoted by Jewish reformers who wish to dissociate themselves from the particularistic dimensions of the Jewish heritage. On the contrary the values of universalism would be championed by various aspects of Judaism's national character. Judaism, he contends, is the root of the modern universalist view of life. Until the French Revolution, the Jewish people were the only nation whose religion was both national and universalist. It is through Judaism that the history of humanity can become sacred, namely a unified development which has its origin in the love of the family. This process can be completed only when the members of the human race are united by the holy spirit.

Such a conception of history is grounded in the Jewish messianic vision of God's Kingdom on earth. From the beginning of their history, Hess notes, the Jews have been bearers of the faith in a future messianic epoch. This conviction is symbolically expressed through Sabbath observance. 'The biblical story of the creation is told only for the sake of the Sabbath ideal', he writes. 'It tells us, in symbolic language, that when the creation of the world of nature was completed, with the calling into life of the highest organic being of the earth – man – the Creator celebrated his natural Sabbath, after the completion of the task of world history, by ushering in the messianic epoch' (Hertzberg, p. 131). Biblical Sabbath precepts thus inspire Jews with a feeling of certainty that a divine law governs both the world of nature and the world of history. This belief, rooted in the spiritual life of the Jewish nation, points to a universal salvation of the world.

What is required today, Hess asserts, is for Jewry to regenerate the Jewish nation and to keep alive the hope for the political rebirth of the Jewish people. In support of this enterprise, Hess cites the work of contemporary French writer Ernst Laharanne, *The New Eastern Question*, which argues for the existence of a Jewish homeland:

No member of the Jewish race can renounce the incontestable and fundamental right of his people to its ancestral land without thereby denying his past and his ancestors. Such an act is especially unseemly at a time when political conditions in Europe will not only obstruct the restoration of a Jewish state but will rather facilitate its realization. What European power would today oppose the plan that the Jews, united through a Congress, should buy back their ancient fatherland? Who would object if the Jews flung a handful of gold to decrepit old Turkey and said to her: 'Give me back my home and use this money to consolidate the other parts of your tottering empire?' . . . You will come to the land of your fathers decorated with the crown of age-long martyrdom, and there, finally, you will be completely healed from all your ills. Your capital will again bring the wide stretches of barren land under cultivation; your labour and industry will once more turn the ancient soil into fruitful valleys, reclaiming it from the encroaching sands of the desert, and the world will again pay its homage to the oldest of peoples. (Hertzberg, pp. 133–4)

In the light of these observations, Hess asserts that a Jewish renaissance is possible once national life reasserts itself in the Holy Land. In the past the creative energies of the people deserted Israel when Jews became ashamed of their nationality. But the holy spirit, he writes, will again animate Jewry once the nation awakens to a new life. The only question remaining is how it might be possible to stimulate the patriotic sentiments of modern Jewry as well as liberate the Jewish masses by means of this revived national loyalty. This is a formidable challenge, yet Hess contends that it must be overcome. Although he recognizes that there could not be a total emigration of world Jewry to Palestine, the existence of a Jewish state will act as a spiritual centre for the Jewish people and for all of humanity. It is, he states, 'the duty of all of us to carry "the yoke of the Kingdom of heaven" until the very end'.

Leon Pinsker: Autoemancipation

The Russian pogroms of 1881 had a profound impact on another early Zionist, Leon Pinsker, driving him from an espousal of the ideas of the Enlightenment to the determination to create a Jewish homeland. Born in Tomaszów in Russian Poland in 1821, Pinsker attended a Russian high school, studied law in Odessa, and later received a medical degree from the University of Moscow. Upon returning to Odessa, he was appointed to the staff of the local city hospital. After 1860, Pinsker contributed to Jewish weeklies in the Russian language and was active in the Society for the Spread of Culture among the Jews of Russia. However, when Jews were massacred in the pogroms of 1881 he left the Society, convinced that a more radical remedy was required to solve the plight of Russian Jewry. In 1882 he published *Autoemancipation*, a tract containing similar themes to those found in Hess's writings. He subsequently became the leader of the new Hibbat Zion movement, and in 1884 convened its founding conference.

In *Autoemancipation*, Pinsker asserts that the Jewish problem is as unresolved in the modern world as it was in former times. In essence, this dilemma concerns the unassimilable character of Jewish identity in countries where Jews are in the minority. In such cases there is no basis for mutual respect between Jews and non-Jews. 'The Jewish people', he writes, 'has no fatherland of its own, though many motherlands; it has no rallying point, no centre of gravity, no government of its own, no accredited representatives. It is everywhere a guest, and nowhere at home' (Pinsker, p. 6).

This situation is aggravated by the fact that the Jewish people do not feel a need for an independent national existence; yet without such a longing, there is no hope for a solution to Jewish misery.

Among the nations of the world, Pinsker asserts, the Jews are like a nation long since dead: the dead walking among the living. Such an eerie, ghostly existence is unique in history. The fear of the Jewish ghost has been a typical reaction throughout the centuries, and has paved the way for current Judeophobia. This prejudice has through the years become rooted and naturalized among all peoples of the world. 'As a psychic aberration', he writes, 'it is hereditary; as a disease transmitted for two thousand years, it is incurable' (Pinsker, p. 8). Such Jew-hatred has generated various charges against the Jewish people: throughout history Jews have been accused of crucifying Jesus, drinking the blood of Christians, poisoning wells, exacting usury, and exploiting peasants. Such accusations are invariably groundless – they were trumped up to quiet the conscience of Jew-baiters. Thus Judaism and anti-Semitism have been inseparable companions through the centuries, and any struggle against this aberration of the human mind is fruitless.

Unlike other peoples, the Jew is inevitably a stranger. Having no home, he can never be anything other than an alien. He is not simply a guest in a foreign country; rather he is more like a beggar and a refugee. The Jews are aliens, he states, who can have no representatives because they have no fatherland. Because they have none, because their home has no boundaries behind which they can entrench themselves, their misery also has no bounds. It is a mistake, Pinsker continues, to think that the legal emancipation of Jewry will result in social emancipation. This, he believes, is impossible. The isolation of the Jew cannot be removed by any form of official emancipation since the Jew is eternally an alien. In summary, he asserts, 'For the living, the Jew is a dead man; for the natives, an alien and a vagrant; for property holders, a beggar; for the poor, an exploiter and a millionaire; for patriots, a man without a country; for all classes, a hated rival' (*Autoemancipation* in Hertzberg, p. 188).

Such natural antagonism between Jew and non-Jew has resulted in a variety of reproaches levelled by both parties at one another. From the Jewish side, appeals to justice are frequently made to improve the condition of the Jewish community. In response, non-Jews attempt to justify their negative attitudes by groundless accusations. A more realistic approach, however, would involve the recognition that the Jewish people have no choice but to reconstitute themselves as a separate people. In recent times, Pinsker points out, there has been a growing awareness of the need for a Jewish homeland:

> Nowadays, when in a small part of the earth our brethren have caught their breath and can feel more deeply for the sufferings of their brothers; nowadays, when a number of other dependent and oppressed nationalities have been allowed to regain their independence, we, too, must not sit even one moment longer with folded hands; we must not admit that we are doomed to play on in the future the hopeless role of the 'wandering Jew' ... it is our bounden duty to devote all our remaining moral force to re-establishing ourselves as a living nation, so that we may finally assume a more fitting and dignified role. (Hertzberg, p. 191)

The Jewish struggle to attain this goal has an inherent justification that belongs to the quest of every oppressed people. Although this endeavour may be opposed by various quarters, the battle must continue – the Jewish people have no other way out of their desperate position. There is a moral duty to ensure that persecuted Jews wherever they live will have a secure home. In this respect, it is a danger, Pinsker states, for Jews to attach themselves only to the 'Holy Land'. What is required is simply a secure land for the Jewish nation:

> We need nothing but a large piece of land for our poor brothers; a piece of land which shall remain our property, from which no foreign master can expel us ... Perhaps the Holy Land will again become ours. If so, all the better, but first of all, we must determine ... what country is accessible to us, and at the same time adapted to offer the Jews of all lands who must leave their homes a secure and unquestioned refuge which is capable of being made productive. (Hertzberg, p. 194)

For Pinsker the present moment is a decisive time for the revival of national aspirations. History appears to be on the side of world Jewry in its longing for a national homeland. Even in the absence of a leader like Moses, the recognition of what Jewish people need most should arouse a number of energetic individuals to take on positions of responsibility. Already, he notes, there are societies who are pressing for the creation of a Jewish nation. They must now invoke a national congress, and establish a national directorate to bring to fruition these plans: 'Our greatest and best forces – men of finance, of science, and of affairs, statesmen and publicists – must join hands with one accord in steering toward the common destination' (Hertzberg, p. 196). Of course not all Jews will be able to settle in this Jewish homeland. Yet, it would serve as a refuge for those who seek to flee from oppression and persecution.

In conclusion, Pinsker contends that the Jews are despised because they are not a living nation. It is an error to believe that civil and political emancipation will raise Jewry in the estimation of other peoples. Instead the only proper remedy for the Jewish problem is the creation of a Jewish nationality, of a people living on its own soil. Jews must reassert their national self-respect, and cease to wander from one exile to another. At present there are forces helping to bring about this vision, and the international Jewish community must work towards this end. No sacrifice, he declares, will be too great to reach the goal which will assure that the Jewish nation's future is secure.

Theodor Herzl: the Jewish state

More than any other figure Theodor Herzl (1860–1904) has become identified with modern secular Zionism. Born on 2 May 1860 in Budapest, Hungary, he was the only son of a rich merchant. After studying at a technical school and high school in Budapest, he went with his family to Vienna where he enrolled in the law faculty of the university. In 1884 he received a doctorate and worked for a year as a civil servant; subsequently he wrote plays, and in 1892 was appointed to the staff of the *Neue Freie Presse*. As its Paris correspondent, he witnessed the Dreyfus Affair and became convinced that the Jewish problem could only be solved by the creation of a homeland for the Jewish people. In May 1895 Herzl requested an interview with Baron Maurice de Hirsch to interest him in the establishment of a Jewish state. When the Baron expressed little sympathy for the project, Herzl hoped the Rothschilds would be more receptive and wrote a 65-page proposal outlining his views. This work was an outline of his *The Jewish State* which appeared in February 1896; this was followed by a utopian study, *Alteneuland (Old-New Land)*, published in 1902.

Herzl's analysis of modern Jewish existence was not original – many of his ideas were preceded in the writings of Moses Hess and Leon Pinsker. Yet what was novel about Herzl's espousal of Zionism was his success in stimulating interest and debate about a

Jewish state in the highest diplomatic and political circles. This was due both to the force of his personality and the passionate expression of his proposals. Convinced of the importance of his views, Herzl insisted that the building of a Jewish homeland would transform Jewish life. The first entry in his diary of 1895 reflects the intensity of this conviction:

> I have been occupied for some time past with a work which is of immeasurable greatness. I cannot tell today whether I shall bring it to a close. It has the appearance of a gigantic dream . . . What it will lead to it is impossible to surmise as yet. But my experience tells me that it is something marvellous even as a dream, and that I should write it down – if not as a memorial for mankind, then for my own delight or meditation in later years. And perhaps for something between these possibilities: for the enrichment of literature. If the romance does not become a fact, at least the fact can become a romance. Title: The Promised Land! ('First Entry in his Diary', in Hertzberg, p. 204)

In the preface to *The Jewish State* Herzl contends that his advocacy of a Jewish homeland is not simply a utopian scheme; on the contrary, his plan is a realistic proposal arising out of the appalling conditions facing Jews living under oppression and persecution. The plan, he argues, would be impractical if only a single individual were to undertake it. But if many Jews were to agree on its importance its implementation would be entirely reasonable. Like Pinsker, Herzl believed that the Jewish question can only be solved if the Jews constitute themselves as one people:

> We have sincerely tried everywhere to merge with the national communities in which we live, seeking only to preserve the faith of our fathers. It is not permitted us. In vain are we loyal patriots, sometimes superloyal; in vain do we make the same sacrifices of life and property as our fellow citizens; in vain do we strive to enhance the fame of our native lands in the arts and sciences, or her wealth by trade and commerce. In our native lands where we have lived for centuries we are still decried as aliens . . . The majority decide who the 'alien' is; this, and all else in the relations between peoples, is a matter of power. (Hertzberg, p. 209)

Old prejudices against Jewry are ingrained in Western society – assimilation will not act as a cure for the ills that beset the Jewish people. There is only one remedy for the malady of anti-Semitism: the creation of a Jewish commonwealth. In *The Jewish State* Herzl outlines the nature of such a social and political entity. The plan, he argues, should be carried out by two agencies: the Society of Jews and the Jewish Company. The scientific programme and political policies which the Society of Jews will establish should be carried out by the Jewish Company. This body will be the liquidating agent for the business interests of departing Jews, and will organize trade and commerce in the new country. Given such a framework, immigration of Jews will be gradual. Initially the poorest will settle in this new land. Their tasks will be to construct roads, bridges, railways, and telegraph installations. In addition they will regulate rivers and provide themselves with homesteads. Through their labour trade will be created, and in its wake markets. Such economic activity will attract new settlers, and thus the land will be populated.

Those Jews who agree with the concept of a Jewish state should rally round the Society of Jews and encourage its endeavours. In this way they give it authority in the eyes of governments, and in time ensure that the state is recognized through international law. If other nations are willing to grant Jews sovereignty over a neutral land, then the Society will be able to enter into negotiations for its possession. Where should this new state be located? Herzl proposes two alternatives: Palestine or Argentina. Argentina, Herzl notes, is one of the most fertile countries in the world, extending over a vast area with a sparse population. Palestine on the other hand is the Jews' historic homeland. If the sultan were persuaded to allow the Jews to repossess this land, the Jewish community could in return undertake the complete management of the finances of Turkey. In this way the Jews could form a part of a wall of defence for Europe and Asia, and the holy places of Christendom could be placed under some form of international extraterritoriality. There are therefore advantages for both these options, and Herzl asserts that the Society should take whatever it is given and whatever Jewish opinion favours.

In the conclusion of this tract Herzl eloquently expresses the longing of the entire nation for the creation of such a refuge from centuries of suffering:

> What glory awaits the selfless fighters for the cause! Therefore I believe that a wondrous breed of Jews will spring up from the earth. The Maccabees will rise again. Let me repeat once more

my opening words: The Jews who will it shall achieve their state. We shall live at last as free men on our own soil, and in our own homes peacefully die. The world will be liberated by our freedom, enriched by our wealth, magnified by our greatness. And whatever we attempt there for our own benefit will rebound mightily and beneficially to the good of all mankind. (Hertzberg, pp. 225–6)

In his novel *Alteneuland* Herzl discusses the social and economic structure of such a state in Palestine. The foundation of the economy, he contends, should be co-operative. Here he sees the New Israel as realizing the social vision of nineteenth-century European utopian socialism. In addition Herzl advocates universal suffrage as well as the full participation of women in the political life of the community. Further, Herzl maintains that schooling be free and universal from kindergarten to university. At the same time both men and women are to give two years' service to the community in such institutions as hospitals, infirmaries, orphan asylums, vacation camps, and homes for the aged. Urban planning is also espoused in the novel: new towns are to be planned in advance so as to ensure that urban sprawl is eliminated. There would also be an electrified system of mass transport, and hydro-electric plants would ensure cheap electricity. Herzl moreover suggests that the Mosaic principle of the jubilee year should be institutionalized into the landowning patterns of society.

These two works – one a passionate call for the building of a Jewish country, and the other a novelistic proposal for Jewish existence in such a future society in Palestine – strengthened the case for political Zionism. In 1903 the British government offered Herzl a large tract of land in Uganda; in the Zionist Congress of that year, he pressed that the offer be accepted as a temporary haven for oppressed Jewry. Although a resolution was passed to investigate this proposal, the Zionists of Russia rebelled. Exhausted by his exertions Herzl died on 3 July 1904. Nearly fifty years later – on 17 August 1949 – his remains were flown on an aeroplane bearing a blue-white flag of the State of Israel to the country which he longed to create.

Ber Borochov: Zionism and Marxism

In nineteenth-century Russia a number of activists in the revolutionary movement were Jewish. Prominent among these figures was Ber Borochov, who attempted to integrate Jewish nationalism with Marxist doctrine. Born in 1881 in a small town in the Ukraine, he was raised in Poltava. After graduating from the local high school, he worked for a year in the Social Democratic Party. During the next decades he was active in a number of Zionist groups; in December 1906 the Poale Zion (Workers of Zion) was established, and Borochov together with Israel Ben-Zvi wrote its manifesto. After 1907 he travelled throughout Europe as a party representative and also engaged in research in Yiddish philology. At the outbreak of World War I, Borochov settled in America where he was an editor, writer and party activist. After the Kerensky revolution in March 1917, he returned to Russia.

Borochov's advocacy of Socialist Zionism was expressed in his first major work, *The National Question and the Class Struggle*, published in 1903. In this study Borochov argues that Marx's own work on the national question was more complicated than usually understood. According to Borochov, both Marx and Engels were concerned with the national struggle. This reading of Marxism enabled Borochov to develop his conception of a horizontal division within society (in addition to the vertical division into classes). These groups are divided into socio-economic organisms (tribes, families, peoples, nations). The class struggle always occurs within these horizontal social-national groupings. Whenever class struggle is integrated into a national struggle, this generates important consequences. If an entire class is conquered by another, the conquering group tries to impose on the vanquished its own class structure. The conquered nation is thus oppressed as a class by the bourgeoisie of the victorious group and subjugated culturally. When this occurs, nationalism among the oppressed peoples appears in a peculiar form:

> These oppressed peoples constantly exist under abnormal conditions of production . . . Such abnormal conditions bring the varying interests of all individuals of the nation into harmonious agreement. It is due to external pressure, which hinders and disorganizes the influence of the conditions of production, that the relations of production and the class struggle itself are hindered in their development. For the proper course of the mode of production is thus hindered, class antagonisms become abnormally dulled, and national solidarity derives greater strength. (Borochov, pp. 42–3)

Out of this situation the national struggle becomes a social struggle of the exploited classes against the exploiting classes of the oppressing national group:

> All feel and all comprehend that the pressure is a national one. It has its origin in a foreign nation and is directed against their own nationality as such ... the national question of an oppressed people becomes sharply divided from the connection it normally has with its basis – with the material conditions of its productive life. Cultural needs then assume an independent importance and all members of the nation become concerned about the freedom of national self-determination. (Borochov, p. 43)

In such contexts both the intelligentsia and the working class can prevent the national movement of the oppressed nation from becoming ethnocentric by emphasizing the people's struggle with universal and international ideals.

For Borochov, once an oppressed people is liberated from foreign oppression, it can begin the class struggle within its own society. In this way Borochov highlights the interconnection between national aspirations for liberation and the class struggle. Orthodox Marxists, he believes, have failed to recognize how national differences affect class structures. In this light, he distinguishes between various forms of nationalism and stresses that nationalism must be given the same consideration as other phenomena of bourgeois society. *The National Question and the Class Struggle* thus provides a general theory of the relationship between the nationalist and the class struggle.

In the following year, Borochov elaborated this analysis in *Our Platform*, in which he applies these observations to the Jewish question. According to Borochov, there are three distinct social units within the Jewish community: the upper bourgeoisie; the middle class and the intelligentsia; and the working class. The first group tends towards assimilation – this is most prevalent among Western Jews. In general the upper bourgeoisie attempts to solve its problems through social integration and economic success, and tries to integrate the Jewish masses into Western culture through philanthropic activity: 'In spite of themselves and despite their efforts to ignore the Jewish problem', he writes, 'the Jewish aristocrats must turn philanthropists. They must provide shelter for the Jewish emigrants and must make collections for pogrom-ridden Jews. Everywhere the Jewish upper bourgeoisie is engaged in the search for a Jewish solution to the Jewish problem and a means of being delivered of the Jewish masses' ('Our Platform', in Hertzberg, p. 361). Yet the persistence of anti-Semitism poses a serious threat to Jewish acceptance, even in the most elevated circles. It is therefore unrealistic to assume that assimilation will enable Jews successfully to find their place in society.

Anti-Semitism is also a serious problem for the Jewish middle class and the intelligentsia. As society becomes more democratic and capitalist, the Jewish middle classes are able to gain respected positions in the community as doctors, lawyers, engineers, journalists and businessmen. However, the more successful they become, the more they are resented by non-Jews as interlopers. Such a situation gives rise to strong feelings of ethnic and nationalist identity: 'Lacking any means of support in their struggle for a market, they tend to speak of an independent (Jewish existence) and of a Jewish state where they would play a leading political role' (Hertzberg, p. 362). Nonetheless as long as this group retains its middle-class position, its centre of gravity is still the diaspora – it does not feel the urgent need for a radical solution to the Jewish problem.

In Borochov's view, neither this middle-class group nor the upper bourgeoisie is able to serve as the bearer of the nationalist cause. Only the oppressed Jewish working class can do this together with the persecuted Jewish lower middle class. These two groups form one social entity capable of pressing for a revolutionary solution. For Borochov, emigration to a Jewish homeland will enable this group to create a new society with an entirely new infrastructure. The Jewish problem, Borochov declares, calls for a territorial solution:

> The impossibility of penetrating into higher levels of production creates the need for concentrated immigration into an undeveloped country. Instead of being limited to the final levels of production, as is the case in all other countries, the Jews should in a short time assume a leading position in the economy of the new land. (Hertzberg, p. 364)

Only Palestine, Borochov contends, will serve as a feasible choice for such a settlement – there Jewry would be able to reconstruct a Jewish society with Jews at the base. Borochov argues that the Jewish proletariat needs such a remedy more than any other class because of its great sufferings. To free Jews from their dependence on non-Jewish economic structures, the Jewish proletariat must struggle for national independence. Such liberation, he believes, is part of the universal struggle of the world proletariat.

By advocating nationhood Borochov did not abandon a universal vision of a better world order; on the contrary, he maintained that only through the establishment of a Jewish state – with Jews controlling their destiny – could the Jewish people be integrated into the universal revolutionary process.

Vladimir Jabotinsky: Jewish self-defence

Among the major figures of modern secular Zionism, Vladimir Jabotinsky was one of the most controversial; his writings and political activity inspired a large number of followers as well as detractors. Born in 1880 in Odessa, he went abroad in his last year of high school as a foreign correspondent. After studying for three years at the university in Rome he joined the staff of another Odessa daily, and in 1901 was recalled to join its editorial staff. In 1903 he helped organize a Jewish self-defence corps in Odessa, and subsequently became a Zionist propagandist.

In the following years he travelled throughout Russia and Europe; after the outbreak of World War I, he worked in northern and western Europe as a correspondent for a liberal Moscow daily. Once Turkey joined on the side of Germany, he became convinced that the future of Jewish interests in Palestine rested with the allies. Opposed to the Zionist leadership who advocated neutrality, Jabotinsky persuaded the British to form three Jewish battalions. Yet after the war Jabotinsky became sceptical of British support for Jewish interests, and during the Arab riots of 1920 he organized a self-defence corps in Jerusalem. Imprisoned by the British military administration and sentenced to fifteen years' imprisonment for illegally possessing arms, he was eventually pardoned. In 1921 Jabotinsky was elected to the Zionist Executive, but quarrelled with Chaim Weizmann. In 1925 he organized the Revisionist Party; several years later this group left the Zionist movement and established the New Zionist Organization. Under his leadership, illegal immigration to Palestine took place and the Irgun engaged in a struggle with the British.

In his autobiography, Jabotinsky notes that he first encountered Zionism as a young man in Berne when he attended a lecture by Nachman Syrkin. At that gathering, he writes, 'I spoke Russian, in the following vein: I do not know if I am a socialist, since I have not yet acquainted myself with this doctrine; but I have no doubt that I am Zionist, because the Jewish people is a very nasty people, and its neighbours hate it, and they are right; its end in the diaspora will be a general Bartholomew Night, and the only rescue is general immigration to Palestine' (Avineri, p. 162). Later in Italy, he was influenced by the national movement and became persuaded that liberalism is irrelevant in the modern world. In an essay written in 1910, 'Man is a Wolf to Man', he emphasizes that it is a mistake to rely on liberal ideas to bring about political reform:

> It is a wise philosopher who said, 'Man is a wolf to man'; worse than the wolf is man to man, and this will not change for many days to come. Stupid is the person who believes in his neighbour, good and loving as the neighbour may be; stupid is the person who relies on justice. Justice exists only for those whose fists and stubbornness make it possible for them to realize it . . . Do not believe anyone, be always on guard, carry your stick always with you – this is the only way of surviving in this wolfish battle of all against all. (Avineri, p. 164)

Such ideas were central to his insistence on Jewish self-defence and self-determination.

Jabotinsky's advocacy of Jewish nationalism was expressed in a wide range of articles dealing with national unity and discipline. For Jabotinsky the essential element of the nation consists in its racial component. It is not territory, religion or a common language that comprises the substance of nationhood; rather its essential character is determined by its racial composition. In 'On Race' Jabotinsky argues that 'a nation's substance, the alpha and omega of the uniqueness of its character – this is embodied in its specific physical quality, in the component of its racial composition' (Avineri, p. 167). In this context Jabotinsky asserts that the Jews are a superior race. In a dialogue between an imaginary Russian and a Jew ('An Exchange of Compliments') published in response to an anti-Semitic tract, the Jewish disputant states: 'But if we are going to make comparisons, everything depends on the criteria to be used, and then, you should know, I will insist on my own criterion: he who is steadfast in spirit – he is superior . . . He who will never give up his internal independence, even when under a foreign yoke – he is superior . . . We are a race that will never be harnessed' (Avineri, p. 169).

In Jabotinsky's view the Jewish people as an emerging nation needs founders and builders who are able to animate its latent potential. 'We need', he writes, 'a generation ready for all kinds of adventures and experiences, a generation that can find its way in the most dense forest. We need young people who can ride horses and climb trees and swim in the water and use their fists and shoot a gun; we need a people with a healthy imagination and a strong will, striving to express themselves in the struggle for life (Avineri, p. 170). In addition, he asserts that it is vital that the Jewish community is disciplined in its commitment to nationhood. In an article describing the organizational structure around which he built Betar (the youth movement of the Revisionists), he writes:

> Betar is structured around the principle of discipline. Its aim is to turn Betar into such a world organism that would be able, at a command from the centre, to carry out at the same moment, through the scores of its limbs, the same action in every city and every state. The opponents of Betar maintain that this does not accord with the dignity of free men and it entails becoming a machine. It suggests not to be ashamed and to respond with pride: Yes, a machine. (Avineri, p. 172)

In his works Jabotinsky advocates the reorganization of social and economic life along the lines of a corporate state. Alongside a Representative Assembly of the Jewish community in Palestine, Jabotinsky proposed another body, a Trades' Parliament. Every person, he maintains, should elect his representative to this Upper Chamber according to his corporation or guild:

> One has to create in the Yishuv [the Jewish community in Palestine] the idea of professional corporations, corporations in which will be associated all those who take part in one of the branches of Jewish economic life in industry, commerce, agriculture, banking and finance, trade, transportation, professional occupations, clerking, etc . . . After such an overall organization has materialized, each corporation will elect its representative to a new National Committee – this will be the Trades' Parliament. Its role will be, first of all, to control all economic life . . . secondly, this Trades' Parliament will establish the Arbitration System from the top downwards, and this system will regulate all the relations between the various economic groups. (Avineri, p. 177)

Regarding the Arab population, Jabotinsky emphasizes that the Jewish people in returning to its ancestral homeland is not returning to oriental culture. In 'The Arabesque Fashion', he maintains that the Jews are a European people:

We the Jews . . . have no connection with that 'Orient', perhaps even less than other European people . . . The spiritual atmosphere of Europe is ours, we have the same rights in it just like the Germans and the English and the Italians and the French . . . And in Palestine this creativity will continue. As Nordau has put it so well, we come to the Land of Israel in order to push the moral frontiers of Europe up to the Euphrates. (Avineri, p. 180)

According to Jabotinsky the Muslims are a backward people, and the Western powers have nothing to fear from the Arab nations if they support Zionist policies. In 1937 Jabotinsky gave evidence before the Peel Commission (the Royal Commission on Palestine), arguing for the establishment of a Jewish state covering all of the original Palestine Mandate, including Transjordan. Aware that this would turn the Arabs in such a state into a minority, he contends this would not be detrimental to the Arab populace:

I have also shown to you already that, in our submission, there is no question of ousting the Arabs. On the contrary, the idea is that Palestine on both sides of the Jordan should hold the Arabs, their progeny, and many millions of Jews. What I do not deny is that in that process the Arabs of Palestine will necessarily become a minority in the country of Palestine. What I do deny is that it is a hardship. It is not a hardship on any race, any nation, possessing so many national states now and so many more national states in the future. One fraction, one branch of that race, and not a big one, will have to live in someone else's state. Well, that is the case with all the mightiest nations of the world. (Avineri, p. 181)

Arguably Jabotinsky's legacy to modern Zionism was his recognition of the importance of power in determining the fate of the Jewish nation. For Jabotinsky it is not morality but power that is of supreme importance in political affairs. In the subsequent history of Israel, this principle has become a central feature of the Jewish state's defence policy. Yet Jabotinsky's inability to recognize the national aspirations of the Arab population was a failure of insight – for a subdued populace the denial of national rights inevitably led to frustration and anger. The bloody history of Arab–Jewish relations in the years following Jabotinsky's death illustrates his lack of perception about Arab aspirations in the Holy Land.

nine

Anti-Zionism

Within the Jewish community ultra-Orthodox critics of Zionism
united in their opposition to what they regard as a betrayal of
traditional Jewish values. According to these opponents, it is forbidden to accelerate divine redemption through human efforts.
Thus the Zionist movement was regarded as a demonic force,
leading the Jewish people astray. Paralleling this critique, liberal
Jews assailed Zionism as a misguided utopian scheme. These
propagandists declared that only emancipation and assimilation
could serve as a remedy to the Jewish problem. Socialists as well
were hostile to the creation of a Jewish homeland. Zionism, they
argued, is a reactionary aberration; instead of this backward-
looking scheme, socialism, they stated, must be instituted in all
countries to bring about the eradication of Judeophobia. In their
espousal of this ideal, a number of propagandists looked to the
Soviet Union as an example of the way in which anti-Jewish attitudes could be eliminated through socialist policies. Within the
Arab world, the formation of Zionist settlements in Palestine promoted fear and hostility. Concerned that the Zionists would over-
whelm the indigenous Arab population, they protested against the
Jewish populace living in their midst. After the Second World
War, such agitation led to the creation of the Palestine Liberation
Organization which promoted armed struggle against the Jewish
state. In their opposition to Israel, Arabs throughout the world
have vilified both Judaism and the Jewish people. Thus anti-
Semitism – previously fostered by the Church – has been absorbed
into Arab culture and transformed into a modern form of Jew-
hatred based on previous stereotypes and myths.

The Orthodox critique

Although some Orthodox Jewish figures endorsed the Zionist
movement, Orthodoxy in Germany, Hungary and Eastern European countries protested against this new development in Jewish
life. To promote this policy an ultra-Orthodox movement, Agudat
Israel, was created in 1912 to unite rabbis and laity against Zionism. Although the Torah maintains that it is the duty of the pious

to return to Zion, these Orthodox Jews pointed out that such an ingathering must be preceded by the messianic redemption. In the nineteenth century the spiritual leader of German Jewish Orthodoxy, Samson Raphael Hirsch, decreed before the advent of Zionism that it is forbidden actively to accelerate divine deliverance. In the light of such teaching, Zionism was viewed by the ultra-Orthodox as a satanic conspiracy against God's will and equated with pseudo-messianism. Prominent among Orthodox critics was Zadok of Lublin who stated that he prayed to the Lord for the day of redemption, but was unwilling to settle in Palestine for fear that such an act would be interpreted as condoning the Zionist movement.

Yet despite such attitudes, Scripture did decree that it was obligatory for Jews to return to the Holy Land, and this prescription called for an Orthodox response. Accordingly, ultra-Orthodox figures differentiated between the obligation to return to the Holy Land and the duty of residing there. Orthodox Jews, they argued, were exempt from actually settling in the land for such reasons as physical danger, economic difficulties, inability to educate the young, etc. In addition, these critics maintained that Zionism was not simply a movement to rebuild Palestine – it was a heretical attempt to usurp the privilege of the Messiah to establish a Jewish kingdom. Further, ultra-Orthodox spokesmen declared that Zionism sought to leave religion out of the national life – as a result the Jewish state would betray the ideals of the Jewish heritage. Throughout its history, the nation had been animated by spiritual principles, and refused to perish because of its adherence to traditional precepts. If Israel endured through thousands of years of persecution, it would be folly to abandon the religious values which kept alive the hope for Jewish survival. Hence, ideologists of the ultra-right such as Isaac Breuer insisted that Zionism was depriving the Jewish people of its religious commitment in a misguided pursuit of modern notions of nationhood. This, he believed, was the most pernicious form of assimilation.

For these reasons Agudat Israel denounced the policies of modern Zionists and refused to collaborate with religious Zionist parties such as the Mizrahi. In Palestine itself the extreme Orthodox movement joined with Agudat Israel in its struggle against Zionism. Frequently its leaders protested to the British government and the League of Nations about the Zionist quest to make a national home in Palestine. Occasionally it even joined forces with Arab leaders. This conflict eventually resulted in the murder of a member of the executive of the Agudat, Jacob Israel de Han. A Dutch Jew by origin, he denounced Zionism in cables to British newspapers, attacking the Balfour Commission and British officers for their seemingly pro-Zionist stance. On 30 June 1924 he was assassinated in Jerusalem by the Haganah (without knowledge of the high command). For the ultra-Orthodox Jews of Jerusalem de Han became a martyr for the glory of God – this incident illustrated the depths of hatred of Zionism among the right-wing Orthodox. According to the ultra-Orthodox spokesman Joseph Sonnenfeld, Zionists were 'evil men and ruffians'; hell, he believed, had entered Israel with Herzl.

Eventually, however, these critics of Zionist aspirations modified their position and began to take a more active role in Jewish settlement. This was due to the immigration of members of Agudat Israel to Palestine, as well as the massacre of Orthodox Jews in Hebron, Safed and Jerusalem during the riots of 1929. None the less the ultra-right refused to join the National Council of Palestinian Jewry which had been established in the 1920s. In the next decades the rise of the Nazis and the events of the Holocaust brought about a split in the movement. In 1934 Isaac Breuer declared: 'Do not leave Jewish history to the Zionists'. If Agudat wished to gain the upper hand against the Zionists, it was obligated to prepare the Holy Land for the rule of God. In the unfolding of God's providential plan for his chosen people, the extreme Orthodox had a crucial role to play. Four years later Breuer asked the General Assembly of the Agudat to decide whether the Balfour Declaration was part of God's providential scheme or satanic in origin. Although some Orthodox leaders in Palestine were sympathetic to Breuer's views, other prominent members remained unconvinced. Such figures as Jacob Rosenheim, the political head of Central European Orthodoxy, maintained that even after the Holocaust the Zionist quest to evacuate Europe and gather up the exiles was misguided since it is impossible to determine what God had planned for his chosen people prior to the arrival of the Messiah.

Between the end of the war and the founding of the Jewish state a zealous extreme group, the Neturei Karta ('Guardians of the City') in Jerusalem accused the Agudat of succumbing to the Zionists. Headed by Amram Blau and Aharon Katzenellenbogen, these extremists were supported by the followers of rabbis in Brisk (Poland) and Szatmar (Hungary) who had emigrated to America and other Western countries. According to Neturei Karta, those who accepted the Jewish state were apostates, and the rabbis who supported Agudat were viewed as leading the new generation away from Torah Judaism. As a result of these policies, these zealots refused to participate in the War of Independence, demanded the internationalization of Jerusalem under the United Nations, rejected Israeli identity cards, and were unwilling to recognize Israel as a state. Yet despite such attacks, the leaders of Agudat continued to support the creation of a Jewish homeland state and a year before its establishment reached an understanding with Palestinian Zionists concerning such matters as Sabbath observance, dietary laws, and regulations regarding education and marriage. Such a conciliatory policy paved the way for Agudat's participation in Israeli politics and its membership in the United Religious Front.

Liberal critics and Zionists

Paralleling the Orthodox critique, liberal Jews attacked Zionism for its utopian character. According to these critics, it was simply impossible to bring about the emigration of millions of Jews to a country which was already populated. In addition, in Western countries nationalism was being supplanted by a vision of a global community – it was thus reactionary to promote the creation of a Jewish homeland. In Eastern Europe on the other hand there was still a Jewish national consciousness. Yet Zionism was unable to solve the problem facing Jewry. Multitudes of Jews in Eastern Europe were enduring hardship; only a small minority of these individuals would be able to settle in Palestine. Hence these liberal propagandists maintained that assimilation alone could serve as a remedy for the Jewish problem.

In response Zionists protested that assimilation was undesirable and inevitably impossible – such a stance was influenced by racial theories published during the first two decades before the First World War. According to these writings, distinctive qualities were inherited regardless of social, cultural or economic factors. For the Zionists, the Jewish people constituted an identifiable ethnic group whose identity could not be manipulated through social integration. Anti-Semitism, they argued, could not be eradicated; it was an inevitable response to the Jewish populace no matter what efforts were made to assimilate Jews into foreign cultures. Further, since Jews were predominantly involved in trade and the professions – rather than agriculture and industry – they were bound to be the first targets during times of crisis. Pointing to Jewish history, the Zionists emphasized that in the past there were rich and powerful Jews, but without warning they lost their positions and were reduced to poverty. There was thus no security for Jews in societies where they were in the minority. Zionism was the only solution.

Liberals viewed this interpretation of Jewish history as a distortion of the past. Previously Jewish emancipation depended on the goodwill of rulers, but in contemporary society, they stated, it would result from global socio-economic factors. The Zionists disagreed. The lessons of Jewish history, they believed, must guide current Jewish thought and action. Judeophobia is an inherent aspect of modern society, and those who championed liberal ideologies such as socialism would be disappointed. In the words of Max Nordeau, the Zionist literary figure and leader: 'Socialism will bring the same disappointments as did the Reformation, the Enlightenment, the movement for political freedom. If we should live to see Socialist theory become practice, you'll be surprised to meet again in the new order that old acquaintance, anti-Semitism' (Laqueur, *A History of Zionism*, p. 388). According to Nordeau, the Jew was rootless, and in his address to the First Zionist Congress he discussed the social exclusion of Jews in Western lands. Although Jews were emancipated and enfranchised, he stated, they were unable to join gentile clubs and organizations. Everywhere Jews encountered the sign: 'No Jews admitted'. Despite the fact that modern Jewry been had assimilated into foreign cultures, they were not fully accepted. Having dissociated themselves from their coreligionists, they were rejected by their Christian neighbours. In spite of fleeing from the ghetto, they were not at home in their adopted countries. These new Marranos were thus strangers alienated from themselves and their tradition.

This depiction of the Jew as a wanderer between two worlds with no home became a dominant theme among Zionist writers. In Germany Moritz Goldstein published an article in 1913 which provoked a storm of controversy. According to Goldstein, the Jews held sway over German culture, yet were rejected by it. Almost all directors of Berlin theatres were Jews; German music was dominated by Jewish artists; literary study was in the hands of Jewish scholars – none the less Jews were viewed as outsiders. What the Jews lacked was a native homeland which would provide the soil from which their true greatness could flower. Not surprisingly Goldstein's opinions were bitterly criticized by the liberal establishment. According to Ernst Lissauer, any attempt to establish a Jewish ghetto on German soil was misguided. Rather, he argued that assimilation must be promoted – this would eradicate any residual anti-Semitic attitudes among the German people.

During this period other voices were also raised against Zionism throughout the Western world. After Herzl issued his summons to the First Zionist Congress, the executive of the German rabbis issued a declaration stating that the desire to create a Jewish state contradicted the messianic longings in Scripture. The Jewish faith, they believed, obligated the community to serve the countries where they lived. In France, Joseph Reinarch declared that Zionism was a trap set by anti-Semites for the naïve. English liberals declared that Judaism is a religion; for this reason British Jews could fully identify with the society in which they resided. Thus Claude Montefiore, the leader of liberal Judaism in Britain, wrote: 'Liberal Jews do not wish or pray for the restoration of Jews to Palestine' (Laqueur, p. 394). Similarly in the United States, liberals denounced Zionist ideology as misreading the modern situation. Speaking at the close of the First Zionist Congress, Isaac Mayer Wise, the spokesman for American Reform Judaism, proclaimed: 'We denounce the whole question of a Jewish state as foreign to the spirit of the modern Jew of this land, who looks upon America as his Palestine and whose interests are centred here' (Laqueur, p. 394).

Some of these liberals were anxious to analyse and refute the principles of Zionism. Felix Goldman, a German anti-Zionist rabbi, contended that Jewish nationalism is a product of the general chauvinistic movement which had poisoned contemporary history, but would be swept away by universalism. The German Jewish philosopher Hermann Cohen stated in a debate with Martin Buber that Zionism rejected the messianic idea, and without this concept there could be no Judaism. The Zionists, he argued, were confused about the national issue. Jews were members of the German nation, even if they had different ethnic origins. Other critics went even further. Ludwig Geiger, the son of one of the founders of liberal Judaism, asserted that Zionists should be deprived of their civic rights.

Despite such criticisms, throughout the 1920s and 1930s Zionism gained many new adherents, and even within the ranks of American Reform Judaism, moves were made to endorse the creation of a Jewish state. Yet resistance to Zionist ideology continued, and in 1942 a number of American anti-Zionists gathered to formulate a programme of action. This body asserted that the political policy of the Zionists was contrary to the universalistic interpretation of Jewish history. Zionism, they believed, was a secularist movement which undermined the religious character of Judaism and was out of touch with the universalistic spirit of the faith. Further, it threatened Jewry since it called into question the loyalty of Jews to the countries where they lived. In the next year the American Council of Judaism was established to promulgate such ideas. Its statement of principles proclaimed:

> We oppose the effort to establish a national Jewish State in Palestine or anywhere else as a philosophy of defeatism . . . We dissent from all these related doctrines that stress the racialism, the national and the theoretical homelessness of the Jews. We oppose such doctrines as inimical to the welfare of Jews in Palestine, in America, or wherever Jews may dwell. (Laqueur, p. 404)

Such opposition did not end with the founding of the Jewish state. Within the ranks of liberal Judaism, a number of writers continued this critique of Zionist ideology. In the 1950s the British reform rabbi Ignaz Maybaum stated that it was a mistake to believe that Israel was the safest part of the Jewish world. Similarly the American Jewish scholar Jacob Petuchowski, writing in the 1960s, maintained that Israel is not the spiritual centre of world Jewry – rather it is one centre among many. Judaism, he believed, is wider than Israel, and an authentic Jewish life is possible elsewhere. Further, he argued that the Jewish tradition has continually been influenced by external influences. Assimilation is thus an inherent aspect of the evolving character of the Jewish faith. In recent years, however, liberal Judaism worldwide has embraced Israel as a Jewish homeland and spiritual centre. The Nazi Holocaust and the embattled situation of a Jewish state in the Middle East has profoundly altered Jewish consciousness, and the liberal critique of Zionism has now been superseded by a sympathetic appreciation of Jewish aspirations in the Holy Land.

The socialist response

Although a number of Zionists were socialist in orientation, socialist theory was hostile to Jewish aspirations to create a Jewish homeland. According to Marx and Engels, economic and social progress was overcoming national exclusiveness – the world was moving towards internationalism. Contemptuous of Moses Hess's views about a Jewish state, Karl Marx saw Judaism as a negative force in society. Many other socialist contemporaries reacted in the same way, regarding themselves pre-eminently as members of the international socialist movement. At the end of the nineteenth century, however, the Jewish issue gained in importance due to the rise of anti-Semitism, and a number of Jewish socialists became increasingly conscious of their Jewish origins. Nonetheless, this did not alter their belief that the coming socialist revolution would solve the Jewish problem. In both Eastern and Western Europe Zionism was viewed as a reactionary aberration, and anti-Zionism became the accepted policy of the socialist movement.

The most influential ideologist of socialist anti-Zionism was Karl Kautsky who maintained that in the past Jews had been an exclusive hereditary caste of merchants, financiers, intellectuals and artisans. Yet with the rise of industrial capitalism, Jews had obtained equal rights and been assimilated into their adopted countries. Anti-Semitism had re-emerged, he believed, by the reaction of the petty bourgeoisie against liberalism. Eastern European Jews had reacted to this threat by calling for national solidarity. But Zionism had no future. Where, he asked, could space be found for a Jewish state? How could Jews be persuaded to engage in agricultural labour or build a massive industry in Palestine? These were insurmountable obstacles to the realization of Zionist aspirations.

After the war Kautsky was impressed by the achievements in Palestine, but he predicted that Jewish capitalists would eventually lose interest in building a Jewish state in the Middle East and the enterprise would collapse. Further, Kautsky was convinced that the Jews would not become more numerous than the Arabs, nor would they succeed in persuading the Arabs that a Jewish state would be to their advantage. According to Kautsky, only the victorious proletariat could bring about the transformation of Jewish life. When the Jews were absorbed through complete emancipation, Jewry would disappear. 'The Jews have become an eminently revolutionary factor', he declared, 'while Judaism has become a reactionary factor. It is like a weight of lead attached to the feet of the Jews who eagerly seek to progress . . . the sooner [this social ghetto] disappears, the better it will be not only for society, but also for the Jews themselves' (Laqueur, p. 420).

Following Kautsky's analysis, Lenin regarded Jewish nationalism as a reactionary movement, asserting that nationalism was incompatible with Marxism. Not only was the demand for national corporate autonomy misguided, it contradicted the international aspirations of the proletariat. Marxists were compelled to struggle against any form of national oppression, but they were at the same time obliged to resist national aspirations. Stalin elaborated Lenin's views by defining a nation as an historically evolved community of language, territory, culture and economic life. According to this stance, the Jews are not a nation since they possess neither a land nor a spoken language of their own. Hence aspirations to found a state are misguided. The solution of the Jewish problem proposed by the Bolsheviks consisted of granting Jews full rights as citizens. After the revolution, a Jewish Commissariat was created to further this aim and encourage assimilation. Its head decreed that Palestine would be built in Moscow through the organization of agricultural communes; later stress was placed on the industrialization of the Jewish populace.

In the Ukraine and the Crimea, Jewish areas were given regional autonomy, and in March 1928 a special area in the Far East – Biro Bidzhan – was reserved for Jewish settlement. By 1937, it was announced that 150,000 Jews would live there. Among Communists abroad, this venture aroused considerable support. Thus Otto Heller wrote:

> The Jews have gone into the Siberian forests. If you ask them about Palestine, they laugh. The Palestine dream will long have receded into history when in Biro Bidzhan there will be motor cars, railways and steamers, huge factories belching forth their smoke . . . These settlers are founding a home in the taigas of Siberia not only for themselves but for millions of their people.
> (Laqueur, p. 427)

This dream of a Jewish settlement in Siberia was not realized – only a few thousand Jews emigrated there, and many soon returned. Yet despite the failure of this enterprise, a number of Western Jews looked to the Soviet Union for protection of the Jewish population. Such writers as Heller declared that Zionism was a harmful illusion. In *Downfall of Judaism* he decreed that the nationalist quest was a product of the European petty bourgeoisie. As a counter-revolutionary movement, it was an historical mistake because it attempted to detach the Jewish question from the problem of commodity production. Further, it contradicted the laws of historical development as well as common sense. Judaism, he believed, was doomed because it had lost its monopolistic position in the capitalist West.

Another author of this period, William Zuckerman, similarly

expressed enthusiasm for the Soviet handling of anti-Semitism. It was an error, he believed, for Jewry to emigrate from the countries where they resided to build a Jewish state. Assimilation is the key to Jewish survival. In *The Jew in Revolt*, written in 1937, he criticized those who sought to rescue Jews from Nazi Germany:

> It is a gross slander on the German Jews whose love for the fatherland is proverbial, to represent them all as being ready to rush in panicky haste from it in a mass exodus at the first approach of misfortune . . . The Jewish acceptance of the Jewish exodus plan from Germany is at the same time the voluntary acceptance of the entire Nazi point of view with regard to the Jews. It is a complete Jewish capitulation to the racial theory of Hitlerism. (Laqueur, p. 429)

According to Zuckerman, the example set by the Soviet Union should be followed in all lands where Jews had settled. If world Jewry were guaranteed civil rights their freedom would be assured.

The emergence of patriotism in the 1930s undermined such internationalist aspirations, and called into question the Soviet Union's belief that assimilation would provide a remedy to the problem of anti-Semitism. Thus in 1937 Leon Trotsky stated that his previous hopes for Jewish assimilation and emancipation were overly optimistic – possibly the Jews would need a territory of their own. A number of Trotsky's followers were preoccupied with the issue of Jewish nationalism. A. Léon, for example, regarded Zionism as incurably reactionary and an impossible dream. The Jewish question, he proclaimed, could only be solved after the victory of world revolution. In the years that followed, such a critique of Zionism continued to be a dominant theme of socialist ideology.

Arab protests

During the decades before the First World War, the foundation of Zionist settlements in Palestine evoked considerable Arab hostility. In 1891 a number of prominent Arabs sent a petition to the Ottoman capital in Istanbul requesting the prohibition of Jewish immigration as well as the purchase of land in Palestine. From 1908 to 1914 anti-Zionist newspapers were published in Haifa, Jaffa, Beirut, and Damascus. During this period Zionism was viewed in the Arab world as a threat to the 1300-year-old tradition of Palestine as a Muslim land.

Before the war, Palestinian Arabs were aggravated by Jewish

settlers whose socialist ideals clashed with their Islamic traditions. In the 1920s and 1930s Arab leaders complained to the British Mandatory Government that Jewish immigrants were advocating Communist principles which led to violence and social change. These radicals, they urged, should be expelled from the country. According to Palestinian critics, Zionism was equated with Communism, and the Jewish character was seen as inherently subversive. Such attitudes were influenced by various anti-Semitic tracts such as the forged *Protocols of the Elders of Zion* which stressed that Communism is part of the Jewish plot for obtaining world domination.

Palestinian arguments against Zionism concentrated on the need to ensure the self-determination of the Muslim community. In their defence, Palestinians appealed to the principle of the right of all peoples to protect their national identity. At the time of the Balfour Declaration, they pointed out, ninety per cent of the population in Palestine were Arabs; Palestine was a Holy Land to millions of Arabs worldwide; the Arabs had lived there since the seventeenth century. Initially the Arab nationalist movement distinguished between the indigenous Jewish populace whom they esteemed, and foreign Zionists who were seen as interlopers. However, this distinction was not long lasting, and in the Arab demonstrations of February and March 1920 all Jews were condemned. In April 1920 Arab mobs in Jerusalem attacked Jewry in the Jewish quarter of the Old City. This massacre was a result of the inflammatory address by the Grand Mufti in Jerusalem, Haj Amin Al-Husseini. From 1920 Haj Amin attempted to provoke Jewhatred by claiming that the Jews wished to occupy the Temple Mount area in order to rebuild Solomon's Temple. In 1929 such agitation resulted in pogroms in Hebron and Safed in which about 100 Orthodox Jews were killed. This uprising was presented as an anti-imperialist revolt and a victory for the Arab world. In the 1930s a popular national movement was founded which brought the Palestinian cause to the forefront of Pan-Arab concerns.

During this period the rise of Nazi Germany intensified Judeophobia in the Arab lands. Hitler was admired in the Arab world as a nationalist leader who had humiliated Britain and France. After Hitler acceded to power, Haj Amin joined forces with the Nazis and planned a boycott against the Jews. After escaping from Palestine, he went to Syria, Iraq and Italy, eventually moving to Berlin where he supported pro-Axis propaganda, organized Muslim SS troops from Bosnia, and collaborated with Berlin intelligence. On 28 November 1941 in a meeting with Hitler he thanked the Führer for his support of the Arab cause. According to Haj Amin, the Arabs were the natural allies of Germany against the British, the Jews and the Communists. In the summer of 1943 he wrote to the foreign ministries of Italy, Hungary, Romania, and Bulgaria, urging them not to allow Jews to emigrate to Palestine.

After the war Palestinian Arabs were silent about the Mufti's involvement in the Holocaust. The Palestinian question was divorced from the plight of European Jewry, and in the 1950s and 1960s Palestinian Arabs continued to admire Hitler for his policy towards the Jewish people. In 1961 during the Eichmann trial, many Arabs viewed Eichmann as a martyr who had benefited humanity by liquidating millions of Jews. Such anti-Semitism was reflected in the Palestinian National Covenant which declares that Zionism is racist and imperialist. The central premise of this document is the rejection of Israel's existence as an independent state. In nearly half of its thirty-three articles, the demand is expressed that Israel cease to exist. All of Palestine is to be restored to the Palestinian people; only those Jews who lived before 1917 in Palestine are given permission to remain; and armed struggle is conceived as the only way of liberating Palestine. For some years however the leader of the PLO, Yasser Arafat, has attempted to utilize diplomatic means in addition to violence to achieve the liberation of Palestine, and in 1988 the Palestinian National Council in Algiers offered a conditional recognition of Israel.

Although the terms of this agreement call for an Arab Palestine on the basis of the 1947 partition resolution and demand that the West Bank and Gaza be handed over to the PLO, this stance is a major departure from previous resolutions. In the 1970s the PLO advocated the creation of a democratic state in Palestine after Israel's demise – such a position was superseded in the 1988 pact by a two-state solution. None the less, the PLO still views Zionism as colonial and expansionist. Further, in the Gulf conflict, the Palestinians under Yasser Arafat supported Saddam Hussein (whose regime befriended such Palestinian terrorists as Abdul Abbas, Abu Nidal and George Habash) and recently the influx of Soviet Jews has intensified the fear that Israel's occupied territory will be flooded with new immigrants. In addition, a number of Palestinians have become concerned that Israel is planning to seize Muslim holy places. Thus since the founding of the Jewish state to the present day the Palestinian populace has adopted a policy of anti-Zionism: the creation of a Jewish state in the Middle East has continuously been viewed as undermining the Palestinian struggle for political independence and self-determination.

Arab anti-Semitism and Zionism

Through the centuries animosity against Jews was fostered by the Church: Jews were accused of deicide and condemned for perpetrating numerous crimes against the Christian population. Following the influx of Jewish pioneers into Palestine, such anti-Jewish attitudes were absorbed and transformed by the Arab world. As early as 1937 King Abd al Aziz ibn Sa'ud of Arabia deplored the influence the Jews had on Britain. 'Our hatred for the Jews', he declared, 'dates from God's condemnation of them for their persecution and rejection of Isa [Jesus Christ] and their subsequent rejection later of his chosen Prophet' (Wistrich 1991, p. 232). For King Sa'ud, it was inconceivable how Britain as a Christian nation could reward those who had condemned Jesus to death. How, he asked, could the British people alienate the Arabs for such a stiff-necked nation? The Jews were the enemies of both Arabia and England, and were committed to seizing all of Palestine, Transjordan and Medina. For these reasons the King opposed any partition of Palestine. Quoting a *hadith*, he proclaimed: 'Verily the word of God teaches us, and we implicitly believe it, that for a Muslim to kill a Jew, or for him to be killed by a Jew, ensures him an immediate entry into heaven and into the august presence of God Almighty' (Wistrich 1991, p. 233).

In 1958 President Nasser of Egypt, who endorsed such attitudes, recommended the anti-Semitic tract *The Protocols of the Elders of Zion* to a visiting Indian journalist: 'It is very important that you should read it. I will give you a copy. It proves beyond the shadow of a doubt that three hundred Zionists, each of whom knows all the others, govern the fate of the European continent' (Cohn-Sherbok 1989, p. 170). Similarly King Feisal, the son of King Sa'ud, customarily gave a free copy of this treatise to visiting officials and delegations, and the Saudis, Iranians, Libyans, and Pakistanis have fostered the myth of the *Protocols* that the Jewry is engaged in a world conspiracy. The Saudis have also fostered anti-Semitic literature which denies that the Holocaust took place, such as *Anti-Zion*, and *The Six Million Reconsidered*, by William Grimshaw. These volumes were sent to all members of the United States Senate and the British Parliament by the World Muslim Congress in 1981 and 1982. This body, which actively encourages anti-Semitism, claimed in 1981 that any settlement with Israel was an act of treason against Muslims. Zionists, it declared, attempt to gain world domination and annihilate the human race. Three years later the President of the World Muslim Congress, Dr Ma'ruf al-Dawalibi, stated to the UN Centre for Human Rights' Seminar on the Encouragement of Understanding, Tolerance and Respect in Matters Relating to Freedom of Religion and Belief, that 'the Talmud says that "if a Jew does not drink every year the blood of a non-Jewish man, then he will be damned for eternity"' (Wistrich 1991, p. 234). This conviction, he stated, was the basis for the persecution of the Jews.

Another factor animating Arab Jew-hatred has been the ancient charge that Jews utilize the blood of Christian children at Passover. This blood libel myth, as well as the concept of secret Jewish cabals that aim to control the world, were prevalent in the Arab world since the 1950s and have been widely conveyed in the Arab press, radio broadcasts, and school text books. On the basis of such Judeophobia, efforts were made in the early 1960s to dissuade the Vatican from clearing the Jews of deicide charges. In particular the document *Nostra Aetate* (which was promulgated by the Second Vatican Council, repudiating Jewish responsibility for Jesus' death) was denounced by the Arab world. According to a number of writers, the removal of this accusation was due to Zionist influence over the Church. In Mecca the Council of the World Muslim League claimed that Vatican II was antagonistic towards Islam and the Arabs. According to Anis Mansour (at one time a leading adviser to President Sadat), Jewish money had purchased exoneration for this traditional Christian allegation. The Vatican, he asserted, was concerned about the anger of American Jewry and their overseas investments; as a result the Catholic Church had given in to Jewish demands. Such anti-Jewish hostility was also expressed by radical fundamentalists in the 1980s who challenged President Sadat in Egypt and President Assad in Syria. For these radicals, the only remedy for the problem of internal decay, Westernization, and imperialism, consists of the Islamization of the entire Middle East.

The Israeli invasion of Lebanon in the 1980s intensified these feelings and led to the crystallization of a new form of anti-Semitism linked to Islamic revolution. Throughout this period to the present day fundamentalist Islam has decreed that it is inconceivable that there could ever be peace with a Jewish state. In the

Occupied Territories the *intifada* has been established in the wake of this resistance to Zionism. According to the ideology of Islamic fundamentalism, Israel represents a demonic, satanic force – no compromise is possible with those who are seen as having usurped Palestine. Thus the Hamas (Islamic Resistance) covenant of August 1988 proclaims that the Jews were behind most revolutions of the past and continue to form a world conspiracy against humanity; such a conspiracy theory serves to mobilize the passions of those Arabs who wish to see Israel destroyed and Islam arise phoenix-like from its ashes.

Such hostile sentiments have generated rampant Jew-hatred. In February 1989, for example, the pro-government Egyptian weekly decreed: 'It has now become clear that perhaps Hitler did have justification for gassing the Jews. Because if the Jews were allowed freedom of action they would have eaten the others' (Wistrich 1991, p. 255). In the same year, Jamal E-Din Muhammad Musa of the Ein-Shamas University stated: 'Jews are deliberately flooding Egypt with drugs and have made contact with the international Mafia in order to bring down the Egyptian society' (Wistrich 1991, p. 256). Again at this time Dr Hamid Rabee of Cairo University claimed that 'Jews are governed by three enemies: self-hatred, fear and provocative behaviour. Zionist leaders have brought drugs, terror and sexual anarchy to America and Western Europe' (Wistrich 1991, p. 256). The existence of Israel in the midst of the Arabs has therefore provoked the most vehement antipathy. The Jewish state is conceived as the embodiment of evil: it symbolizes an infringement of national and human rights by a colonial, occupying force. Not surprisingly during the Gulf War of 1991 Saddam Hussein saw himself as a modern Nebuchadnezzar who would be able to liberate Palestine from this foreign aggressor.

ten

Modern Israel

Despite the views of anti-Zionists, at the end of the nineteenth century concrete steps were taken to bring a Jewish state into existence. In August 1897 the First Zionist Congress took place under the leadership of Theodor Herzl. Subsequently Herzl engaged in extensive negotiations with political leaders throughout the world. By the time Herzl died, Zionism had become an organized movement and Zionists continued to press for the creation of a Jewish homeland. Eventually the British government approved of such a plan although Britain insisted that the rights of the Arabs be safeguarded. After the First World War, Herbert Samuel was appointed High Commissioner in Palestine to oversee this policy, but he met with considerable resistance from the Zionists who did not wish to appease the Arab populace. Although the British government initially allowed free immigration to Palestine, this policy was superseded by increased restrictions on the number of Jewish immigrants. In May 1939 a White Paper was published which limited the number of immigrants to 75,000 over the next five years, and none thereafter except with Arab permission. This policy evoked widespread Jewish resistance, and the Jewish military forces engaged in conflict with the British. After a campaign of terror, Britain handed over the Palestinian problem to the United Nations, and a special committee was appointed to formulate a plan for the future of the country. On 29 November 1947 a recommendation that there be both an Arab and a Jewish state was passed by the UN General Assembly. Immediately the Arabs began to attack Jewish settlements, and the Israelis were forced to defend their new state. On 14 May 1948 Prime Minister David Ben Gurion read out the Scroll of Independence in the Tel Aviv Museum. In subsequent years Arabs and Jews have repeatedly engaged in battle. The Sinai War of 1946 was followed by the Six-Day War in 1967 and the Yom Kippur War in 1973. In 1978 Egypt signed a peace agreement with Israel; however, other Arab neighbours refused to follow this precedent. In recent years Arab–Israeli conflict has intensified in the Occupied Territories where the Arab population has supported resistance (*intifada*) against the Israeli government. Arab–Israeli conflict thus continues to undermine the Jewish quest for a secure existence in the Holy Land.

The early struggle

The quest for a Jewish state was set in motion by the events of the nineteenth century. Following the inspiration of early Zionist leaders, the First Zionist Congress met on 29 August 1897 in the Great Hall of the Basel Municipal Casino under the leadership of Theodor Herzl. Subsequently Herzl cultivated important figures in Turkey, Austria, Germany and Russia to further his plans. In 1902 a British Royal Commission on Alien Immigration was appointed with Lord Rothschild as one of its members. On 7 July 1902 Herzl appeared before the Commission, declaring that further Jewish immigration to Britain should be accepted but that the ultimate solution to the refugee problem was the recognition of the Jews as a people and the finding by them of a legally recognized home.

This appearance brought Herzl into contact with the Colonial Secretary, Joseph Chamberlain, who subsequently suggested to Herzl that a Jewish homeland could be established in Uganda. Fearful of the plight of Russian Jewry, Herzl was prepared to accept the proposal. As a result Lord Lansdowne, the Foreign Secretary, wrote in a letter:

> If a site can be found which the (Jewish Colonial) Trust and His Majesty's Commission consider suitable and which commends itself to HM Government, Lord Lansdowne will be prepared to entertain favourable proposals for the establishment of a Jewish colony of settlement, on conditions which will enable the members to observe their national customs. (Sanders, pp. 37–8)

After Herzl read Lansdowne's letter to the Zionist Congress, a number of Russian delegates who viewed the Uganda Plan as a betrayal of Zionism walked out. At the next Congress, Uganda was formally rejected as a place for a national homeland.

At the time Herzl died, Zionism had become an established movement, yet it expressed a minority view in the Jewish world. Until the First World War all branches of Judaism were generally opposed to secular Zionism, and assimilationists saw no attraction in a Jewish state in the Middle East. After Herzl's death, David Wolffsohn became the leader of the Zionists and continued to agitate for the creation of a Jewish national home. In Britain Chaim Weizmann pressed for the acceptance of this plan with the support of the liberal MP Herbert Samuel. In a meeting with the Foreign Secretary, Sir Edward Grey, on 9 November 1914, Samuel asked about a homeland for the Jewish people. In reply Grey said that the idea had always had a strong sentimental attachment for him, and he would be prepared to work for it if the opportunity arose. Later in the day Samuel attempted to enlist the support of Lloyd George, the Chancellor of the Exchequer. When Samuel later put his plan to the Cabinet, it was resisted by his cousin Edwin Montague. In a letter to Venetia Stanley written on 28 January 1915 the Prime Minister referred to Samuel's plea for a Jewish homeland in Palestine: 'We might plant in this not very promising territory about 3 or 4 million Jews and this would have a good effect on those (including I suppose himself) who were left behind' (Brock, pp. 406–7). During this period Weizmann pressed on with his proposals. On 18 August 1916 Lord Robert Cecil recorded his meeting with Weizmann:

> He [Weizmann] said with great truth that even in this country a Jew always had to give an explanation of his existence and he was neither quite an Englishman nor quite a Jew, and that the same thing was equally true with much more serious results in other countries . . . Perhaps a phrase he used may convey something of the impression which he made. He said: 'I am not romantic except that Jews must always be romantic, for to them reality is too terrible.' (Sanders, pp. 313–14)

Later in the year when Lloyd George became Prime Minister and Arthur Balfour was appointed Foreign Secretary, the Zionist cause was given a more sympathetic hearing. In January 1917 British troops began the assault on Palestine; at the same time the Tsar was overthrown and the provisional Prime Minister Kerensky ended Russia's anti-Semitic code. At the end of the month Germany engaged in U-boat warfare, thereby drawing America on to the Allied side. In the light of these events, the US government became a supporter of a Jewish home in Palestine. In the same year Balfour as Foreign Secretary wrote to Lord Rothschild, the head of the English Jewish community, promising British commitment to a Jewish homeland in Palestine. The original draft of this letter (the text of which was agreed on by both sides beforehand) stated that Palestine should be reconstituted as a whole as a Jewish national home with internal autonomy, and that there should be

an unrestricted right of Jewish immigration. This document was
not approved by the Cabinet until 31 October 1917, but substantial
changes were made. Palestine was not equated with the national
home, nor was there any reference to unrestricted Jewish immigration. Further, the rights of the Arabs were safeguarded. The
central passage of the letter, subsequently known as the Balfour
Declaration, read:

> His Majesty's Government view with favour the establishment
> in Palestine of a national home for the Jewish people, and will
> use their best endeavours to facilitate the achievement of this
> object, it being clearly understood that nothing shall be done
> which may prejudice the civil and religious rights and political
> status enjoyed by Jews in any other country. (Johnson, p. 430)

A month after the Balfour Declaration was published, General
Allenby captured Jerusalem. When Weizmann went to meet him
in 1918, Allenby was overwhelmed by military and administrative
difficulties. Weizmann was told the time was not propitious to
implement the British plan: 'Nothing can be done at present', he
stated. 'We have to be extremely careful not to hurt the suscepti-
bilities of the population' (Johnson, p. 431). Yet despite such
obstacles as well as opposition from various quarters Britain
secured the Palestine mandate at the peace negotiations and steps
were taken to create a national Jewish homeland.

Aftermath of the First World War

At the end of the nineteenth century a number of agricultural
settlements, funded by such philanthropists as Moses Montefiore
and Edmund de Rothschild, were established in Palestine by Jewish settlers (the first Aliyah). At the beginning of the twentieth
century in the wake of Russian pogroms, a second wave of Jewish
immigrants (the second Aliyah) emigrated to the Holy Land.
These pioneers set up the new garden suburb of Jaffa (later Tel
Aviv) and founded kibbutzim as well as agricultural settlements.
In 1909 the young men of the second Aliyah, who had previously
participated in Jewish defence groups in Russia, established the
Society of Shomerin (Watchmen) to protect these new settlements.
Under the leadership of the Russian-born writer, Vladimir Jabotin-
sky and the Russian war hero Joseph Trumpeldor, a Jewish regi-
ment (Zion Mule Corps) was founded, and participated in the
First World War. After the war neither the Zionist authorities nor

the British showed any desire to keep the Jewish Legion in existence. Jabotinsky, however, believed its continuation was necessary
for Jewish survival and formed a self-defence organization (which
later became the Haganah).

With the rise of Arab nationalism, the Jewish settlements in
Palestine came increasingly under threat. In March 1920 the Arabs
attacked Jewish settlements in Galilee when Trumpeldor was killed;
this was followed by Arab riots in Jerusalem. In response, Jabotinsky's self-defence force went into action and Jabotinsky and others
were arrested, tried by a military court, and given fifteen years' hard
labour. Arab rioters were also convicted and imprisoned. Following these events, Lloyd George sent out Herbert Samuel as High
Commissioner, to the fury of the Arab population. Intent on im-
plementing the Balfour Declaration – which aimed to safeguard
the civil and religious rights of non-Jewish communities – Samuel
criticized the Zionists for failing to recognize the importance of
Arab nationalist aspirations. On 10 August 1921 he wrote to
Weizmann: 'It is upon the Arab rock that the Zionist ship may be
wrecked'. To the Palestinian Jewish leaders, he cautioned:

> You yourselves are inviting a massacre which will come as long
> as you disregard the Arabs. You pass over them in silence . . .
> You have done nothing to come to an understanding. You know
> only how to protest against the government . . . Zionism has
> not yet done a thing to obtain the consent of the inhabitants
> and without this consent immigration will not be possible.
> (Johnson, p. 437)

Despite such cautionary advice, the Zionists had little resources
for appeasing the Arab population in the early 1920s and were
therefore not anxious to heed Samuel's words. Nonetheless Samuel
pursued a policy of even-handedness, pardoning the Arab extremists who had started the riots of 1921. Following this act, he confirmed Sheikh Hisam, who was elected Grand Mufti of Jerusalem
by the electoral college of pious Arab Muslims, in preference to
the extremist Haj Amin Al-Husseini. Subsequently the Al-Husseini
family and the nationalist extreme wing who had led the 1920 riots
embarked on a campaign against the electoral college. Throughout
Jerusalem they put up posters which proclaimed: 'The accursed
traitors, whom you all know, have combined with the Jews to have
one of their party appointed Mufti.'

Within the British staff an anti-Zionist, Ernst T. Richmond
(who acted as an adviser to the High Commissioner on Muslim

affairs) persuaded Sheikh Hisam to step down and urged Samuel
to allow Haj Amin to take his place. On 11 July 1921 Samuel saw
Haj Amin, who gave assurances that he and his family would be
dedicated to peace. Three weeks later riots occurred in Jaffa and
elsewhere in which forty-five Jews were killed. This error of judgement was compounded when Samuel fostered the creation of a
supreme Muslim Council which was transformed by the Mufti and
his followers into a means of terrorizing the Jewish population.
Further, Samuel encouraged Palestinian Arabs to contact
their neighbours to promote Pan-Arabism. As a result the Mufti
was able to generate anti-Zionist feeling within the Pan-Arab
movement.

Despite these setbacks the British were insistent on implement-
ing the intention of the Balfour Declaration to create a homeland
for the Jewish people in Palestine. In this quest egalitarian principles were paramount. Thus in a meeting of the Imperial Council
on 22 June 1921 the Canadian Prime Minister Arthur Meighen
asked: 'How do you define our responsibilities in relation to Palestine under Mr Balfour's pledge?' In response, Winston Churchill,
the Colonial Secretary, stated: 'To do our best to make an honest
effort to give the Jews a chance to make a national home for themselves.' Meighen then asked if this meant they would take control
of the government. Churchill replied that they could do so if they
became a majority in the country. Meighen then asked if this meant
pro rata with the Arab population. To this Churchill said: 'Pro
rata with the Arab. We made an equal pledge that we would not
turn the Arab off his land or invade his political and social rights'
(Johnson, p. 440).

Although the British government initially agreed that all Jews
should be free to emigrate to Palestine, immigration eventually
became a pressing issue. After the Arab riots, Samuel suspended
Jewish immigration, and three boatloads of Jews fleeing from
Poland and the Ukraine were sent back from Israel. According to
Samuel, mass migration could not be allowed; not surprisingly this
policy led to vehement Jewish protests. Under Samuel's successor
Lord Plumer the country prospered, yet Jewish resentment continued. Although Weizmann adopted a moderate stance towards
Palestinian development, other leaders such as Jabotinsky were
more impatient. In 1922 Churchill ended the ban on immigration,
but his White Paper none the less insisted that immigration must
reflect the economic capacity of the country. Unwilling to accept
British policy Jabotinsky believed that immigration should be the

sole concern of Jewish authorities. On this basis, he left the Zionist executive in 1923, and in 1925 founded the Union of Zionist–Revisionists which sought to attract the largest number of Jews in the shortest possible time. This movement was hailed in Eastern Europe where its youth wing Betar wore uniforms and received military training.

Despite such efforts to encourage Jewish immigration, the Jewish population in Palestine grew gradually. By 1927 only 2,713 immigrated whereas 5,000 left the country. Three years later the number of arrivals and departures were about the same. But from 1929, as the economic and political situation grew worse throughout Europe, a large number of Jews sought to enter the country. In 1929 a massacre took place in Palestine in which 150 Jews were killed; this led to a further limit on immigration despite the fact that hundreds of thousands of Jews sought entry into Palestine. As more and more Jews were allowed to settle, Arab resentment intensified. Each year there were more than 30,000 arrivals, and in 1935 the number grew to 62,000. In response, in April 1936 a major Arab uprising took place. On 7 July 1937 a commission headed by Lord Peel recommended that Jewish immigration be reduced to 12,000 a year, and restrictions were placed on land purchases. In addition a three-way partition was suggested: the coastal strip, Galilee and the Jezreel valley should be formed into a Jewish state, whereas the Judaean hills, the Negev and Ephraim should be the Arab state. This plan was rejected by the Arabs and another revolt took place in 1937. In the following year, the Pan-Arab conference in Cairo adopted a policy whereby all Arab communities pledged they would take action to prevent further Zionist expansion.

After the failure of the tripartite plan in London in 1939 the British abandoned the policy of partition. In May 1939 a new White Paper was published stating that only 75,000 more Jews could be admitted over five years, and thereafter none except with Arab agreement. At the same time Palestine should proceed with plans to become independent. Although there were then about 500,000 Jews in Palestine, the Arabs still constituted the majority in the country. As a result the Arabs would be in a position to seize control of Palestine and expel the Jewish people.

The establishment of a Jewish state

The 1930s witnessed various divisions within the Zionist ranks. In 1931 Weizmann was forced to give up the presidency of the World Zionist Congress due to pressure from the Mizrahi. In the same year elections to the Zionist Assembly resulted in a split between Mapai (with 31 seats), the Revisionists (16 seats), and Mizrahi (five seats). In the military sphere the Revisionists, Mizrahi and other Zionists split from the Haganah to form the Irgun. At this time the Revisionists accused Mapai of collusion with the British; the Revisionists were condemned by Mapai as fascists. On 16 June 1933 the head of the Political Department, Chaim Arlosoroff, was murdered; two extreme Revisionists were arrested, charged with murder, but later acquitted. Yet despite such internal divisions, after the outbreak of war in 1939 the establishment of a Jewish state became the central concern of all Zionists.

Although the Jews supported the allies, Jewry was committed to overturning British policy as enshrined in the 1939 White Paper. During this period the British attempted to prevent illegal immigrants from landing in Palestine: if their ships got through they were captured and deported. In November 1940 the *Patria* which was about to set sail for Mauritius carrying 1,700 deportees was sabotaged by the Haganah; it sank in Haifa Bay with the loss of 250 refugees. Two years later the *Struma*, a refugee ship from Romania, was refused landing permission, turned back by the Turks, and sunk in the Black Sea with the death of 770 passengers. Such events, however, did not alter Britain's determination to prevent the entry of illegal immigrants.

In 1943 Menahem Begin, formerly chairman of Betar, took over control of the Revisionist military arm, the Irgun. With 600 agents under his control, he blew up various British buildings. On 6 November 1944 the ultra-extreme group, the Stern Gang (which had broken away from the Irgun), murdered Lord Moyne, the British Minister for Middle Eastern Affairs. Outraged by this act, the Haganah launched a campaign against both the Sternists and the Irgun. While he was fighting the British and other Jews, Begin organized a powerful underground force in the belief that the Haganah would eventually join him in attacking the British. In 1945 a united Jewish Resistance movement was created which embraced the various Jewish military forces, and on 31 October it began blowing up railways. In retaliation the British made a raid on the Jewish Agency on 29 June 1946, arresting 2,718 Jews. Begin, however, persuaded the Haganah to blow up the King David Hotel where a segment of the British administration was located. When Weizmann heard of this plan he was incensed, and the Haganah was ordered to desist. Begin refused, and on 22 July 1946 the explosion took place, killing 27 British, 41 Arabs, 17 Jews and 5 others. In consequence the Haganah commander Moshe Sneh resigned, and the resistance movement divided. The British then proposed a tripartite plan of partition which was rejected by both Jews and Arabs. Exasperated by this conflict, the British Foreign Secretary, Ernest Bevin, declared he was handing over this dispute to the United Nations.

Despite this decision, Begin continued with his campaign of terror, insisting on the right of the Irgun to retaliate against the British. In April 1947 after three members of the Irgun were convicted and hanged for destroying the Acre prison fortress, Begin ordered that two British sergeants be hanged. Such an act of revenge provoked worldwide condemnation, and anti-Jewish riots took place throughout Britain. These incidents encouraged the British to leave Palestine as soon as possible, and also coincided with the succession of Harry S. Truman as President of the United States. Sympathetic to the Jewish cause and anxious for the support of American Jewry in the 1948 election, Truman pressed for the creation of a Jewish state. In May 1947 the Palestinian question came before the United Nations, and a special committee was authorized to formulate a plan for the future of the country. The minority recommended a binational state, but the majority suggested that there be both an Arab and a Jewish state as well as an international zone in Jerusalem. On 29 November this recommendation was endorsed by the General Assembly.

After this decision was taken, the Arabs began to attack Jewish settlements. Although the Jewish commanders were determined to repel this assault, their resources were not considerable compared with the Arab side. The Haganah had 17,600 rifles, 2,700 sten-guns, about 1000 machine guns, and approximately 20,000–43,000 men in various stages of training. The Arabs on the other hand had a sizeable liberation army as well as the regular forces of the Arab states including 10,000 Egyptians, 7,000 Syrians, 3,000 Iraqis, and 3,000 Lebanese as well as 4,500 soldiers from the Arab Legion of Transjordan. By March 1948 over 1,200 Jews were killed; in April Ben Gurion ordered the Haganah to link the Jewish enclaves and consolidate as much territory as possible under the United Nations plan. Jewish forces then occupied Haifa, opened up the route to

Tiberias and eastern Galilee, and captured Safed, Jaffa and Acre.
On 14 May Ben Gurion read out the Scroll of Independence in the
Tel Aviv Museum:

> By virtue of our national and intrinsic right and on the strength
> of the resolution of the United Nations General Assembly, we
> hereby declare the establishment of a Jewish state in Palestine,
> which shall be known as the State of Israel. (Johnson, p. 527)

War between Jews and Arabs

On 11 June a truce was concluded, but in the next month conflict
broke out and the Israelis seized Lydda, Ramleh and Nazareth as
well as large areas beyond the partition frontiers. Within ten days
the Arabs agreed to another truce, but outbreaks of hostility continued. In mid-October the Israelis attempted to open the road to
the Negev settlements and took Beersheba. On 12 January 1949
armistice talks took place in Rhodes and an armistice was later
signed by Egypt, Lebanon, Transjordan and Syria. These events
created the ongoing Arab–Palestinian problem: 656,000 Arab
inhabitants fled from Israeli-held territories: 280,000 to the West
Bank; 70,000 to Transjordan; 100,000 to Lebanon; 4,000 to Iraq;
75,000 to Syria; 7,000 to Egypt; and 190,000 to the Gaza Strip.

On the basis of the 1949 armistice, the Israelis sought agreement
on the boundaries of the Jewish state. The Arabs, however, refused
to consider this proposal – instead they insisted that Israel return
to the 1947 partition lines without giving any formal recognition
of the new state. Further, despite the concluding of the armistice,
fedayeen bands continued to attack Israeli citizens, and boycotts
and blockades sought to injure Israel's economy. After King
Abdullah was assassinated on 20 June 1951, a military junta ousted
the Egyptian monarch; on 25 February 1954 President Gemal
Abdul Nasser gained control of the country. From September
1955 the Soviet bloc supplied weapons to the Arabs, and this
encouraged Nasser to take steps against the Jewish State. From
1956 he denied Israeli ships access to the Gulf of Aqaba (they
had already been prevented from using the Suez Canal). In
April 1956 he signed a pact with Saudi Arabia and Yemen, and
in July he seized the Suez Canal. Fearing Arab intentions, Israel
launched a pre-emptive strike on 29 October, and in the war
that followed Israel captured all of Sinai as well as Gaza, and
opened a sea route to Aqaba.

At the end of the Sinai War Israel undertook to withdraw from Sinai as long as Egypt did not remilitarize it and UN forces formed a protective cordon sanitaire. This arrangement endured for ten years, but attacks still continued during this period. In 1967 Nasser launched another offensive, and on 15 May he moved 100,000 men and armour into Sinai and expelled the UN army. On 22 May he blockaded Aqaba; several days later King Hussein of Jordan signed a military agreement in Cairo. On the same day Iraqi forces took up positions in Jordan. In the face of this Arab threat, Israel launched a strike on 5 June, destroying the Egyptian air force on the ground. On 7 June the Israeli army took the Old City, thereby making Jerusalem its capital. On the next day the Israeli forces occupied the entire Left Bank, and during the next few days captured the Golan Heights and reoccupied Sinai.

Despite such a crushing defeat, the Six Day War did not bring security to the Jewish state. Nasser's successor President Anwar Sadat expelled Egypt's Soviet military advisers in July 1972, cancelled the country's political and military alliance with other Arab states, and together with Syria attacked Israel on Yom Kippur, 6 October 1973. At the outbreak of war the Egyptians and the Syrians broke through Israeli defences, but by 9 October the Syrian advance had been repelled. On 10 October the American President Richard Nixon began an airlift of advanced weapons to Israel; two days later the Israelis engaged in a counter-attack on Egypt and moved towards victory. On 24 October a cease-fire came into operation.

Later after the Labour coalition lost the May 1977 election and handed over power to the Likud headed by Menahem Begin, Sadat offered to negotiate peace terms with Israel. On 5 September 1978 at the American presidential home Camp David, the process of reaching such an agreement began and was completed thirteen days later (although another six months were required before a detailed treaty was formulated). The treaty specified that Egypt would recognize Israel's right to exist and provide secure guarantees for her southern border. In return Israel would hand over Sinai. In addition she would undertake to negotiate away much of the West Bank and make concessions over Jerusalem as long as a complementary treaty was agreed with the Palestinians and other Arab countries. This latter step, however, was never taken – the proposal was rejected by the Palestinian Arabs. This meant that Israel was left with the responsibility for overseeing Arab occupied territories.

In the years that followed, Arab influence grew immeasurably, due to the Arabs' control of oil in the Middle East. As the price of oil increased, Arab revenue provided huge sums for the purchase of armaments. At the UN the Arab world exerted its power, and in 1975 the General Assembly passed a resolution equating Zionism with racism. Further, Yasser Arafat, the leader of the Palestine Liberation Organization, was accorded head of government status by the UN. Fearing the growing threat of Palestinian influence and terrorism, Israel launched an advance into southern Lebanon in June 1982, destroying PLO bases. This Israeli onslaught and subsequent occupation served as the background to the killing of Muslim refugees by Christian Falangist Arabs in the Sabra and Shatilla camps on 16 September 1982. Throughout the world this atrocity was portrayed as Israel's fault. In response to this criticism, the Israeli government ordered an independent judicial inquiry which placed some blame on the Israeli Minister of Defence, Ariel Sharon, for not having prevented this massacre.

The *intifada*

After the Israeli conquest during the Yom Kippur War, the State of Israel took control of the Occupied Territories. In the following years the Palestinians staged demonstrations, strikes and riots against Israeli rule. By 1987 the Palestinians in the West Bank and Gaza were largely young educated people who had benefited from formal education. Yet despite such educational advances, they suffered from limited job expectations and this situation led to political radicalism. Such frustration came to a head on 9 December 1987 in Jabaliya, the most militant of the Gaza refugee camps. An Israeli patrol was trapped there during a protest about the death of four Jabaliya residents who were killed in a road accident the previous day. The soldiers shot their way out, killing one youth and wounding ten others. This event provoked riots throughout the Occupied Territories. By January 1989, the Israeli Defence Forces declared that 352 Palestinians had died, more than 4,300 were wounded, and 25,600 arrested. In addition, 200 Arab homes had been sealed or demolished. As hostilities increased, the *intifada* (resistance) demonstrated that occupying the West Bank and the Gaza Strip would be a perpetual problem.

The Jewish state was unprepared for such a situation, and the army was forced to improvise. As time passed, the *intifada* became more resilient and its tactics changed to ambushes, small-scale conflicts, and selective strikes. In addition the technology of modern communications (including radio, telefax and photocopying) were used to apply pressure against the Israelis. In the view of many observers, this uprising had transformed the Palestinian people. Thus Dr Eyad Sarraj, the Arab director of mental health services in the Gaza Strip, declared:

> The uprising has dramatically transformed the Palestinian self-image. They have regained their self-respect. They feel they have scored a significant victory over the Israelis. For the first time they feel equal, even more powerful. The national identity has been strengthened and sharpened, there is a new cohesion. A high level of aspiration is replacing hopelessness. People are now talking of an end of the occupation as a matter of fact. (E. Silver, p. 5)

Again, Dr Ali Kleibo, an anthropologist at Bethlehem University, emphasized that the *intifada* was being used to change the nature of Palestinian existence:

> People are using it to question the traditional institutions of Palestinian life, be it the educational system, the importance of community action (something that has never happened before), the reorganization of the village into an educational, political and economic unit that goes beyond the *hamula* [extended family]. The level of solidarity that you see now never existed before. We are totally involved in questioning relations that before seemed sacrosanct, that appeared to us as absolute. The system is being reshuffled – with the Israelis, with our village, with our family, the whole system. And we are the ones who are reshuffling it. (E. Silver, p. 6)

Despite having such an impact, the *intifada* created tensions within the Palestinian community. As the resistance developed, Islamic revivalism spread from the Gaza Strip to the West Bank and Jerusalem and posed a serious threat to secular Palestinian nationalism. Such a division was aggravated when the PLO endorsed a two-stage solution to the Palestinian problem. Such a policy was bitterly condemned by fundamentalists. Hamas, the Islamic Resistance Movement, insisted on a Muslim Palestine from the Mediterranean to the Jordan. Clause 11 of its Manifesto declared:

> The Islamic Resistance Movement believes that all the land of Palestine is sacred to Islam, through all the generations and

forever, and it is forbidden to abandon it or part of it, or to yield it or part of it. No Arab state individually has this right, nor do all of the Arab states collectively, nor does any king or president individually, nor do all the kings and presidents collectively. No organization individually has the right, nor do all the organizations collectively, whether they are Palestinian or Arab. (E. Silver, p. 7)

Yasser Arafat, however, adopted a more pragmatic approach and abandoned such maximalist formulations of the Palestinian position in favour of a policy which took into account the reality of Israel's existence.

From the Israeli side, the Israeli Defence Forces viewed the *intifada* in the context of Israel's relationship with its Palestinian neighbours and the world in general. As a result, General Shomron ruled out the use of massive force in dealing with this issue. 'The *intifada*', he stated, 'will end at some point.' But the question remains what legacy it will leave. 'I am saying', he claimed, 'that the residents of the territories will always be our neighbours. I therefore do not think that we have an interest in causing a great deal of suffering, even though we can do so the moment we make such a decision' (E. Silver, p. 9). Similarly, Brigadier-General Zvi Poleg, who took over as commander of the Israeli Defence Forces in the Gaza Strip in 1988, stressed that the *intifada* was not a war: 'I'm a military commander', he declared, 'but you must be able to see a number of aspects of the problem, and not just see it through the gunsights, because you're working with human beings. If a local person gets hurt, gets killed, you must first of all remember that he is a human being. He wasn't born in order for someone to kill him. He was born to live. So if there's no absolute need to shoot, don't' (E. Silver, p. 9).

Despite such a stance, the *intifada* was generally regarded as more than a local skirmish, and throughout the world Israelis were viewed as guilty of brutality. As a result, there was a growing feeling that Israel should abandon the Occupied Territories. Thus a poll conducted by Professor Elihu Katz, Director of the Hebrew University's Israel Institute of Applied Social Research, in January 1989, revealed considerable sympathy towards the idea of a Palestinian state. Concluding his findings, Professor Katz wrote:

Some 30 per cent of Israeli Jews (half of the left and 10 to 20 per cent of the right) are willing to grant the essential prerequisites for a Palestinian state: negotiations, substantial territorial concessions and recognition. If questions are worded to make evident that security and peace might be obtained in exchange for these concessions, the favourable proportion increases substantially to 50 per cent or more. (E. Silver, p. 12)

Thus after several years of Palestinian revolt in the Occupied Territories, the Israeli population appears more prepared to settle its dispute with its Arab inhabitants, as has been evidenced by the peace talks beginning in 1992 between Israel and the Palestinians.

eleven

Concluding Reflections

During the period of Emancipation reformers argued that a Jewish state is no longer necessary. For these assimilationists, liberalism provides the first step towards the realization of the messianic era. This survey of the Jewish longing for a homeland has demonstrated that this view was a fundamental error: the quest for a return to Zion is a central feature of Jewish life and thought. Yet the desire for a Jewish presence in the Holy Land was at all times inspired by a utopian conception of the future. In ancient times this took the form of an ideal theocracy; this was eventually superseded by the belief in the coming of the Messiah and an ingathering of the exiles in Zion; in modern society such ideas have been replaced by Zionist notions of human liberation and freedom. Now as the Jewish state confronts the dilemmas of political empowerment, it must not lose sight of the moral and spiritual dimensions of the faith. This is the ultimate challenge facing Israel in the third millennium: to balance political, social, and economic concerns with the idealistic vision of creating God's Kingdom on earth.

The quest for a homeland

With the onset of Jewish emancipation in the late eighteenth and early nineteenth century, Jewish assimilationists argued that human beings were progressing towards a one-world culture. In all countries economic and social developments led to the diminution of national characteristics. Hence it was a mistake to return to Jewish nationalism. In particular, spokesmen from Reform Judaism maintained that although it was imperative to have a Jewish state thousands of years ago, this was now no longer required. Such a view led to the elimination of all references to a personal Messiah in the Reform liturgy; instead Reform Jews prayed for the realization of the messianic era in modern society. According to these early reformers, the emancipation of the Jews and the new liberalism in the West constituted the first steps in the fulfilment of this vision. Championing Jewish enlightenment, progressives urged Jewry to discard all particularistic and national elements in the tradition. No longer, they stated, should Jews yearn for a restoration in Palestine; rather, they should encourage the advancement of liberal ideas in the countries where they reside.

Such a vision was a betrayal of a fundamental dimension in the Jewish heritage. As we have seen, from its very earliest history the Jewish people yearned for a homeland of their own. In the Book of Genesis Abraham was promised by God that he would be the father of a multitude and that his progeny would inherit the land: 'To your descendants I give this land, from the river of Egypt to the great river, the river Euphrates, the land of the Kenites, the Kenizzites, the Kadmonites, the Hittites, the Perizzites, the Rephaim, the Amorites, the Canaanites, the Girgashites, and the Jebusites' (Genesis 15.18–19). This land was to be entrusted to Abraham's descendants by divine authority, and this promise was repeated through the patriarchal narratives. In the thirteenth century BC Moses led the Israelites out of captivity in Egypt, and finally under Joshua's leadership the Israelites subdued the inhabitants of Canaan. Ruled over by the judges, the nation prospered, and eventually a monarchy was established with Saul as the first king. In the tenth century BC the nation divided into two rival kingdoms with Israel in the north and Judah in the south. As time passed, a succession of northern kings incorporated Canaanite practices into the cult – such apostasy led the prophets Elisha and Elijah to remonstrate against the rulers' corruption. In the eighth century other prophetic voices in both the north and the south were raised against the iniquity of the nation, predicting that God would unleash his anger unless the people turned aside from their evil ways. Unwilling to listen to these words of caution, the Israelites continued to abandon God's laws, and in time both Israel and Judah were devastated by foreign powers.

Following the Assyrian and Babylonian conquests, the exiles despaired of their fate. Their iniquity had brought about this tragedy, and the scattered Jewish populace seemed condemned to exile. Yet despite these events, the nation arose from the old kingdoms. In the sixth century BC King Cyrus of Persia permitted the Jews to return to their former home; there they rebuilt the Temple and the nation underwent a transformation. None the less, such national restoration ended when Jerusalem and the Temple were devastated in 70 AD by the Romans. For a second time the Jewish people were cast into exile. Bereft of their home, the people longed for a kingly figure who would lead them back to Zion and renew earthly life in accord with the messianic expectations found in Scripture. With fervent anticipation they foresaw a future redemption when earthly life would be transformed and all peoples would worship the one true God. According to rabbinic scholars, this event would be an integral part of God's eschatological plan for his chosen people and all humanity. This utopian vision of the future was animated by the belief that God would not abandon his people; instead he would lead them back to the land of their fathers.

In the years following the destruction of the Temple, a number of messianic figures appeared on the Jewish scene. During the period after Herod's death, Jews from Galilee and elsewhere believed that Jesus, the son of Joseph and Mary, was the promised Messiah. Although mainstream Judaism rejected such claims, the Jewish community continued to yearn for redemption, and in AD 132 a revolt against the Romans was led by Simon bar Kochba who was widely viewed as the Messiah ben David. In the mid fifth century another messianic pretender from Crete declared that he would redeem the Jews from exile and lead them back to the Promised Land. When this plan failed, Jewish scholars attempted to calculate the date of messianic deliverance – these reflections are recorded in a variety of midrashic works of the next few centuries. Later other pseudo-Messiahs emerged within the Jewish world, claiming that they had been sent to free Jewry from the bondage of exile.

The failure of these messianic figures did not crush the Jewish hope for redemption. In the fourteenth and fifteenth centuries Jews continued to yearn for the Messiah who would return the Jewish people to their ancestral home. Messianic treatises were accordingly produced, and numerous writers in these and later centuries continued to speculate about his arrival. During this period other false Messiahs alleged that they had come to inaugurate a new age. Undaunted by the failure of these individuals to bring about the transformation of Jewish existence, messianic calculators of the sixteenth century persisted in their computations. Eventually the arrival of Shabbatai Tzevi was heralded throughout the Jewish world as the Redeemer. Yet when he converted to Islam his followers were overcome with despair. In the wake of these events, many Jews became disillusioned with centuries of messianic anticipation and disappointment; as a result most post-enlightenment Jews have ceased to believe in a Messiah who will lead the nation to the Holy Land and bring about the end of history. Rather most of the Jewish community have come to accept that the return to Israel must be accomplished through human effort.

Thus at the beginning of the nineteenth century Zionists such as Moses Hess, Leon Pinsker, and Theodor Herzl argued that Jewry must reconstitute itself as a separate people in its own country. Only in this way, they believed, would the Jewish community be able to escape from anti-Semitism. Although this quest to create a national homeland was initially opposed by both Orthodoxy and Reform Judaism, the events of the twentieth century illustrate that the creation of a Jewish state is necessary to ensure the survival of Judaism and the Jewish people. The quest for a Jewish home has therefore been a constant feature of Jewish existence through the ages. Inspired by the prophetic vision of a land flowing with milk and honey, the Jewish nation has yearned for a return to the Promised Land and this aspiration inspired centuries of messianic speculation as well as the foundation of a modern Jewish state.

A utopian vision

Through the centuries the quest for a Jewish homeland was inspired by utopian ideals. The Book of Genesis records that God had declared to Abraham that he would give him a fruitful land for his descendants to occupy; this Promised Land was later occupied by the ancient Israelites who had been freed from Egyptian bondage. There they were to create a theocracy under God's law. Yet once a monarchy was established, the people strayed from the Torah, and it became the prophets' duty to draw them back to the God of their fathers. Repeatedly prophetic voices were raised against the iniquity of the nation. As God's chosen elect, the Israelites were obligated to keep the covenant and thereby serve as a light to the nations.

Initially, the prophets Elijah and Elisha rebuked the leaders of the northern kingdom: in later centuries they were followed by prophets in both the northern and southern kingdoms who inveighed against idolatry and sin. The earliest Hebrew prophet whose book was dedicated to the proclamation of God's ethical requirements was Amos, a shepherd from Tekoa, who was active in about 760 BC. Israel, he declared, had sinned

> because they sell the righteous for silver,
> and the needy for a pair of shoes –
> they that trample the head of the poor
>   into the dust of the earth,
> and turn aside the way of the afflicted;

a man and his father go in to the same maiden,
  so that my holy name is profaned;
they lay themselves down beside every altar
  upon garments taken in pledge;
and in the house of their God they drink
the wine of those who have been fined. (Amos 2.6–8)

Several decades after Amos began his ministry in Israel, Isaiah embarked on a prophetic mission in Judah. God had chosen Israel to produce justice, Isaiah proclaimed, but insisted that the nation had produced bloodshed (Isaiah 5.7). Like Amos, Isaiah protested against the indifference of the rich to the poor and oppressed:

It is you who have devoured the vineyard,
  the spoil of the poor is in your houses.
What do you mean by crushing my people,
  by grinding the face of the poor? (Isaiah 3.14–15)

A century later the prophet Jeremiah emphasized that God demands righteousness from the people. In a sermon delivered in about 609 BC, he insisted that it was wrong to assume that Jerusalem was immune from attack because God's presence in the Temple provided protection:

Do not trust in these deceptive words: 'This is the temple of the Lord, the temple of the LORD, the temple of the LORD...' Will you steal, murder, commit adultery, swear falsely, burn incense to Baal, and go after other gods that you have not known, and then come and stand before me in this house, which is called by my name, and say, 'We are delivered!'? (Jer. 7.4, 9–10)

These classical prophets, as well as later post-exilic prophets who carried on and elaborated their message, became the conscience of the nation. They attacked the people's iniquity and their exploitation of the rich. God's covenant, they insisted, demanded compassion, justice and righteousness. Such ideals, they believed, must be at the centre of the national life.

Once the Jews had been exiled by the Romans in the first century AD, the Jewish people had lost its home. Yet the idealism that animated the prophets was transformed into a messianic vision of a future age. Drawing on Scripture, rabbinic sages depicted God's Kingdom on earth. The Messiah, they believed, would usher in a period of peace and tranquillity. Citing the Book of Isaiah, they declared that after a catastrophic upheaval, the end of days will ensue when the house of the LORD will be established on the top of the mountain, and all peoples will stream there for spiritual nourishment. During the Messiah's reign God's sovereignty would be accepted by all, and justice would rule the earth. From century to century this messianic hope inspired the nation to long for a return to Zion, and numerous would-be Messiahs claimed to inaugurate this new age. The biblical hope for God's reign on earth was in this way reinterpreted as an other-worldly yearning for the end of history when peace would be established through God's representative, and the word of the LORD would go out from Jerusalem.

In the nineteenth century this theme of messianic deliverance was linked by religious Zionists with the establishment of Jewish settlements in Palestine. The writings of such writers as Yehuda hai Alkalai, Zwi Hirsch Kalischer and Abraham Isaac Kook were animated by fervent idealism. Alongside such a mystical vision secular Zionists advanced the Zionist cause with equal fervour. According to a number of early Zionists, the creation of a Jewish state would advance the cause of human liberation and freedom. Thus Moses Hess wrote in *Rome and Jerusalem*:

> I believe that the national character of Judaism does not exclude universalism and modern civilization; on the contrary, these values are the logical effect of our national character. If I none the less emphasize the national root of Judaism rather than its universalist blooms, that is because in our time people are too prone to gather and deck themselves out with the pretty flowers of the cultural heritage rather than to cultivate them in the soil in which they can grow. Judaism is the root of our whole contemporary universalist view of life. (Hertzberg, p. 128)

For Leon Pinsker, the creation of a Jewish state would serve as the remedy to the problem of anti-Semitism. In *Autoemancipation* he stated:

> The Jews are not a living nation; they are everywhere aliens; therefore they are despised. The civil and political emancipation of the Jews is not sufficient to raise them in the estimation of the peoples. The proper and the only remedy would be the creation of a Jewish nationality, of a people living upon its own soil, the auto-emancipation of the Jews; their emancipation as a nation among nations by the acquisition of a home of their own. (Hertzberg, p. 198)

Echoing such sentiments, Theodor Herzl in *The Jewish State* confidently expected the Jewish nation to liberate the Jewish people and all humankind: 'Let me repeat once more my opening words: The Jews who will it shall achieve their state. We shall live at last as free men on our own soil, and in our own homes peacefully die. The world will be liberated by our freedom, enriched by our wealth, magnified by our greatness' (Hertzberg, pp. 225–6). Such optimism and dedication became the hallmark of Jewish pioneers who settled in Palestine, tilled the soil and created a Jewish presence in the Holy Land. They and their descendants sacrificed themselves in the quest to regain their ancient home. Though beset by enemies on all sides, the State of Israel they created has prospered and developed, becoming the most powerful state in the Middle East.

This saga of Jewish aspirations for a homeland in the land of their ancestors reveals the utopian aspects of the nation's yearning. Through four millennia, Jewry was guided by the belief that it was possible to create God's Kingdom on earth. In ancient Israel, the state was to be a theocracy. Continually the prophets reminded the nation of its divine obligations. With the destruction of Jerusalem and the Temple, the desire for a Jewish home was transformed into an eschatological vision of messianic redemption in Zion. The Jews were to return triumphally with the Messiah at their head. As time passed, this dream faded, yet the longing for a Jewish home did not diminish. Increasingly Jewry came to believe that this eternal quest could be realized only through the labours of the Zionists. Yet despite this shift in religious conviction, the early Zionists were infused with hope and enthusiasm. Their task was to create a Jewish society which would be a light to the nations.

Political empowerment and the Palestinians

With the establishment of Israel, the Jewish nation has become a major power after 2000 years of exile. Having endured the horrors of the Holocaust, world Jewry today is united in its commitment to Jewish survival: the rallying call of the Jewish people has now become: 'Never Again!'. But how is the Jewish community to respond to the social responsibilities of political empowerment? In discussing this issue, a number of conservative Jewish writers from across the religious and political spectrum have stressed that pragmatic considerations must be paramount as the State of Israel struggles to endure against formidable odds. Such a policy of *real-*

politik, they maintain, will inevitably countenance the occasional use of immoral strategies to achieve desired ends – this is the price of empowerment. According to these pragmatists, if Judaism and the Jewish people are to continue into the twenty-first century, there must be constant vigilance about those forces which seek to undermine the existence of Jewry: anti-Semitism must be countered wherever it exists, no matter what the political, economic, social, spiritual or moral cost may be.

This survey of Jewish aspirations to create a Jewish homeland, however, reveals that such a stance is inherently flawed. As we have seen, the idea of Israel was at all times animated by an idealistic vision of the Jewish future. It was not enough simply to ensure a Jewish presence in the Holy Land: what is required instead is the attempt to create God's Kingdom on earth. Such utopianism is at the heart of the ancient, medieval and modern quest to return to Zion. Hence contemporary Israeli society is under an obligation to live up to the moral prescriptions of the Torah – Jewish life in Israel must be infused with the ethical values of the faith. Jewish survival as an end in and of itself is insufficient.

As an empowered people the Israelis thus have the duty to consider the plight of all those (Jews and non-Jews alike), who are currently undergoing hardship and deprivation in the Jewish state. As God's suffering servant through the ages, the Jewish people should find this message of solidarity with the underprivileged of paramount significance. As we have observed, the prophets of ancient Israel condemned every kind of abuse. Scripture speaks of positive action to prevent exploitation and oppression from becoming widespread. Israelis should thus feel an obligation to take steps to eradicate human suffering within the Holy Land. In particular, they should address themselves to the economic deprivation that affects all those who are disadvantaged: the young, who are often frustrated by the lack of opportunity to obtain training and work; manual labourers, who are often ill-paid and find difficulty in defending their rights; the unemployed, who are discarded because of the harsh exigencies of economic life; and the old, who are often marginalized and disregarded. In all such cases, the Jewish nation – which has constantly endured hardship – should feel drawn to the downtrodden of modern Israel, sharing in their distress. Defending the Jewish state against aggressors must not overshadow these social concerns.

In this context the State of Israel must also give heed to the Palestinian quest for human dignity. A number of early Zionists were acutely aware of the need of the Arab population in Palestine. Thus Ahad Ha-Am warned about the dangers of ignoring the Arab presence and trampling on their rights:

> One thing we certainly should have learned from our past and present history, and that is not to create anger among the local population against us . . . We have to treat the local population with love and respect, justly and rightly. And what do our brethren in the land of Israel do? Exactly the opposite. Slaves they were in their country of exile, and suddenly they find themselves in a boundless and anarchic freedom, as is always the case with a slave that has become king; and they behave toward the Arabs with hostility and cruelty, infringe upon their boundaries, hit them shamefully without reason and even brag about it. (Avineri, p. 123)

Again, the Jewish philosopher Martin Buber stressed that the Jews must attempt to live in peace with their Arab neighbours and respect them as human beings. In an 'Open Letter to Mahatma Gandhi' written in 1939, he stated:

> I belong to a group of people who from the time Britain conquered Palestine have not ceased to strive for the concluding of a genuine peace between Jew and Arab. By a genuine peace we inferred and still infer that both peoples should develop the land without the one imposing its will on the other . . . We considered it a fundamental point that in this case two vital claims are opposed to each other, two claims of a different nature and a different origin which cannot objectively be pitted against one another and between which no objective decision can be made as to which is just, which unjust. We considered and still consider it our duty to understand and to honour the claim which is opposed to ours and to endeavour to reconcile both claims. (Hertzberg, p. 463)

This study has chronicled the tragic inability of both the Arab and Jewish communities to reach such reconciliation. For five decades these two rival peoples have sought to conquer one another. This terrible chapter in the history of modern Judaism must come to an end. Now that the desire of the Jewish people for a homeland has been fulfilled, the nation should turn its attention to the plight of Palestinian refugees who have been dispossessed of their national heritage. The Palestinian people, like the Jews, deserve to have a home of their own on the soil of their ancestors.

Over the last few years the Palestinian uprising has emphasized the urgency of this task of reconstruction. As we have seen, the Jewish state has understandably been wary of any negotiated settlement with the Palestinian people – Palestinian Arabs are regarded as the enemy and a grave threat to Jewish survival. Yet the horrors of the Holocaust must not be allowed to eclipse the needs of others to achieve communal autonomy.

In seeking this goal the Jewish people need to recognize that just as the quest to return to Israel is deeply rooted in the Jewish psyche, so too does a similar need exist for Palestinian Arabs. Arguably Jews over the years have misused their newly found power – this must now be rectified by granting the Palestinian population a territory of their own. Political empowerment in Eretz Israel thus brings with it the social duties to the dispossessed. Such a shift in attitude calls for a profound change of heart on the part of both Israel and world Jewry. Recent events – such as the Palestinian defence of Saddam Hussein in the Gulf War – make this reversal painfully difficult. However, Jewish ideals demand nothing less than solidarity with Palestinian aspirations. Only by joining in common cause with those Palestinians who seek liberation and freedom can contemporary Jewry echo the ancient words of Isaiah:

> I will rejoice in Jerusalem,
>> and be glad in my people;
> no more shall be heard in it the sound of weeping
>> and the cry of distress . . .
> The wolf and the lamb shall feed together,
>> the lion shall eat straw like the ox;
>> and dust shall be the serpent's food.
> They shall not hurt or destroy
>> in all my holy mountain, says the Lord. (Isaiah 65.19, 25)

The problem of anti-Semitism

As we have seen, the early proponents of secular Zionism were convinced that Judeophobia is unavoidable in Western society. Thus Moses Hess in *Rome and Jerusalem* decreed that it is impossible for Jews to escape from Jew-hatred no matter what steps are taken towards emancipation and liberation: neither Jewish reform nor conversion to Christianity can provide a means of overcoming such sentiments. For Hess, only the restoration of Jewish nationalism can enable Jewry to gain social, political and economic equality.

Similarly, Leon Pinsker in *Autoemancipation* argued for the creation of a national homeland in the wake of the Russian pogroms of 1881. Although initially a fervent supporter of the Enlightenment, Pinsker asserted that the Jewish problem can only be solved through Jewish statehood. In the diaspora the Jews are like the dead among the living, but with the creation of a Jewish society they will be able to regain their self-respect and communal integrity. Again, in *The Jewish State*, Theodor Herzl espoused Zionism as a remedy for anti-Semitism. Convinced of the necessity of a home for those who are oppressed, Herzl maintained that the building of a Jewish state would transform Jewish life; no longer would Jews be vulnerable to attack.

These prognostications about the elimination of Jew-hatred have not been realized in this century. On the contrary, Arab anti-Semitism has been intensified by the establishment of a Jewish state. Today Arab writing is penetrated with anti-Semitic motifs, images and stereotypes drawn from the past. In Egypt for example the press frequently castigates Jews for their crimes against humanity. In political cartoons Israel is personified by hooked-nosed and hunchbacked figures with wispy beards, skull caps, and black hats. Headlines call for the destruction of the Jewish state. In addition books and articles reiterate the traditional account of Muhammad's betrayal by the Jewish people. Such Arab recycling of Western Judeophobia is also found in international forums. Thus the Libyan representative of the United Nations declared on 8 November 1983:

> It is high time for the United Nations and the United States, in particular, to realize that the Jewish Zionists here in the United States attempt to destroy Americans. Look around New York. Who are the owners of pornographic film operations and houses? Is it not the Jews who are exploiting the American people and trying to debase them? If we succeed in eliminating that entity, we shall by the same token save the American and European peoples. (Wistrich, p. 257)

This theme of sexual permissiveness is a constant feature of the Arab media. Israel is regarded as a society dominated by an ethos of sexual freedom which if introduced into Muslim culture would lead to widespread degeneracy. In this context Israel, Zionism and the Jews are portrayed as seeking to destroy the Muslim faith by advancing moral corruption. Some prominent writers in Egypt have even alleged that the Jews become obstetricians in order to perform abortions and thereby eradicate the gentile population and that they desire to introduce AIDS into Arab countries through drugs and sexual immorality. Such accusations – reminiscent of heinous medieval charges against the Jewish populace – portray Jewry as corrupt and inhumane, intent on undermining the foundations of civilized society.

Similar anti-Jewish agitation has also been a central motif of Soviet policy since the Second World War. During the war anti-Semitism existed in the Red Army, and as the war ended many Jews were removed from government departments. In September 1948 an article in *Pravda* denounced Israel as a bourgeois tool of American capitalism; the Jewish anti-Fascist committee was eliminated; and Yiddish schools were closed. This was followed by an attack on Jewish writers, painters, musicians and intellectuals. The campaign extended to Czechoslovakia, and on 20 November 1952 the Czech Communist Party General Secretary as well as other communist leaders including eleven Jews were accused of a Trotskyite–Titoist–Zionist conspiracy and executed. In 1953 nine doctors including six Jews were accused of plotting to poison Joseph Stalin in conjunction with British, American and Zionist agents. This trial was to have been a prelude to the deportation of Jews to Siberia but Stalin died before the doctors were tried. Stalin's successor Nikita Khrushchev changed the orientation of anti-Jewish propaganda from spying to economic criminality; many Jews were convicted and sentenced to death. Furthermore, during Khrushchev's reign the number of synagogues was reduced from 450 to 60, and he permitted the publication of the anti-Semitic tract, *Judaism without Embellishment*. After Khrushchev's fall there was a brief respite, but following the Six Day War in 1967 the campaign against Jews was resumed. In 1971 Leonid Brezhnev decided to allow a large number of Jews to leave the Soviet Union, and during the next decade 250,000 emigrated. But accompanying this large-scale exodus there was an increase in trials of Jews and the procedure for obtaining an exit visa became more complicated. In the 1980s even fewer visas were granted as the Soviet campaign against Zionism intensified.

After Gorbachev's accession to power, chauvinist anti-Semitism has flourished, particularly within Pamyat which spearheads the Movement for the Restoration of Monuments of Russian Culture, and the Russian Republic Culture Fund. Among the ranks of those who support Pamyat are intellectuals whose ideology is grounded in their disillusionment with communism. Advocating patriotism and traditional values, they have attacked what they believe to be the destructive influences of Western cosmopolitanism. Symbolic of this new movement was an incident that occurred in January 1990 when members of Pamyat besieged the Moscow Writers' Club, shouting: 'You dirty Jewish mongrels, you're not writers! Get out to Israel!'

Turning to other countries in Europe, Polish Jewry has recently suffered from a wave of anti-Jewish sentiment. Despite the disappearance of the Polish Jewish community, anti-Semitism has continued to serve as a vital factor in Polish political life. In 1980–1 the Communists attempted to discredit Solidarity and the dissident organization KOR. In the Communist press Jews were accused of influencing Solidarity, and anti-Semitic pamphlets caricatured the Solidarity adviser Bronislaw Giermek as a Hasidic Jew. A number of labour activists were also falsely accused of being Jewish. In the elections of 1990 the liberal Catholic prime minister Tadeusz Mazowiecki was smeared as a crypto-Jew, and his government was depicted as being controlled by the Jews rather than authentic Poles.

Recent events in France have also raised fears about the growth of anti-Semitism. In 1980 a bomb exploded outside a Paris synagogue on Rue Copernic which was possibly the work of Palestinian terrorists or neo-Nazis. This was followed by attacks on synagogues, schools, and other institutions. According to an opinion poll taken at the time, over half the respondents believed that anti-Semitism had become widespread. The 1982 terrorist assault on a Jewish delicatessen in the Rue des Rosiers resulted in six deaths and twenty-four injuries. During this period Jewish graves were desecrated throughout the country, resulting in the outrage which took place at Carpentras on 9 May 1990: thirty-four graves were damaged or destroyed and a corpse was exhumed and impaled on an umbrella. This desecration was followed by a series of anti-Semitic incidents throughout the country, ending in a protest in Paris by prominent Jews as well as Christians and Muslims.

Similar hostility has also been expressed in post-war Germany. According to the researches of Werner Bergman six to seven million Germans could be classified as anti-Semitic; approximately two million of that number were characterized as hard-core anti-Semites. Post-war Austria has also witnessed the continuation of anti-Jewish attitudes. Such animosity surfaced when the former Secretary General of the United Nations, Kurt Waldheim, was attacked for his activities during the war. The campaign against

Waldheim provoked a backlash of Jew-hatred, and after 1986 it was widely believed that international Jews based on the east coast of the USA manipulated the media to defame Waldheim's character.

Recent outbursts of Judeophobia have also taken place in Britain. From the 1970s neo-Nazi and ultra-right groups promulgated Jewish conspiracy theories of the pre-war years. The National Front, for example, has promoted fascism and racial bigotry. Its anti-Semitic publication, *Holocaust News*, attempts to demonstrate that the murder of European Jewry did not take place. In addition, there have been assaults on Jewish cemeteries, the proliferation of anti-Semitic graffiti, assaults on Orthodox Jews in north London, and verbal abuse directed at pupils of Jewish schools.

Such examples of contemporary hostility to the Jewish people illustrate that the flames of anti-Semitism have not been quenched by the creation of a Jewish state. In fact the founding of a Jewish homeland in Israel appears to have had precisely the opposite effect. Diaspora existence did not disappear once Israel was established: there was simply not enough space in Palestine to accommodate world Jewry, and in any case the majority of Jews did not wish to emigrate. Thus Jews continue to live as aliens in foreign lands where they continue to be the target of persecution, and the existence of a Jewish homeland in the Middle East has exacerbated hostility towards the Jewish people who are characterized, particularly in Arab lands, as usurpers and exploiters.

Israel and the future

For nearly 4000 years the Jewish people have longed for a homeland of their own. From the time of Abraham to the present this yearning has been at the centre of the Jewish faith. As God's chosen people, the promise of a return to Zion sustained them through persecution and suffering. Now that the Jewish nation has re-established itself in Israel after centuries of exile, what of the future? In the light of the events of the twentieth century, it has become extremely difficult for many Jews to believe that God will stand by his people in times of disaster. Increasingly for Jewry a void exists where once the Jewish people experienced God's presence, and as a result modern Israel has been invested with many of the attributes previously reserved for the Deity. Hence in the post-Holocaust world the traditional conception of a divine redeemer and deliverer has been eclipsed by a policy of Jewish self-protection. It is the Holy Land which is viewed as ultimately capable of providing a safe haven for those in need: Israel – not the God of history – is conceived as the protector of the Jewish people.

Such a shift away from theological commitment poses profound difficulties for the future, given the perilous situation of the Jewish state. Over the years Arab anti-Semitism has intensified; even if a Palestinian homeland were created in the Middle East, this would be no guarantee for the survival of modern Israel. The threat of a nuclear holocaust would in all likelihood continue as an ever-present reality. What if Israel were destroyed, and the Jewish state wiped off the map? How could the Jewish community endure yet another tragedy of this order without belief in God and redemption? For those Jews who have substituted the Holy Land for God himself, the destruction of Israel would be the ultimate tragedy.

In substituting the political Israel for traditional religious belief, modern Zionism has turned the story of Jacob wrestling with the angel on its head. According to the Book of Genesis, the patriarch Jacob wrestled with a messenger of God until dawn at the ford of Jabbok. When this messenger saw that he could not prevail against Jacob, he touched the hollow of Jacob's thigh which was thereby put out of joint. As dawn appeared the messenger said: 'Let me go for the day is breaking.' But Jacob replied: 'I will not let you go, unless you bless me.' And he said: 'What is your name?' He said, 'Jacob.' Then the angel said: 'Your name shall no more be called Jacob, but Israel, for you have striven with God and with men, and have prevailed' (Genesis 32.26–9). This incident was the origin of the name Israel (meaning 'he who struggles with God') which subsequently became the designation of Jacob's twelve sons, and eventually of the entire nation.

Here Jacob struggled, and through God, he became Israel. Yet in the contemporary world it appears that political Israel has prevailed and has become a substitute for God. In the quest to provide a refuge for all who are oppressed and persecuted, the State of Israel has eclipsed religious faith. Such an altered perspective is profoundly disturbing because it provides no religious sustenance for the nation. In the past Jews viewed God as an all-powerful creator: he is the omnipotent Lord of the universe, capable of doing everything. In his omniscience he is aware of all things that take place in the universe including the human heart. In addition God is active in the world's affairs. Not only is he the source of all, he chose the Jews, guides their destiny, and directs all history to its final consummation. As holy, righteous and merciful Lord, he is a loving father to all who call upon him. This view of the Deity, enshrined in the Jewish tradition, has animated the faithful from earliest times.

Through the centuries this belief in the God of Abraham, Isaac and Jacob sustained generations of Jews who suffered persecution and death. As martyrs were slaughtered, they glorified God through dedication to the Jewish faith. These heroic Jews who remained steadfast did not question the ways of God; rather their deaths testified to their firm belief in a providential Lord of history. In Judaism this conviction gave meaning to the struggle of Jewish warriors, strength of endurance under cruel torture, and a way out of slavery through suicide. By believing in God, the Jewish people have managed to endure millennia of suffering with the assurance of divine deliverance.

Israel may not survive, and if the Jewish people forget God in their passion for the land, then they also will disappear from history. The State of Israel is not an ultimate insurance policy – it is simply a human attempt to bring about the realization of the Jewish yearning for a homeland. Through centuries of hardship, the nation remained faithful to their hope of return. Year by year in the Passover service, they promised themselves: 'Next Year in Jerusalem'. Through their religious faith, the sense of destiny and nationhood was preserved. Since 1948 when Israel became a Jewish state, the hope of a return to the Promised Land became a reality. Yet if Israel is a state like any other, it is subject to the political vicissitudes of all other earthly institutions. The true Israel can only prevail if it continues to wrestle with God. If the Jewish people are to survive into the third millennium, it is not enough for them to assert their identity merely through supporting the State of Israel. The patriarch Jacob himself knew that more was necessary all those years ago when he wrestled with God by the ford of Jabbok. As he limped away from the encounter, he declared: 'I have seen God face to face and still my life is preserved.'

Bibliography

Works cited in the text

Avineri, S. *The Making of Modern Zionism*. New York 1981.
Borochov, B. *The National Question and the Class Struggle*. Chicago 1935.
Brock, M. and E., eds *H. H. Asquith: Letters to Venetia Stanley*. Oxford 1952.
Cohn-Sherbok, D. (1989) *The Jewish Heritage*. Oxford.
Cohn-Sherbok, D. (1991) *Issues in Contemporary Judaism*. London.
Davidson, I., ed., *Selected Religious Poems of Solomon ibn Gabirol* 1923.
Ha'am, A. *Nationalism and the Jewish Ethic*. New York 1962.
Harkavy, A. A., ed. *Judah Halevy: Poems*. 2 vols. Warsaw 1893–4.
Hertzberg, A., ed. *The Zionist Idea: A Historical Analysis and Reader*. New York 1959.
Johnson, P. *A History of the Jews*. London 1987.
Klausner, J. *The Messianic Idea in Israel*. London 1956.
Laqueur, W. *A History of Zionism*. New York 1972.
Pinsker, L. *Autoemancipation*. London 1932.
Sanders, R. *The High Walls of Jerusalem: A History of the Balfour Declaration and the Birth of the British Mandate for Palestine*. New York 1984.
Silver, A. H. *A History of Messianic Speculation in Israel*. New York 1978. (= Silver)
Silver, E. 'The Intifada and After', *Survey of Jewish Affairs 1989*. Oxford 1989. (= E. Silver)
Wistrich, R. *Anti-Semitism: The Longest Hatred*. London 1991.

Further reading

Ackroyd, P., *Exile and Restoration*. London 1968.
Agus, J., *Modern Philosophies of Judaism*. New York 1940.
Anderson, B. W., *The Eighth Century Prophets*. London 1979.
Baile, D., *Power and Powerlessness in Jewish History*. New York 1986.

Baron, S. W., *A Social and Religious History of the Jews*. New York 1952–76.

Begin, M., *White Nights*. New York 1977.

Ben-Sasson, H. H., *A History of the Jewish People*. Cambridge 1976.

Braybrooke, M., *Time to Meet: Towards a Deeper Relationship Between Jews and Christians*. London 1990.

Bright, J., *A History of Israel*. Philadelphia 1972.

Brueggemann, W., *The Land*. Philadelphia 1977.

Buber, M., *Zion: The History of an Idea*. Edinburgh 1985.

Cohn, N., *Pursuit of the Millennium*. New York 1970.

Cohn-Sherbok, D. *On Earth as it is in Heaven: Jews, Christians and Liberation Theology*. New York 1987.

—— *The Crucified Jew: Twenty Centuries of Christian Anti-Semitism*. London 1992.

Davies, W. D., *The Territorial Dimension of Judaism*. Berkeley 1982.

Dawidowicz, L., ed., *A Holocaust Reader*. New York 1976.

de Lange, N., *Judaism*. Oxford 1986.

Drane, J., *The Old Testament Story*. London 1973.

Dubnow, S., *History of the Jews in Russia and Poland*. New York 1973.

Ellis, M., *Beyond Innocence and Redemption: Confronting the Holocaust and Israeli Power*. San Francisco 1990.

Encyclopaedia Judaica. Jerusalem 1972.

Epstein, I., *Judaism*. London 1975.

Flannery, E. H., *The Anguish of the Jews*. New York 1985.

Frankel, W., *Survey of Jewish Affairs 1989*. Oxford 1989.

Freischner, E., ed., *Auschwitz: Beginning of a New Era*. New York 1977.

Friedlander, A., *Out of the Whirlwind*. New York 1976.

Gilbert, M., *The Holocaust*. London 1986.

Ginzberg, L., *The Legends of the Jews*. Philadelphia 1954.

Grant, M., *The History of Ancient Israel*. New York 1984.

Gubbay, L., *Quest for the Messiah*. Sussex 1990.

Halkin, A. S., ed., *Zion in Jewish Literature*. New York 1961.

Halpern, B., *The Idea of the Jewish State*. Cambridge 1969.

Heschel, A., *Israel: An Echo of Eternity*. New York 1969.

Husik, I., *A History of Medieval Jewish Philosophy*. Philadelphia 1958.

Jacobovits, I., *The Timely and the Timeless*. London 1977.

Jacobs, L., *Principles of the Jewish Faith*. London 1964.

—— *A Jewish Theology*. New York 1973.

Jewish Encyclopaedia. New York 1901–5.

Katz, J., *Exclusiveness and Tolerance*. New York 1962.

Katz, S., *Post-Holocaust Dialogues: Critical Studies in Modern Jewish Thought*. New York 1983.

Kohler, K., *Jewish Theology*. New York 1968.

Kumar, K., *Utopia and Anti-Utopia in Modern Times*. Oxford 1989.

—— *Utopianism*. Buckingham 1991.

Lindbloom, J., *Prophecy in Ancient Israel*. Oxford 1962.

Littell, F. H., *The Crucifixion of the Jews*. Georgia 1986.

Marcus, J. R., ed., *The Jew in the Medieval World*. New York 1965.

Margolis, M. L., and Marx, A., *A History of the Jewish People*. Philadelphia 1927.

Montefiore, C. G. and Loewe, H., eds, *A Rabbinic Anthology*. New York 1974.

O'Brien, C. C., *The Siege: The Saga of Israel and Zionism*. London 1986.

Petuchowski, J., *Zion Reconsidered*. New York 1966.

Plaut, G. W., ed., *The Rise of Reform Judaism*. New York 1963.

—— *The Growth of Reform Judaism*. New York 1965.

Poliakov, L., *The History of Anti-Semitism*. London 1974.

Rubenstein, R. L., and Roth, J., *Approaches to Auschwitz*. London 1987.

Rubenstein, W. D., *The Left, The Right and the Jews*. New York 1982.

Ruether, R. R., *Faith and Fratricide: The Theological Roots of Antisemitism*. London 1975.

Sachar, A. L., *A History of the Jews*. New York 1973.

Sachar, H., *Israel: The Establishment of a State*. London 1957.

—— *The Course of Modern Jewish History*. New York 1958.

—— *A History of Israel*. New York 1976.

Schechter, S., *Aspects of Rabbinic Theology*. New York 1961.

Scholem, G., *Major Trends in Jewish Mysticism*. New York 1954.

—— *The Messianic Idea of Judaism*. New York 1971.

—— *Sabbatai Sevi: The Mystical Messiah 1626–1676*. Princeton 1973.

Schweid, E., *Israel at the Crossroads*. Philadelphia 1973.

Selzer, M., *Zionism Reconsidered*. New York 1970.

Seltzer, R., *Jewish People, Jewish Thought*. New York 1980.

Sigal, P., *Judaism: The Evolution of a Faith*. Grand Rapids 1988.

Sokolow, N., *History of Zionism*. London 1919.

Trepp, L., *A History of the Jewish Experience*. New York 1973.

Vital, D., *The Origins of Zionism*. Oxford 1975.

Wigoder, G., *Jewish–Christian Relations Since the Second World War*. Manchester 1988.

Wistrich, R. S., *The Left Against Zion: Communism, Israel and the Middle East*. London 1979.

—— *Anti-Zionism and Antisemitism in the Contemporary World*. London 1990.

Zeitlin, S., *The Rise and Fall of the Judaean State*. Philadelphia 1962–8.

Index